MY MELODIOUS MEMORIES

THE AUTHOR

MY
MELODIOUS MEMORIES

By
HERMAN FINCK

With 46 Illustrations

SECOND IMPRESSION

NOVERRE PRESS

First published in 1937

This facsimile reprint published in 2012 by
The Noverre Press
Southwold House
Isington Road
Binsted
Hampshire
GU34 4PH

© 2012 The Noverre Press

ISBN 978-1-906830-52-6

TO
COLLIN BROOKS

CONTENTS

CHAPTER		PAGE
I.	EARLY DAYS	15
II.	MUSIC HALLS AS I KNEW THEM	30
III.	THIRTY YEARS AT THE PALACE THEATRE	44
IV.	COMEDIANS AND COMEDIENNES	72
V.	TEN YEARS AT DRURY LANE	87
VI.	MY PANTOMIME DAYS	116
VII.	THOSE PLAY PRODUCERS	126
VIII.	COMPOSERS AND CONDUCTORS	141
IX.	MUSIC—AND MODERNISM	170
X.	CABIANA	188
XI.	IN CLUBLAND	195
XII.	KINGS AND QUEENS	222
XIII.	"IN THE SHADOWS"	230
XIV.	MEN WHO DRAW	242
XV.	AUTHORS AND OTHERS	254
XVI.	DEAR OLD PALS	284

LIST OF ILLUSTRATIONS

THE AUTHOR, BY G. L. STAMPA	*Frontispiece*
	FACING PAGE
IMPORTANT PHOTOGRAPH OF THE AUTHOR	24
A SOMEWHAT LATER PORTRAIT OF THE AUTHOR	25
HOMMAGE À PAVLOVA	48
CHARLES MORTON	49
H. G. PÉLISSIER	64
PÉLISSIER OFF DUTY	65
ARTHUR ROBERTS	84
GEORGE ROBEY	85
ARTHUR COLLINS	104
E. T. REED HAS A JOKE	105
HERMAN AND GERMAN	124
SIR ALEXANDER MACKENZIE	125
THE OLD DINING-ROOM AT THE SAVAGE CLUB	144
GEORGE WHITELAW'S CARICATURE OF THE AUTHOR	145
THE A.C.M. CLUB	164
IN THE CHAIR AT THE SAVAGE	165
"IT'S ALL RIGHT, OFFICER"	184
"I WAS THE FIRST MOVING PIANIST"	185
"IT'S FOR YOU, SIR"	185
IRVING, BY PHIL MAY	204
TOM WEBSTER	205
DAVID WILSON'S PORTRAIT OF MARK HAMBOURG	232
"I THOUGHT YOU SAID YOU DIDN'T GO TO NEVINSON'S PARTY," MY WIFE REMARKED	233
JIMMY PRYDE'S PORTRAIT OF IRVING IN "LYONS MAIL"	248
LANCE THACKERAY'S PORTRAIT OF SIR SEYMOUR HICKS IN THE DRUNKEN SCENE FROM "DAVID GARRICK"	249
GEORGE R. SIMS	264
WHAT I REALLY LOOK LIKE	265
MY GREAT FRIEND, GEORGE BULL	288
ARTHUR WIMPERIS	289

LIST OF ILLUSTRATIONS

In the Text

	PAGE
ONE OF MY INNUMERABLE PALACE PROGRAMMES	60
SIGN FROM MY DOOR AT DRURY LANE	107
PAUL WHITEMAN ALARMED SOME OF THE SERIOUS "BROTHERS"	161
A SATURDAY NIGHT MENU	197
BUCOLIC NIGHT AT THE SAVAGE CLUB	199
A.C.M. CLUB MENU	206
STANLEY LOGAN DID THIS	211
PROGRAMME FOR A ROYAL COMMAND PERFORMANCE	225
EXAMPLE OF WHAT GEORGE STAMPA WILL DO WHEN ROUSED	245
THIS DRAWING CURED INFLUENZA	252
E. V.'S NOTE	258
LETTER FROM STAMPA ABOUT FAREWELL TO E. V. LUCAS	267
LETTER FROM BASIL MACDONALD HASTINGS	269
SIR JAMES BARRIE'S LETTER	273
THE LENGTH OF HARLEY STREET	293

MY MELODIOUS MEMORIES

CHAPTER I

EARLY DAYS

THE normal literary man who has achieved sufficient years of indiscretion to write memoirs has one stock anecdote which he produces—thereby spoiling the effect of many an artistically cooked dinner—for his annoyed friends at an hour when they demand nothing of life but to be left in peace to appreciate their host's excellent port. This anecdote is about childhood days. It tells how he (the normal literary man aforesaid) saw Charles Dickens; and, in the really acute cases where the story has taken a serious grip on the teller's mind, it goes on to relate how the Great Author patted the child on the head. It may even end (the raconteur is approaching dementia if it does) with an alleged remark by Mr. Dickens, starting, " Ah, my little man . . ."

It may be argued that if all these stories were true, Charles Dickens must have passed his life walking in front of long files of little boys (drawn up in marching order for the purpose), giving each boy a hurried pat on the head as he passed. Just like Napoleon: how he ever made all that brandy I cannot think—especially when he had to dash away in the middle of operations to fight Austerlitz, Jena, Eylau, Friedland, Eckmuhl, Essling, Wagram, Borodino, Dresden, Leipzig, Ligny and (as you may have heard) Waterloo. And people would keep worrying him about First Coalitions and Second Coalitions and Third Coalitions and Fourth Coalitions : I can never remember which is which and I expect Napoleon found it very difficult—unless he tied knots in his handkerchief to remind him which Coalition was causing all the bother. Incidentally, an eminent historian I have consulted about the Great Brandy Mystery thinks the brandy may not have been made by Napoleon, but by another man of the same name.

However, to return to Charles Dickens. The truth or otherwise of the anecdotes does not matter much. If a man has the effrontery to tell his friends that it happened to him, and to tell them so repeatedly, he will undoubtedly also put the story in his reminiscences. And if he does that it gives a him a most impressive start for the book. Something like this:

> " One of the earliest memories of my childhood is the sight of the stately figure of the late Mr. Charles Dickens, his hands folded behind his back, as he walked in an attitude of genial contemplation along the rose-bordered gravel path which led to the front door of my home. . . ."

Musicians of ripe, or ripening, age have in many cases dodged the ubiquitous Mr. Dickens in their childhood years. But instead of meeting Charles Dickens they were singing their hearts out as choirboys. This, too, has its uses. It enables you to begin your reminiscences with a splendid flourish, as:

> " The pale yet rich glow of sunshine glinting through stained-glass windows across the Cathedral's noble Gothic nave seemed to suffuse with a tender mellowness the long-past years of my boyhood. . . ."

I not only never met Charles Dickens, but, though this may sound exaggerated, I was never a choirboy either. Neither of these things have worried me much till this moment when, anxious to start my " Melodious Memories," I find myself feeling much as the late John Hollingshead, the man who first rented—and made—the Gaiety Theatre, felt when he wrote the opening words of his life story:

> " The man who sits down with a light heart to write his autobiography, of course for a pecuniary consideration, and says that he regards the task as a pleasant one, must be a

fool and a liar. He must be a fool, because he must think that his utterances will be regarded as of some importance, and he must be a liar because he must know that the very paper he is writing on has a taint of Kensal Green; that the room in which he is writing assumes, for the time being, the aspect of a family vault, and that every slip of paper he scrawls over only provides another brick for the building of the great book 'Finis'."

Now, having given the matter consideration which it would be sheer unseemly levity to describe by that inadequate word "earnest," I have decided to start in the good old-fashioned way:

I was born in 1872 (not 1527, as you might think; do not confuse me with my namesake composer born then).

A great many other things happened in that year of 1872—less important to me, but then I am prejudiced. Early closing—midnight in London, eleven o'clock in the Provinces—was introduced. Great Britain paid America £3,250,000 for damage done to shipping during the Civil War. Japan decided to tolerate missionaries.

Still, as I said, the really important thing, from my point of view, is that I was born that year, in a house two doors from Waterloo Bridge. My father was then a conductor in the West End, or leader of the orchestra at Drury Lane Theatre. When I was young I was sometimes taken to see shows when he was conducting or leading the orchestra. There was a turnstile just outside our house, at the end of Waterloo Bridge, and I was so small that on these occasions I used to be lifted over the turnstile to save a penny.

I went to a school in Roupell-street, opposite to Waterloo Station. The schoolmaster was a very generous kind-hearted man; he liked music and so he liked me because I liked music. I think he wanted me to go into the Church! This schoolmaster had one peculiarity; he always, morning, noon and night, wore a white evening-dress tie. I could never find out why. Perhaps it was because he was growing old. He may have thought that a

B

man in the evening of his life should be always dressed for the part.

On Sundays I was given the choice of having a three-hour violin lesson, or going to church. One Sunday, when I had chosen to go to church, I foolishly decided that I ought to have at least as much liberty as other boys; so I squandered a penny on an artificial rose and wandered about until it was time to go home for lunch. As soon as I arrived home, my rose was noticed and I was asked where and when I had acquired it. "Oh, I bought it after church," I replied, but my deception was soon found out: after that I went to church *and* had a three-hour violin lesson.

When I was fourteen, and still at school, my father came home one evening and said: "Get your violin out. You are going to play in an orchestra to-night." I was taken off to the Princess's Theatre, in Oxford Street. At this theatre, which has since disappeared, *The Noble Vagabond*, a play which had a good long run, was being produced, and my father was leader of the orchestra. In the cast there were several people who afterwards became famous—Charles Warner, Charles Cartwright and Dorothy Dene. The comedian in the play was a brother of Wilson Barrett.

I had never been in an orchestra before the night my father took me to the Princess's, but I was told to play the violin. My father wanted to "give the boy a chance," to teach me the routine of orchestra work, and provide me with experience. Besides, my presence added another to the three or four violins in the orchestra—without payment.

Within a week one of the violinists left the orchestra at the Princess's, either owing to illness or because he had been offered a better engagement. I became a member of the orchestra with a salary of thirty shillings a week.

After that I never knew whether I was supposed to be at school or earning a livelihood. I used to go to school, play in orchestras, and work at home practising the violin and piano. When I was about sixteen, I went to the Guildhall School of Music. I worked very hard writing music, and sometimes I

EARLY DAYS

played at balls very late at night. I was doing a tremendous amount of work at that time—I still am, when I come to think of it. In fact, looking back on my boyhood days reminds me of the story a famous London hotelier tells about himself. "My father," the hotelier relates, "used to say, ' My boy, I am a broad minded man. I don't trouble myself about what you do out of working hours.' My working hours were 7 a.m. to 11.30 p.m."

My father, who was a pupil of the great Polish violinist, Henri Wieniawski, was not only a fine violinist, he was a good teacher of the violin; he had patience and knew how to bring out the best of his pupils' abilities. One of his pupils was Lord Harrington, who lived in Whitehall in those days. He loved the violin passionately, and used to pay my father half a guinea to go to his home in the morning and give him a lesson or play a duet with him. Sometimes Lord Harrington, a charming venerable old man, would say to my father, "You know, I don't feel like playing the violin to-day. Let's drink a glass of sherry and smoke a cigar together." And they did.

Charlie Rolls—of Rolls-Royce—was also taught by my father. The Hon. C. S. Rolls, to describe Charlie properly, was destined for the Army. But he did not want to go into the Army, so he said to his father: "If I went into the Army you would give me an allowance. Suppose you give me as a lump sum the capital that would be necessary to provide the allowance you would give me if I received a Commission." His father agreed and soon afterwards Charlie started the business of C. S. Rolls and Co. Before long he met a young engineer named F. H. Royce. They went into partnership: hence Rolls-Royce. Charlie was the first Englishman to fly the Channel. He did it twice in one day in 1910; received congratulations from the King and from famous people all over the world; and then asked in surprise: "What's all the fuss about?" Only a few weeks later, ni July, 1910, Charlie entered for the alighting prize at the Bournemouth Air Rally. He used the same Wright biplane in which he had flown the Channel. When he was descending, and his machine was still about fifty feet up in the air, the side of the tail-plane and part of the rudder broke away. The biplane crashed upside down and Charlie was killed. (You may wonder how I know all these details; but then, I read so much!)

Another of my father's pupils was Charlie Perkins—his family were the Perkins of Barclay and Perkins, the brewers—a close friend of Charlie Rolls. The Perkins family compelled Charlie to learn the violin, but for a time he took none too kindly to his lessons and the necessary practice. My father, believing in a little healthy competition, said to him: " My son practises regularly. He plays the violin better than you do; you must not let him beat you." The truth was, however, that my father was not satisfied with me either. He would come home, listen to me —I was about twelve years old when this happened—and say: " You played that piece pretty badly. You should hear Charlie Perkins play it . . ." By arousing the natural, if concealed, rivalry of two boys, my father made very good violinists of both of us.

In those early days, I played the violin in all kinds of places —in the Canterbury, a famous old Music Hall in Lambeth; at Sanger's Circus, and at the Surrey Theatre. I nearly became conductor at the Elephant and Castle Theatre at the age of fifteen; but they decided I was too young for the post. The same thing happened to me again a year later.

I was then studying at the Guildhall School of Music in the morning and going on to the Comedy Theatre to play there later in the day. Jimmy Glover soon afterwards left his job as conductor at the Comedy to take up a better engagement, and left the post of conductor at the Comedy apparently in my hands. He wanted me to be his successor and thought there would be no difficulty in the way of my having the post. But I looked too young to be the conductor of a men's band—they were all, compared to me, old men in it in those days. So I lost the job.

That, by the way, was a great season at the Comedy (apart from the fact that they did not have me as conductor when they might have done!). Among the people appearing there were Charles Hawtrey, Lottie Venne, Charles Brookfield and many others ... but of all of these more anon. That famous old actor Harry Kemble—" the Beetle "—was there too. Harry had an attractive but most unusual deep voice, and it was so distinctive that everyone who knew him would imitate him at some time or other. I and a number of other friends were sitting, a few years ago, in the Café Royal with Stanley Logan, who is now in America, when suddenly Stanley began a perfect imitation of Harry Kemble's voice. Since Stanley was too young ever to have heard Kemble we were all astounded ; but we found that the habit of imitating his peculiar way of speaking had become so widespread that Stanley had picked it up from the imitators— and so gave us a most life-like imitation of Kemble's voice.

One night, when I was a boy, I went to play at a party at the house of Alma Tadema, the great Dutch-born painter. It was a terribly wet night, and I had a long way to go, so I was damp and bedraggled by the time I rang the bell at his house.

Alma Tadema, apparently thinking I was the first of his guests to arrive, came to open the door himself; he was a curious-looking little man with a beard.

He led me across a vast hall (his house was magnificently furnished), and then said suddenly : " Ah, a very vet night. Did you vipe your feet ? "

" Is there a mat ? " I asked.

" Yes," replied Alma Tadema.

" Then I wiped my feet on it," I said.

This pert answer apparently amused him, for he then said : " What is your name ? Finck ? I know that name. . . ." And it turned out that he knew my father. As soon as I was thus identified Alma Tadema made a great fuss of me, and took me round the house.

When the party was finished he came over to the band and said : " We all go and have some nice supper now." He was indeed a charming host.

I also made an appearance on the stage. It was at the Criterion in *She Stoops to Conquer*, and I was, as far as I remember, sixteen at the time. I was really in the orchestra but someone was wanted in one scene to play among the actors, and I was chosen and put into costume—with a red nose. For my short appearance on the stage I was paid more than for a whole evening's playing in the orchestra. This annoyed the other orchestra players and they would peer up at me—the orchestra was under the stage in that play—through a hole in the boards. Sir Charles Wyndham and Mary Moore, a fine comedienne who afterwards became Lady Wyndham, were in the play, with George Giddens who played Tony Lumkin. Giddens could not whistle, but was required to do so in the play. So he had to screw up his mouth and blow silently while the real whistling was done by a man at the side of the stage.

(I once saw a man in a worse predicament than that at the Palace Theatre. He was an amateur siffleur and although he had had plenty of experience at parties, he had never been on the stage before. When he appeared, he pursed his lips, but you could hear nothing. Suddenly I realised what had happened and said down the speaking-tube : "Drop the curtain. They have put so much make-up on his lips that he can't make a sound.")

Three years after that, aged nineteen, I was working at the Palace Theatre. For years I was the youngest member of the orchestra, and conductor there. The Palace was then run by old Charles Morton, who thought a great deal of me. One night he said: "You ought to grow a moustache, Herman." I resented that; music, I thought, should be above mere considerations of hairiness. So I replied: "Why, you haven't a moustache yourself, Mr. Morton." It was true, for although luxuriant white whiskers frilled the sides of his face, the front was clean shaven. "Ah, but you're not as old as I am," Morton said, and wandered away with his hands folded thoughtfully behind his back. He was over eighty at the time.

I wrote violin sonatas, fugues, and all types of serious music in the years immediately preceding my twentieth birthday. And every Wednesday afternoon my father gave a string-quartette party. He was so good with this type of music that he could play many Beethoven quartettes from memory— a rare feat. On these Wednesday afternoons we played Beethoven, Mozart and Haydn—we always started with Haydn.

EARLY DAYS

There were the two violins, a viola and a 'cello. We two violins and the viola several times waited patiently—but in vain—for the 'cellist. He would eventually make excuses on the ground that his 'cello was locked up at the theatre, or that he could not bring it for some other reason. This went on for so long that my father became very tired of it. So he bought a 'cello and said to our friend: "Whenever you want to play it, this 'cello is in my house waiting for you. So when we have a quartette party, turn up punctually—and no more excuses!" I still have that 'cello.

I had an uncle, named Herman like me, who lived in Amsterdam in those days. He was a teacher of the piano, and a very well-known and successful one; he had much more money than my father, and was inclined to take the attitude: "Why did you go to England, when you could have done much better for yourself if you had stayed in Holland?" This uncle of mine had no son, and one day when he was talking to my father he asked: "What are you going to do with young Herman?"

"I am teaching him the fiddle and he is having good experience in orchestras," my father explained.

"Listen," said my uncle, "I know you cannot afford to send him to Leipzig, but I will send him there for you, as I have no son of my own." Leipzig was the University where everyone who could afford it, and those, who, like Sullivan, won the Royal Academy's Mendelssohn scholarship, then went to study music.

My father thought over the offer carefully; then he thanked my uncle and refused it. "It is very kind of you," he said, "but, after all, Herman is my own son. I think I should keep him with me and do the best I can for him myself."

I have often thought over the queer way in which my career hung in the balance while my father was deciding his reply to his brother's offer. If I had gone to Leipzig anything might have happened to me; and certainly none of the things that have happened would have happened. I should, without a doubt, never have written, "In the Shadows. . . ."

Another scheme nearly altered my whole life too. My

mother's brother held a post of some importance with the firm of S. Morden and Co., in the City Road, who made gold and silver pencils and things like that. It was suggested that I should go into that business. If I had done so, I might now have been writing my memoirs with a pencil I had made myself. As it is, I use a pencil which Gertie Millar, now Countess of Dudley, gave me. It is a Morden pencil too: the letters " S. M. & C." are stamped into the gold of the case.

I was also once in danger of becoming a soldier. Regimental bands, including the Coldstream Guards, used, as now, to take private engagements. When they played at balls, they found it essential to have a pianist, but none of the guardsmen could play the piano sufficiently well. So on a number of occasions the highly irregular practice of dressing a civilian pianist in uniform for the evening was adopted. Meanwhile, they were looking for a young man who could play the piano and whom they could persuade to join the Coldstream Guards' band. I was approached; but I was puzzled. " What do I do when you march along the Mall ? " I asked, " I can't march with a grand piano strapped to my stomach, like the man who plays the big drum."

" Oh, no," was the reply. " You would play the triangle when we were marching."

I did not feel that the idea of marching along the Mall hitting a triangle was as dignified as it might have been. Still, my boyish head was filled with thoughts of magnificent uniforms —and a busby, especially the busby. I went home and told my father all about the scheme that I should join the Coldstream Guards. He was horrified, and was far too sharp a man not to squash the project very flat.

So I did not go to Leipzig and I did not take to making pencils or become a soldier. I took to writing comic songs and band parts. I continued to play the violin at balls late at night from time to time—and in clubs where I wore band uniforms of every cut and colour and nationality you can imagine, as well as some I sincerely hope you can't imagine. Usually we appeared as Hungarians. King Edward VII liked Hungarian bands and

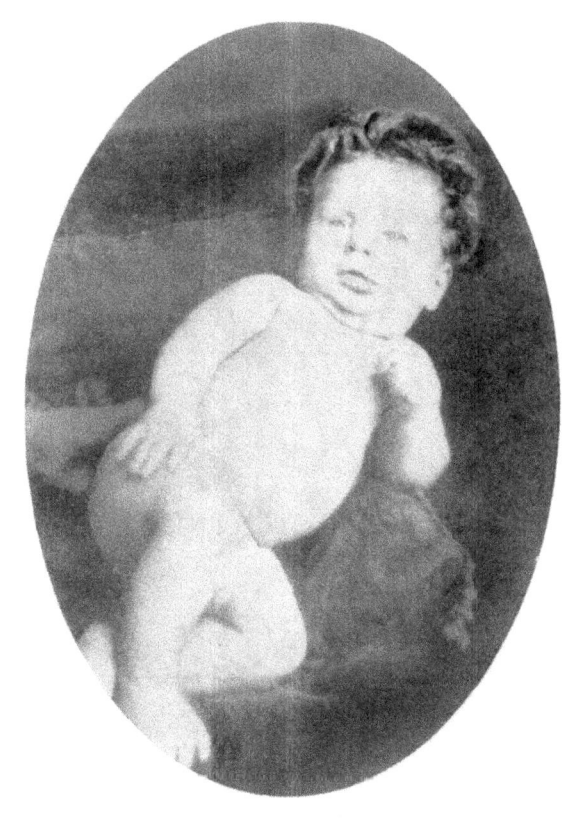

IMPORTANT PHOTOGRAPH OF THE AUTHOR

A SOMEWHAT LATER PORTRAIT OF THE AUTHOR

EARLY DAYS

this had made them fashionable, so we had to masquerade as Hungarians in order to earn a livelihood. This meant we had to have someone in the band who could speak German, and he was supposed to act as an "interpreter" whenever necessary. One night, when I and the other members of the band were decked out in dazzling Hungarian costumes, a young man—one of those infernal people who must always stick their noses in where they are most inconvenient—asked me: "Why are you playing Offenbach? Why don't you play something Hungarian?"

Feeling horribly un-Hungarian, I replied: "We can't play Hungarian music all the time. Some of the people don't like it." Then better pseudo-Hungarians came between us, and after that I was kept out of the way of stray members of the public given to asking awkward questions.

The biggest piece of early fame that came to me was unearned —and embarrassing. Dennys, the booksellers, had a shop in Holywell Street, usually called Booksellers' Row, at that time. Every Saturday, after the matinée, I would go to this shop to buy a book. One Saturday, when I reached the shop for my usual visit, a curious little man who had been an assistant there for many years hailed me with: "Oh, Mr. Finck, your book is splendid; it's sure to be a great success. . . . I have been telling *everyone* how brilliant it is for such a young man to write a book like that."

And sure enough, about half the centre of the shop was devoted to a dazzling display of copies of *The Life of Wagner*, by H. Finck.

I didn't reply to the assistant. I couldn't. It was one of those "moments when you would rather be dead." I bought a book without noticing what it was and hurried away from the shop.

Alas! "H. Finck" was not Herman Finck, then well under twenty, but Henry Finck, a distinguished musical critic in New York.

There used to be a very fine orchestra at the Crystal Palace which regularly gave morning concerts, and the members of the orchestra usually did well for themselves because the morning concerts enabled them to squeeze in one more engagement a day than other players could. On a certain day one member of the orchestra I knew played at the Crystal Palace in the morning and afternoon, at a theatre in the evening, and then went on to play at a ball. After that it is not surprising that when he awoke the following morning he was too ill to go to work.

The result was that I received a telegram telling me to go to the Crystal Palace to act as the invalid's deputy at the morning concert. I was then living at Streatham and as soon as I received the telegram I put my violin case under my arm and hurried off to the station. But I had received notice so late that I could not reasonably be blamed if I failed to reach the Crystal Palace in time.

However, when I entered the concert hall—it is, incidentally, a very large one—I could hear nothing.

" Thank goodness," I thought, " they have not started yet."

So I went forward and was going to take my place when there was a terrific crash from the instruments in the orchestra. I was so surprised that I tripped over a step.

What I had taken for silence was a long-sustained note by the violas! The piece they were playing was the Overture to Weber's *Oberon*.

Manns, the conductor, was startled—and furious. He glared at me; then he stopped the orchestra, and he refused to continue the overture until I had taken my place in the orchestra.

That was one of the cases in which the sending of a deputy could not be avoided, but the practice of sending deputy players to represent members of the orchestra who want to take other engagements is most annoying, and I shall refer to it more than once in the course of this book.

On one occasion I severely reprimanded a member of the orchestra for sending a hopelessly inefficient deputy.

" You have no right to send a man like that," I said, " apart from the damage done by his own bad playing, he upset the people all around him."

" Oh, I'm sorry, Mr. Finck," the culprit replied, " but he's such a nice chap."

"Yes," I said, "and so is our milkman—but he can't play the 'cello."

One of the jobs I did when a young man was to act as reader to a firm of music publishers. I was working on the music of a comic opera they were publishing when I noticed that the opening number was a "Brewers' Chorus," and the opening words were, curiously enough, "All hail!" This delighted me, and I said to the German head of the firm who had just come in: "Look here, this is wrong, you know! Surely it should be 'All Ale!'"

"Vell, vell," he snapped out angrily, "if zat is so vy you not correct it? Vy come bozzering me vith it, Finck? It has nozzing to do vith me."

That was the last joke I tried on him.

My first engagement as a conductor was at the Duke of York's theatre. I was already sub-conductor at the Palace when I received this post. I also used to play the piano in the afternoon at the old Aquarium—I never saw a fish there in all the times I visited the place—which was in Westminster, not far from the Houses of Parliament. At various times, I can remember almost every possible form of entertainment at the Aquarium —except, of course, fish. Sir Arthur Sullivan conducted there a number of times; there were promenade concerts, and variety shows. At one period a man and his two daughters did trick swimming in a tank there, and an old clown—he had retired from deliberate clowning—would announce the turn to all and sundry by waving a kind of baton and shouting out the world's worst rhyme. It ran:

> "Have you seen the Beckwith family in the water?
> If not, well then you oughter!"

Another time I had to play in the dark—not "In the Shadows!"—for a Serpentine Dance. As I had written the music myself it was not very difficult to remember it, even in the dark. Masses of gossamer stuff used to float down on to the stage during this dance and mirrors were arranged so that, with only one girl dancing, you had the effect of a whole ballet pirouetting round the stage.

One day, while this was running—it was in the early days of the cinema—I was just leaving the theatre when the manager ran after me in a high state of excitement. " We have just got a picture of the fight between Fitzsimmons and Corbett," he shouted. " It's the first time a fight has ever been shown on a cinematograph. For heaven's sake come back and play some music while we're showing it."

The boxing kangaroo appeared at the Aquarium. They solemnly fastened boxing gloves on to the animal's paws, hoofs, feet, hands or whatever kangaroos have at the end of their front legs ; but it did not box at all. The man with the kangaroo would put on boxing gloves too and walk up to the animal and hit it. The kangaroo, very naturally anxious to ward off these absurd blows, would tumble on top of the man that was hitting it. But of boxing there was not a sign.

One particular set of incidents always springs to my mind when I think of the Duke of York's Theatre as it was in the days when I first knew it. When I became conductor there, a very famous—and very beautiful—actress named Mrs. Cora Brown-Potter was appearing in the play then being produced ; it was an adaptation of *Francillon*, by the younger Dumas—the man who wrote *La Dame aux Camélias*. The play was not a success ; as far as I know none of the younger Dumas' plays except *La Dame aux Camélias* has been really successful in this country. Anyway, the success or otherwise of the play has only an indirect bearing on this story. Appearing with Mrs. Brown-Potter was a famous actor named Kyrle Bellew, the son of a clergyman (the Rev. John Montesquieu Bellew, who eventually unfrocked himself and became a Roman Catholic), and a person very appreciative of his own abilities and importance. Mrs. Brown-Potter and Kyrle Bellew were fast friends.

Besides these two, Arthur Elwood, a very fine young actor, had a part of some prominence in the play. When the daily newspapers reviewed the piece the next morning, this young man received far more flattering notices than any of the other players—and he deserved to do so, for he had acted his part remarkably well. In the Sunday papers a few days later, Arthur

Elwood was also given a great deal of praise and space, at the expense of the more established favourites; and again he deserved it, for he received all this attention purely on the merits of his performance. He was a delightful man, quiet and rather retiring—and most certainly no publicity hunter.

Still, merit or no merit, the praise Elwood received caused much heart-burning and unpleasantness. There is no occupation in the world where there is so much petty professional jealousy as on the stage.

When I was leaving the theatre a night or two later, I heard a terrible noise at the stage door: voices raised in anger—all the sounds of a first-class quarrel.

I saw Kyrle Bellew, young Elwood, and Mrs. Brown-Potter standing in a group—a very animated group, as a gossip-writer would say. Kyrle Bellew was being extremely rude to the younger man, and was making loud and boastful offers to fight him—or threats to hit him; it was difficult to disentangle the finer points of the row from the general din that was going on. And (though I hate to suggest such a thing of a very beautiful woman) Mrs. Brown-Potter had every appearance of deliberately throwing oil on to the flames by encouraging Kyrle Bellew.

Another minute or two, and hard words (which break no bones, says the proverb) had given away to blows and knocks which were going very near to breaking bones. Elwood may have been a meek, quiet fellow in ordinary conversation, but he had certainly learned somewhere how to look after himself when it was a question of a bout of fisticuffs. Before the battle finished, he had given Kyrle Bellew a thorough hiding—of which a hard blow over the eye was the climax.

Next day Kyrle Bellew arrived at the theatre with an eye so black that its blackness was visible when he was on the stage, do what he would to hide it.

And (of course, things always happen like that) King Edward VII—then Prince of Wales and very fond of going to the Duke of York's—came to see the play that night. I think he must have had a quiet laugh as he sat alone in a little box and watched that black eye.

CHAPTER II

MUSIC HALLS AS I KNEW THEM

THE Music Hall, like a great many other people who have since achieved remarkable success, came of poor but not particularly honest parentage. This is, after all, a very good start in life, for it means that the child is faced with the necessity of getting on without being burdened by any inherited scruples—scruples which have been a confounded nuisance to most of us on our way through the world—about methods of doing so. The poor but not-too-honest parent of the Music Hall was a sing-song held behind or inside a public house; you could have drinks or meals while you listened to a man singing or, at a later date, watched a conjuror do strange things with hats, rabbits, sovereigns, watches and other valuables and invaluables with which conjurors have always been addicted to doing strange things.

From these beginnings grew the old-fashioned Music Hall—places like the Old Mogul Tavern which turned into the Middlesex Music Hall, and which was once where the Winter Garden Theatre now stands.

Once the Music Hall became properly organised, with a real stage, a whole cast of assorted entertainers and an orchestra (very badly paid and consisting of a pianist and four or five other players—cornet, trombone and drums. Noise by percussion was beginning to creep in even in those days). They invariably had a Chairman. This Chairman was the hub—or tub, if you go by his shape and capacity—of the Music Hall universe. He sat at the head of a table with his back to the stage, and, although he was normally a most disreputable person, all the young bloods considered it was a privilege to sit at his table and to buy him all the drinks and cigars he could absorb (the answer,

MUSIC HALLS AS I KNEW THEM

according to Euclid and experience, was infinity). The ostensible reason for having a Chairman was to keep the noisy people in the gallery or at the back of the hall quiet; of course, he was completely unable to do anything of the kind, despite bangings on the table with his hammer. The Chairman, too, used to start the programme by himself singing a song; it had to be the first item because he was never sufficiently sober at any other time.

One evening a particularly magnificent Chairman was presiding at a Music Hall show. Vast diamonds glittered and twinkled in his studs; they must have been worth quite fourpence as solid glass. A mighty expanse of false shirt-front dazzled all who were not near enough to see that its return from the laundry was an event already historical. Across the wide steppes of waistcoat was slung in noble curves a watch-chain that would have provided a brass-foundry with enough raw material for a month's work. He was, in fact, as the audience of the day would have said, "a deuce of a swell."

This all-powerful and alcoholic Chairman rose, banged the table with his hammer and proclaimed in a beautiful hops-and-malt voice:

"Ladies and gentlemen, Madame Campobellino will now sing that dear old song, 'Home, Sweet Home.'"

He sat down. From the back of the hall a raucous voice dynamited with the most searing contempt, shouted:

"What? 'Er? Why, she ain't no better nor what she oughter be!"

The Chairman rose again. His chest swelled till the waistcoat hovered perilously along the edges of his dickey, and the audience were in infinite risk of seeing revealed the unspeakable mysteries of the soft shirt beneath. His hammer crashed down on the table in stern demand for order.

"Nevertheless," he shouted. "*Nevertheless*, she will sing, 'Home, Sweet Home!'"

The great Péllisier of the Follies, when a young man, was taken with a passionate ambition to go on to the stage. He thought that the best way to start would be to try to persuade some Music Hall proprietor to give him a chance to sing—even if he had to pay, instead of being paid, to go on. So Péllisier wrote what he hoped would be a suitable song—he thought they would like songs about drink—and called it, "Booze, booze, booze." It had a lilting chorus which, Péllisier dreamed, would be taken up by the enthusiastic audience and sung till the skylights were forced open.

Eventually, Péllisier was given a chance to sing his song in an obscure Music Hall. He went through the first verse and eventually reached the chorus. There was a horrid silence from the gallery. It lasted through the second verse, but at the second chorus there was a " certain liveliness " (to use a highly technical term) among the audience. Half-way through the third verse a man in the gallery shouted : " When are they going to burn yer ? " That ended Péllisier's career as a Music Hall solo singer.

In the subsequent days of his—and the Follies'—greatness Pélissier would often send me completely ridiculous notes and postcards. One of his postcards which I still have, reads :

>'Erman 'Inck,
>   207 Adelaide Road,
>   N.W.
>
>" I think there must have been too much champagne in the ice ! H. P."

Another one showing him with a curious glassy look, is addressed :

>27 Fort Crescent Esq.,
>   Margate,
>   H.F.
>" Sunday morning. H. G. P."

When we wanted something from me which I had not had time to attend to, he sent me a reminder couched thus :

>" Dear Herman,
>   Yrs sincerely,
>   H. G. Pélissier.
>Please reply."

The old Canterbury Music Hall was in the Westminster Bridge Road, near to Finck Street—a mysteriously named thoroughfare which I suspect may have been so called after my father, for we lived nearby. I remember the Canterbury in the days when they used to stage big-scale tableaux there, things like "The Battle of Plevna." The Canterbury and a Hall named Lusby's in the Mile End Road were bought by the same proprietors who ran them together, renaming Lusby's the Paragon, regularly exchanging turns. If a man doing a turn at both Halls the same night was one of the worse paid artistes, or had a large family to support, he would go by the underground. If, however (as most of the entertainers did), he aspired to "cut a figure," he would hire a brougham and drive in style from the Canterbury to Lusby's to repeat his show. The journey took about an hour.

A team of three or four Americans came over from the United States and were such a success that they were given engagements at both Halls. They were, apart from success on the stage, amusing companions, and usually found that three of four people wanted to accompany them on their drive from the Canterbury to Lusby's; but a brougham would not hold so many passengers. So the Americans began to "think big" in the grand transatlantic style; they hired an enormous pantechnicon which arrived with the words "Must not be slung" (whatever that may mean) in large letters along the side. So, with swinging oil lamps above them, the Americans and their friends would sit in the middle of the pantechnicon and, as it rumbled and bumped slowly along, they would have supper and then play cards. I went with them one night; but when they started to play cards I just watched. I can make out the red suits without any difficulty, but I have never been able to discover which are the spades and which are the clubs.

A paper called the *Entr'acte* was then popular and its two middle pages were always occupied by two drawings by a brilliant cartoonist, Alfred Bryan, or Charles Grineau, to give him his real name. He was a tremendously hard worker; he drew a cartoon for a different paper every day of the week, and turned out so much work that no one appreciated how good he was, and he was always badly paid in consequence. Max Beerbohm wrote of him :

"I cannot help calculating in an idle moment that I see every year more than 1100 new examples of Mr. Bryan's work. . . . His profusion has blinded the eyes of the art-critics to his great merit. . . . His profusion has tired and glutted the public which associates his name with nothing in particular. There is something sad about his profusion. . . . In his theatrical sketches nobody, I think, can approach him, nor can any of my superlatives do them full justice. . . . His sketches of all the *dramatis personæ*, even of those who only appear on the stage for a few minutes, are miracles of acute observation and spontaneous humour."

At the Canterbury the programme was put in place of one of the two Bryan cartoons in the middle of the paper, and so faced a political drawing or a picture of a variety star. A man who was a cheap bookmaker during the day would come round during the performance, shouting, " Programme. . . .*Entr'acte*. . . . *Entr'acte*. . . . Programme." He never allowed the performance to interrupt his programme-peddling, so just when you were laughing at a comedian's best joke, or repressing a lump in the manly throat during a sentimental ballad, a yelp of " Programme. . . . *Entr'acte*," would make you jump almost into the row of seats in front.

One frequent turn at the Canterbury was " Jolly John Nash." His only form of jollity was to come on to the stage laughing and to sing laughing songs. He would laugh and laugh—far more than the audience did. Then he would suddenly begin a sentimental cornet solo ; and that was where *I* began to laugh.

A fine pantomimist was Paul Martinetti, who was half-Italian and half-American. He did a sketch called, *Duel in the Snow*, the story of two famous French robbers, Jacques Strop and Robert Macaire, and another called *The Terrible Night*. The music for this was written by Oscar Barrett, a fine old English gentleman now aged eighty-nine, who was for years conductor at Drury Lane. The scene of *The Terrible Night* was in a restaurant and it was acted on two floors at once—without words, mime throughout. I remember well seeing this sketch at the Canterbury when I was a boy and went there once a week. Years and years later Alfred Butt (now Sir Alfred Butt) came to me at the Palace Theatre. It was when he had just become manager, on the death of Charles Morton, and he said: " I have a lot of ' back number ' turns that have been booked by Charles Morton. One of them is a man named Martinetti. Do you know anything about *The Terrible Night?* They're going to do it here."

" It made me laugh twenty years ago," I replied, " but I should not like to say whether it would make me laugh now." The sketch was played at the Palace, but it did not suit our audiences.

Schalkenbach, the " one-man orchestra," was another Canterbury turn. He was a flat-nosed, extremely ugly man, but he sat in the corner of the stage—always in the corner, for some reason or reasons unknown—and played a little organ from which he could obtain the most amazing effects. Had he lived at a later date he would have been a sensation as organist in one of the bigger West End cinemas.

Years later, a famous sketch called *Humanity* was produced at the Canterbury. It was a true story, founded on events which happened one night in a house in Craven Street in the Strand, where two men had a terrible fight lasting for hours, hitting each other with pokers or anything else they could grab. Everyone knew the story of this fight in Craven Street, so it was a sensation when it was reproduced as a stage scene; it was a tremendous favourite. C. B. Cochran was then a Music Hall agent, and he persuaded Hickory Wood, then well known as an author of pantomimes, to write a burlesque called *Inhumanity*. I wrote the music.

Humanity was such strong-meat melodrama that it was like a piece of burlesque itself; but it had become a classic in the minds of the audiences, or those in the cheaper seats, anyway. Not merely was *Inhumanity* a flop; it was howled off the stage!

The proprietors of Gatti's restaurant, in the Strand, at one time owned two Music Halls. One was in Villiers Street, leading from the Charing Cross end of the Strand down to the Embankment, and near the Adelphi Arches—it is now the Gate Theatre. The other was in the Westminster Bridge Road. And the variety artiste of that day would greet his professional friend with the question: "Hello, George, are you on at the 'Road' or the 'Arches' this week?"

I remember being taken to "The Arches" as a boy. You paid sixpence or a shilling for admission, but that included a refreshment ticket, which you presented at the bar and received a glass of beer—or, in my case, since I was very young, I had ginger beer or lemonade.

The first time I saw Herbert Campbell was at "The Arches." He was singing a song called, "The Josser's Cricket Club"; naturally he knew nothing about cricket, but it was a glorious sight to see this vast and rotund man, with a tiny cricket cap on his head and swinging a bat in his hand, singing:

> "If you want to be gay and learn to play,
> On a Saturday afternoon . . ."

My first recollection of the site of the Tivoli Music Hall—it stood in the same position as the Tivoli Cinema does to-day—was a German restaurant which was there. It was an extremely good restaurant, though I am afraid that I did not then appreciate the excellence of the cooking as much as I should do to-day.

Dan Leno, Wilkie Bard, Joe Elvin, George Robey, Vesta Tilley, Marie Lloyd and Albert Chevalier were appearing at the Tivoli Music Hall during the earlier years of my recollections of it. It was run in conjunction with two other Music Halls belonging to the same proprietors—the London Pavilion and the Oxford. The conductor at the Tivoli was a great character, Angelo Asher, the man who first orchestrated "Ta-ra-ra-boom-de-ay."

The Bedford Music Hall, like the Tivoli, has been turned by time into a cinema, but the Metropolitan is still a Music Hall.

A pantomimist and acrobat I remember well is Boisset, an exceptionally handsome man, who eventually died as a result of eating half a dozen oysters in Glasgow. He was a man who lived at night, hating to go to bed and hating to get up—no doubt he had developed these habits through being on the stage for so many years. I wrote the music for several of Boisset's acts, and he would ask me to meet him, to discuss what I should write, at an hotel which stood where the Green Room Club is now. Boisset was a generous, hospitable man and fond of company. It was his habit to order a whole leg of mutton (restaurants were then less afraid of allowing you to see what you were eating than they are to-day). One night he made the order, " A leg of pork, please, to keep the Jews away ! " When his joint arrived, Boisset would insist on everyone present being his guest for supper, even if he had never seen them before.

One night Boisset, who was staying in the hotel, was giving an even better party than usual. Dan Leno, Little Tich, and half the planets—they were too important to be described as merely stars—in the Music Hall firmament were there. I was sitting next to Boisset talking about the musical arrangements for his next show. Suddenly a policeman swung the door open, stalked in, and arrested everyone in the room ! We were led away—we all went (fairly) quietly and without gyves—to Marlborough Street Police Station. The majesty of the Law finally decided to spare our lives, and we were fined half a crown each. The charge, by the way, was "consuming intoxicating liquor on licensed premises during prohibited hours." As it was Boisset's party and he was a guest at the hotel, it always seemed to me that we were unjustly mulcted and amerced of those half-crowns. But the truth behind the whole matter was, as we found out afterwards, that the police were hot on the track of the proprietor of the hotel because he had, in the upper stories, allowed people to have " done those things which they ought not to have done." He was well and truly caught in due course and fined £250, which brought his business, both legitimate and otherwise, to an unholy and unhappy end.

Little Tich was, as I said, at that unlucky party given by

Boisset. The innumerable other evenings we spent together passed off more peacefully, I am thankful to say.

I deplore the appalling popularity of the saxophone, but, taking the saxophone for what it is, Little Tich was a very fine amateur player. One evening, rather late, I went home with him and he played to me and I played the piano to him. We had some asparagus when we arrived, and every time I suggested that it was late and I ought to go home, he said: "No, don't go just yet. Have some more asparagus." He afterwards sent me a photograph inscribed, "To the asparagus king."

Little Tich also played the 'cello well, and had curious artistic ideas; he was a highbrow in his own way. One evening he sent a message to the theatre saying that he had hurt his foot, so it was impossible for him to appear to do his famous "big boot" dance. Later, he was found in the front row of the stalls at the Lyceum watching Henry Irving. He had paid for his seat, too; that was one of his whims; he would never allow anyone to give him a seat in a theatre. (Harry Lauder is the same.)

When he went to Paris for a fortnight's engagement, Little Tich was such a sensation that he stayed there for three years and returned at various times after that. He acquired a first-class knowledge of French and could sing songs in several other languages too.

The real name of Little Tich was Harry Relph. He first called himself Little Tich in humorous contrast to the burly Tichborne claimant who had created such a stir, and H. Chance Newton wrote the famous bill line:

"One Tich of Nature Makes the Whole World Grin."

James Fawn, who so often sang comic duets with Arthur Roberts, was much addicted to singing "drunk" songs, but he managed to do so without being offensive or vulgar. In one highly successful turn at the Metropolitan he appeared as a drunken and hiccuping solicitor in a wig and gown. Such details as the fact that it was a barrister's wig and gown, and that anyway a solicitor could hardly be drunk so early in the day, spoilt no one's amusement. "The Postman" was another of his clever turns. He came on in a postman's uniform and read the postcards which he took from his bag. Two I thought especially good. One was: "Dear George. I am sending your coat by parcel post. To save weight and make it travel more cheaply I have cut off all the buttons. You will find them in the left-hand pocket." The second read: "Dear Harry, I have taken in a young lodger. God bless you and keep you from your loving wife."

Music Hall songs were revolutionised by the Cockney ballads of Albert Chevalier. At first he sang his songs—he wrote them himself—only at parties or after dinners, but it was soon recognised that they were very good, and Hugh Jay Didcott, the famous variety agent, brought Chevalier on to the Music Hall stage. Chevalier was an instantaneous success at the London Pavilion, so much so that even the other people in the same programme would crowd into the wings to watch him when he was singing. It was not that they were jealous, as you might think; it was a spontaneous tribute to a great artist. Chevalier was a great sentimentalist: I heard him sing "My Old Dutch" twice in one day at Eastbourne and both times tears streamed down his cheeks as he sang.

At the end of the War, Chevalier wrote to me:

"I am sending herewith my play *Cupid and the Cure*. Don't throw it aside simply because it may not, at first, appeal to you as a possible musical piece. Read it carefully and try to see what *I* see: a new kind of *musical* play containing humour, romance and a direct human touch—as much an innovation, *in its way*, as 'Lincoln' was, in drama, so far as *form* is concerned. In the case of 'Lincoln' the form used was old enough to appear new. I am not for one moment disputing the excellence of 'Lincoln.' It is a fine play. I am only trying to point out that it owed much of its attractiveness to its apparent fresh form, and in *Cupid and the Cure*—as a *musical* play—in a prologue and three acts, the form would be fresh enough to appear novel, apart from any merit you may see in the story....

"Should the play appeal to you, you would of course let me

know, and we could then come to some arrangement. Anyway, don't hesitate to say exactly what you think. I shall be curious to hear your views."

Needless to say, I did not " throw it aside," but *Cupid and the Cure* is still among that infinite number of plays which have never been produced.

That most lovable little man, Edmund Gwenn, admired Chevalier so much that he learned to copy his voice and manner. But that is only one of the infinite number of things the versatile Gwenn can do. He sings comic songs or plays Hamlet with equal ease. It was with Gwenn that I went to Wimbledon three or four years ago to hear a number of our old friends in *Veterans of Variety*. We went down in a third-class railway carriage, and it cost about one and sixpence for the two of us. All the other passengers were men going home from work in the City. I was alarmed to see that some of them looked up from their evening papers and gave me most piercing glares. My conscience was all in a turmoil and I was busily trying to remember whether I had murdered anyone or robbed a bank, when one of the men folded back his *Evening News*. On the page that swung round to face me was a picture of myself with an article of reminiscences. I was immensely relieved to find that the passengers' glares were only normal curiosity. Of course, had I realised that that was the day fixed for my article to be published, I should have been spared those soul-searching minutes.

After watching the show we went round behind the stage to see the " Veterans of Variety." Among them were a ventriloquist named Fred Russell, who was also the Editor of a technical paper, and Harry Champion, now over seventy. We sat round, chatting and drinking bottled beer, and I made Gwenn sing Harry Champion's songs in front of him! The result of all that was that we lost the last train back to Town. After some trouble we managed to hire a car. It only cost us one and sixpence to be taken down to Wimbledon, but being brought back turned out to be an expensive matter!

George Chirgwin (" The White-Eyed Kaffir ") was one of the greatest characters that ever appeared on the Music Hall stage. He had a splendid voice and played the one-stringed fiddle remarkably well. One of his favourite turns was to take a tin tray and make two clay pipes dance a hornpipe on it—breaking the pipes at the end of the " dance." Chirgwin was on the stage one night when I was sub-conductor at the Palace; I was due to be relieved, but the man who should have done so had not arrived, so I could not leave the orchestra. I had a long and difficult piece of conducting ahead of me and I was feeling extremely annoyed that the other man had not arrived to give me a rest. It was just then that Chirgwin leaned over and said to me: " Mr. Finck, have you got a pin ? " " No," I replied, " but I have got the needle ! " (the old-fashioned equivalent of the modern slang, " I am fed up "). There was a roar of laughter from the front row of the stalls.

Chirgwin, by the way, became the " White-Eyed Kaffir " by accident. He was appearing as a nigger minstrel, and one night after being made-up with burnt cork, he thoughtlessly rubbed his right eye. When he walked on to the stage with a big patch of the burnt cork rubbed off round his right eye there was a great burst of laughter. After that, Chirgwin would have all his face blacked except a diamond-shaped patch round his right eye, and before long he came to be described on the bills as " The White-Eyed Kaffir." Still, he would often say (he was notorious for his puns): " You know, I don't Kaffir it much."

A pair of Irish comedians—they were brothers, although one was much older than the other—were known as " The Two Macs," and used to quarrel with great regularity and vehemence off the stage. But I always persisted in calling the turn " The Three Macs," because there was another brother of whom little was heard. He acted as dresser to the two comedians. As I was leaving the theatre I saw a mass of arms and legs in vigorous action, with grunts, groans and impolite remarks coming from the same direction. I had just begun to count the assorted limbs, when I saw the tangle was the three Mac brothers. Apparently the dresser had been growing more and more annoyed by the publicity and big salaries which his two brothers were earning, and I should think they had probably been treating him in a high-handed way. Anyway, a good hearty family fight was in progress when I arrived. It was the comedians against the dresser, and although two against one is supposed to be winning odds, the dresser dressed down the other two brothers with vigour and dispatch.

So much for Music Hall stars; now a word about the most neglected and badly treated people in the Music Hall business—the writers of songs. They never received any credit for their work, and usually found it difficult to persuade people to give them the other kind of credit either. People would say to one another: "Have you heard Dan Leno's new song? It's magnificent, tremendously funny." They gave all the credit to the man who sang the song and forgot about the poor fellow who wrote it.

High among the song writers was Joseph Tabrar, author of " Daddy Won't Buy Me a Bow-Wow," and brilliantly clever at that kind of work, though he never learnt to write, and always had to dictate his innumerable songs.

George Le Brunn, who was given by the paper *To-day* the well-meant, if somewhat silly, title " The Beethoven of the Music Halls," was a rollicking fellow. He would write a song, walk into a publisher's office and sell it for any sum he could—cash down.

George had a brother who had the misfortune to have paralysed legs, but was a teacher of dancing in Kennington, for all that. When this man was not teaching dancing he wrote songs. One day he brought some of his songs to the Palace, propelling himself on one of those tri-cycles which are worked by hand, to see if he could sell them. Blake, the famous stage-door keeper, carried him into the theatre and sat him down on the piano stool. He played a tune that was much better than the usual run, and someone smacked him enthusiastically on the back and knocked him of the piano stool. The man who did this had not a leg to stand on, of course, and the song was duly bought and paid for.

A certain manager was notorious for being most particularly friendly to his employees when he contemplated getting rid of them.

" You're not looking well, my boy," he would say. " Why not try a fortnight at Margate? Splendid place! Wonderful air! Go to the cashier and get your money and go and enjoy yourself. Have a good time and take your wife with you. Yes, yes; it'll do you a lot of good. Let me hear how you get on. Good-bye, my boy, good-bye!"

And he would grasp the employee's hand, shake it fervently, show him to the door, and, after giving him another cordial grip, repeat that he must have a good time.

But after a time it became notorious that a friendly farewell like this only meant that a note would be received during the holiday, intimating that the employee's return was not required.

When one official went to the manager to ask for a holiday, he received his immediate consent. " And I hope you will have a very good time," said the manager as he rose from his desk. " You must write and let me know how you get on. Good-bye, my boy, good-bye!"

The manager held out his hand, but the official dodged to the door, saying, "No you don't, guv'nor, no you don't! I know what that means. No, thank you!"

That employee was not given the sack during his holiday!

CHAPTER III

THIRTY YEARS AT THE PALACE THEATRE

THE statement that I sat in the conductor's *chair* at the Palace Theatre for more than twenty years is one which, I feel strongly, adds insult to discomfort. All the players in the orchestra, except the drummer, can work sitting down at their ease, but the conductor has to stand. Even the little chair for him to sit on when he is not conducting is more a mockery than a kindness; he so seldom has a chance to sink on to it.

Still, it was not always like this. Once upon a time conductors really did have chairs to sit on. I used to conduct sitting down in my earlier days at the Palace; my chair was not in the position where a modern conductor stands; it was close to the footlights. The result was that you were directing a large number of musicians without being able to see what was going on among the few behind you. You had to rely entirely on what you heard of their playing and I should have found a reflecting mirror like the ones in motor cars most useful.

Once during my sitting-down era a troupe of trick-cyclists came to the Palace. The clown of the troupe had a heavy cycle which fell to pieces at the climax of his turn. As I was, from my chair, close against the footlights, watching this troupe wheeling at high speeds about the stage, the clown's cycle fell to pieces—but not in the way it should have done. I saw a heavy wheel whizzing across the stage, straight for me. For about three-one hundred and twenty-fifths of a second I had a horrid vision of this wheel crashing into the orchestra, knocking me backwards and devastating the landscape far and wide. I threw away my baton, stood up, thrust my arm over the edge of the stage—and caught the wheel. I spun it back across the stage, picked up my baton and went on conducting, thinking no more of the incident.

Among the audience that afternoon was the famous George Jacobi, writer of more than a hundred ballets and conductor at the Alhambra. Matinées were rare in those days, and as there was not one at the Alhambra that day, George had come to see the Palace show. Afterwards, I met him and he said, "Herman, that was wonderful."

I was always fond of Jacobi, but at that moment my heart really warmed to him. "What a compliment," I thought, "praise of my orchestra and conducting from a man so much older than myself, who does the same job; an authority on music. . . . I wonder which particular piece we played he is referring to?"

So I asked: "What was wonderful, George?"

"Why, the way you caught that wheel, Herman!" he replied.

It's a hard life for those that follow the arts.

Old Charles Morton managed the Palace for many years. I say "old" partly as a term of affection, but chiefly because I cannot remember him when he was anything but old. He was a great character, wearing a white wig and a top-hat, and given to walking about with his hands clasping a programme and folded behind him. During matinées he always wore the conventional frock coat and a bow-tie with black and white spots.

At every performance, Morton sat at a little table behind the stalls, looking down the centre aisle. There was an extra chair at his table and, if you were of sufficient importance, he might invite you to take a seat with him.

Morton was kind-hearted, but always had a somewhat austere dignity, and well knew how to be firm when necessary. One evening he saw a man standing at the back of the stalls (a favourite place for men at a loose end, and conveniently near the bar, which was more or less a club) throw down a cigarette-end and stamp it out. Morton walked up to the man, clapped him on the shoulder, and said sternly: "Would you do that on your own carpet?" Then, he asked the offender to leave the theatre.

Somewhere Morton had a house and a wife, who rarely came to the theatre and who probably did not know anything about her husband's life there, for I should not imagine that he was the kind of man to chat over the business affairs of the day when he arrived home. Every night at nine o'clock he used to have a pot of tea made for him from special little packages prepared by himself and brought from his house.

Morton's business methods would appear a little curious to people accustomed to high-powered modern "efficiency." Being an old man he would not use such ultra-modern gadgets as telephones or typewriters. He would sit down at his desk and write all his letters himself. When he had written a letter he would carefully address an envelope, put the letter inside, stick down the flap—and throw the completed letter on to the floor. Eventually an employee would come into the room and collect up the Palace correspondence from the floor around the manager's desk.

It was only when Morton came to the Palace that the place really "took on," though two ballets produced there by 'Gus Harris had been successful successors to an unsuccessful venture as an opera house with a Grand Opera specially written by Arthur Sullivan, *Ivanhoe*.

One of the features introduced into the programme by Charles Morton in those early days was the *tableau vivant*. *Tableaux vivants* were not, of course, new, but they took on a new lease of life and popularity as they were produced by Morton, and for some years they were a regular part of the Palace programme. There were representations of many famous pictures, beautifully carried out; some of them were posed by girls apparently in a state of undress, but actually most decorously covered with the tights which were then thought essential on the stage.

While the revived vogue for *tableaux vivants* was in progress, one of the periodical exhibitions at Earl's Court was held, and I was asked to go down there to provide music for some *tableaux vivants* which were being presented out of doors in the grounds of the exhibition building.

It rained practically every day and so what should have been a big success turned out to be a lamentable failure. After three days we got rid of the orchestra and I was left alone with an eccentric harmonium-ist, to play the music arranged specially for piano and harmonium. We alternately played the overtures "Ruy Blas" and "Egmont." But if I said "Ruy Blas," he would start "Egmont."

One of the programme girls at Earl's Court was not bad looking, but she was most infernally fat. One day she came up to me and said: "I hate wandering about with programmes. Do you think I could get a job in the *tableaux vivants*?"

"Can you stand still?" I asked, "or keep a pose?"

"Oh, yes, I'm sure I could do that," she replied.

"Very well," I said, "I'll speak to the manager about you."

Shortly afterwards the manager arrived and I said: "One of the programme girls wants to know if you can give her a job in the *tableaux vivants*."

"Which one is it?" he asked. "Oh, that fat one? She's no good."

"I wish you'd have a word with her," I said, "and then she won't blame me for the fact that she doesn't get a job."

So the girl was sent for and told to pose on the stage.

"See how long you can stand still," said the manager.

Just then both he and I were called away to answer an urgent telephone call from the Palace; and then we went away to have lunch.

When I went into the "orchestra" half an hour or more afterwards, I was amazed to see the fat programme girl standing on the stage in a ridiculous pose.

"Hello, what are you doing up there?" I enquired.

"I was *told* to stand here," she replied wearily.

"Great Scott, so you were," I thought—but it would have broken the poor girl's heart to tell her that she had been completely forgotten, so I gently intimated that I thought she had stood there long enough.

Once, before he came to the Palace, Morton made a mistake: he did not take the trouble, when manager of the Alhambra, to hear Vanoni, the French artiste, sing. Vanoni turned out to be a very popular turn, and Morton was angry with himself for having lost the opportunity of engaging her. We were reminded of this incident every Monday morning at the Palace, for then we had to endure the " trial turns "—and trials they were, I can assure you. After the Vanoni incident, Morton decided : " In future I will never let anything go by ; I will see anyone who wants me to see them." That was his rule, but while the unhappy " trial turns " were showing their paces or arpeggios, Morton would have people carrying great advertisements past for him to see and would, between seeing to other things, just give the turns a quick glance and decide whether they had any hope. They seldom had.

One weird-looking woman, very badly dressed—an alleged singer, although she looked as though she had stepped out of one of Belcher's drawings of charwomen—came towards me and said : " I am sorry, I have no music. Will you play for me ? "

" Certainly," I replied, " what would you like me to play ? "

" The Death of Nelson," replied the woman, in a tone of sepulchral majesty.

One good thing that came out of the trial turns was Jimmy Dunn—not to be confused with the noted journalist of the same name—whose friendship I enjoyed for many years. Jimmy was the son of a Tasmanian banker, but found himself in London, ruined, as the result of a financial crash. So he put his banjo underneath his arm, came along to the Palace, sang comic songs, and was given a job.

A great friend of his was a doctor, and one evening Jimmy introduced me to him. After the guest's departure, I said : " He's a very amusing companion, but is he a good doctor ? "

" Good doctor ? " said Jimmy. " Him ? Why, I wouldn't put my tongue out to him ! "

Wet days were the worst for " trial turns." People anxious for shelter walked into the Palace and recited bad verse badly or sang worse songs worse, just to pass the time. It passed our time, too ; often I had the orchestra there until four o'clock on a Monday afternoon. That could, of course, never happen now,

HOMMAGE À PAVLOVA

With praise of Paulhan ev'rywhere
The universe resounds
He's heavier than is the air
By just ten thousand pounds
But if the Daily Mail could spare
A sum of equal size
For one who's lighter than the air
Pavlova wins the Prize

M.T.P.

Café Royal
June 9th
1910

CHARLES MORTON

because rehearsals of more than three hours mean that the players have to be paid extra.

In those days, however, the orchestra could be kept any length of time, and on a Monday, before the "trial turns" started, we had an ordinary rehearsal first of music only and then of the current turns, beginning at about ten o'clock. Conscientious artistes like Vesta Tilley, Gaby Deslys, Gus Elen, Marie Lloyd, R. A. Roberts and many more, arrived punctually for rehearsals and worked hard at them, only staying away if they were ill, but other performers were less devoted to work—especially early on a Monday morning. The normal excuse was that they had been travelling from somewhere—travelling from a party a few hours before, that usually meant. They even tried the outrageous trick of sending chauffeurs, valets or coachmen to represent them—and sing their songs for them!—at rehearsals. Before long, I had these practices stopped. In one case a famous woman star did not trouble to attend a rehearsal, and Morton very rightly refused to let her go on to the stage.

Annoying, though not quite so bad, was the habit of orchestral players of sending a deputy (who had not attended the rehearsals), while the man who belonged to the orchestra went somewhere else to play at a higher fee. I put my foot down about this at the Palace, and there was a tussle. I gave the whole orchestra a month's notice. Nominally the month was to allow the players to think the matter over; actually I wanted time to engage another band in case they really did leave. In the end I lost only one man—and the "deputy" system had been killed in one orchestra at least.

Another practice to which I objected when I was at the Palace was the habit of sending bouquets to performers, and expecting the conductor of the orchestra to hand them up. I maintained that if anyone wished to pay a tribute to a performer, they should pay it privately, and I would never allow bouquets to be passed up on to the stage.

On the last night of one of her seasons, when Pavlova had just finished her amazing Ballet, and the walls of the theatre were bulging outwards with applause, I was amazed to see my music boy (assistant librarian) crawling towards me, holding an extraordinary contraption—a thing that looked like a mixture between a bower of roses and a laurel wreath for an outsize Roman emperor, with festive ribbons trailing from it in all directions. As soon as I saw the boy I gave him a forty-five-horse-power frown and said: " Take it away ; " but on he crawled, closer and closer. My growls of " Take it away " rose in a wild crescendo to shouts of " Go away . . . Go away," which were drowned among the tumult in the theatre. Still, the boy knew my ideas about bouquets, and my looks told him plainly enough what I meant. He was obviously terrified, expecting the sack forthwith, but had received orders to win through, even at the cost of his life. When he was about two feet away from me he screamed out through the din : " Please, sir, it's for you, sir ! " And so it was, inscribed, " To the Maestro," by Pavlova. In half a minute someone had put it round my neck, and there was nothing for me to do but bow to the audience and the harassed boy.

I was summoned to serve on a Grand Jury at ten o'clock one Monday morning—our busiest morning—when Pavlova was appearing at the Palace. All the way to the Old Bailey I was wondering how I could avoid serving, and when I arrived I asked a policeman.

The policeman's advice was : " Directly you hear your name called, go into the well of the Court and say ' Excuse ! ' "

So I went down steps into the well of the Court, and with each step I descended the Court grew bigger and I grew smaller. All the pantomime of legal dignitaries stalking solemnly in, holding bouquets, and the emblems of pomp and circumstance completed the undermining of my morale—that and the thousands of eyes which gazed down on me, with inexorable hostility, it seemed. It was just like a terrible nightmare, pervaded with the obsession, " I shall never reach the theatre in time for the rehearsal with Pavlova. Finally, I squealed out, " Excuse ! "

" And what is your excuse, sir ? " asked a portentious voice.

My nerve came back to me then ; I seemed to grow again till I nearly reached my normal height, and I replied : " I am the

Musical Director at the Palace Theatre, and all the orchestra and the company of artists are waiting for me to begin a rehearsal—including Madame Pavlova...."

" Ah, charming artist, charming artist," said the Recorder, a little irrelevantly I thought, at the mention of Pavlova's name. " Very well, Mr. Finck, your excuse will be accepted."

At this I began to grow taller and expand, even beyond my normal size, but just as I was leaving the Court, the Recorder said: " Ah, Mr. Finck, you will understand that you will have to appear on another occasion for jury service."

By that time I was feeling so top-of-the-morning that I foolishly said: " Of course, I shall be *delighted* to do so."

So I had no one but myself to blame when I was called again for Grand Jury service on a Tuesday a few weeks later, and was in court for two and a half days. I remember that a very pompous man was elected foreman of the Grand Jury, and he began to behave like a coroner—cross-examining everyone in the most fierce and senseless way imaginable. We should have been stuck in that jury-box for weeks if we had not snubbed that foreman into keeping quiet.

However, to revert from the Grand Jury to Pavlova, as I should like to have done then and am at liberty to do now: I have her to thank for the fact that if I want to know the time I never have to ask a policeman. In 1912, when all London was flocking to the Palace to see her and her Russian ballet company —a great novelty and a real theatrical sensation at that time— she gave me a gold watch and chain. The watch was inscribed, " To my dear Conductor, Herman Finck. Gratefully, Anna Pavlova," and has gone perfectly ever since. So it was, you see, a real watch from a real artist.

Pavlova, who later took a house at Hampstead, with swans all over the place, was a charming woman, but I cannot say that I ever liked her first partner Mordkin. How could you like a man who came to the theatre for rehearsals in a top-hat, a frock coat and brown boots?

Mordkin was unknown in England when the company came to London, but he made a hit with his dancing, and success had the effect upon him that it has upon so many people, especially people connected with the theatre. He began to grumble and squabble about the way he was billed in the advertisements. Pavlova would not give way to him, and this led to one of the most extraordinary scenes I have ever seen in a theatre—and I have seen a good many.

As an item in the programme, Pavlova danced Rubinstein's "Valse Caprice," and Mordkin had to catch her at the finish as she threw herself into his arms. One night he appeared to make no attempt to catch her, and Pavlova fell on to the stage. This naturally caused much excitement, but nothing to the excitement when she got up and slapped him on the cheek. The curtain was at once rung down, and the "Bioscope," as the "moving pictures" of those days were called, put on. I continued playing, but presently I became aware that an extra "moving figure" was present. It was Mordkin, bobbing about in front of the pictures, trying to shout explanations—in Russian—of his side of the case to those of the audience who were not already outside discussing what they had seen. I stopped him. I made the orchestra play so loudly that not a word could be heard in Russian or any other language.

An ambitious young man once confided in me that he would like to have my job at the Palace, not because he was a musician, but because a conductor's chair must be such a good place from which to study feminine legs. I was sorry to disillusion him, but the sad fact is that the opportunity can never be fully taken. For one thing, you are far too busy with the band; for another, you do not look at the legs of the dancers when you are playing for them. What you are most intent upon is the *time*, so you have to watch their *feet*. All the same, I must admit that I have looked up at many thousands of lovely legs, both old style—the peg-top variety which were once worn by principal boys—and new style—the more slim (perhaps I should say slimming) kind which are nowadays in fashion.

I have seen legs reputed to be insured for a million dollars, and I have found that legs of infinitely less theatrical value may nevertheless be theatrical signposts. It happened like this: We were getting up a benefit matinée for Courtice Pounds. One of the principal items was the Gilbert and Sullivan opera, *Trial by Jury*, and although the performance was to be at His Majesty's Theatre, we were to hold our rehearsals at the Carlton Theatre (now a cinema) nearby in the Haymarket. The stage door is presumably always at the side or back of a theatre, but I did not know my way about, and as I did not see it at once, I went into the theatre by the ordinary front entrance to make enquiries. While I was doing so, a little lady came up to me and said: " I want to find the stage door, too. . . ." It was Jessie Bond, who successfully played so many comedy parts in Gilbert and Sullivan operas, and we set out together to find the stage door.

As we turned the corner we saw three young girls wearing very short frocks and displaying much shapely leg.

" Mr. Finck," said Jessie Bond, " we can easily find the stage door now."

" How ? " I asked.

" By following those legs."

And it was so!

I remember when Maud Allan burst upon a considerably startled, not to say scandalised, London, about thirty years ago, and danced with bare legs. It was a furore. All these years afterwards, it is amusing to look back and think what a stir Maud Allan caused because she danced with bare limbs. Tights were essential things in those days, and there was an outcry—and also a large incoming of audience—over Maud Allan. She " got away " with it—or them—because the cloak was classical dancing. She wore hardly any clothes—but she danced Mendelssohn's " Spring Song " and " Salome," and cavorted about the stage with a " property " head of John the Baptist. The brother of the great author George Moore, " Gus " Moore, did some very clever publicity over Maud Allan.

I believe that King Edward VII was not at all pleased when, later, Lady Constance Stewart Richardson followed Maud Allan with an even more daring undress " classical dancing " turn. I was told that His Majesty did not approve of a member of such a family going on the Variety stage. I fear that I was partly to blame. I recommended the turn, and it was due to me that it was booked. But I never got the usual agent's fee of ten per cent on the artiste's salary: all I got was a pair of sleeve links—and links does not even rhyme with my name.

After that I may as well tell you about Mr. Volny, who occupied different managerial positions at the Palace. He was a remarkably, in fact, extraordinarily thin man, and one day I remarked of him: " Volny ! His name ought to be Beaune ! "

My first acquaintance with Gaby Deslys was when she played in a little thing called *À La Carte*, at the Palace, by Dion Clayton Calthrop, and the music arranged by myself. Now, all sorts of stories were told about Gaby, but my own experience of her was that she was an extremely nice woman, a very hard worker in the theatre, and that she was a very good Catholic. She had a prie-dieu in her house in Kensington Gore.

Her partner in those days, Harry Pilcer, was very jealous of her, and I think he was economical by nature. I found out afterwards that when Gaby thought she would like to make me a present of some sort, she asked Pilcer to find out how many studs I wore in my dress shirts. Every night of the last week of their engagement he used to be hanging about the stage door when I came in, and I could not make out why, as he said : " Ah, good evening, Herman," he always fixed his eyes on my shirt-front. Finally, I found out. He reported to Gaby that I wore one " stud." So I did—about one evening a week. On the other four or five nights I wore two studs. Gaby did not know this, of course, and so she gave me one pearl stud.

When a turn called " Humpsti-Bumpsti " appeared at the first Royal Command Music Hall Performance (which I conducted, as I shall relate later on), they got a big laugh by ending the act by falling on to the drum. But I have never encouraged artistes to come into the orchestra—any more than I have, as I explained, encouraged the practice of handing up flowers to the stage by way of the orchestra—and when I was conducting for Regine Flory (who shot herself at Drury Lane some years ago) in one of the Palace revues she fell into it.

She had a dance to do, finishing on twirls down stage, and

I repeatedly said to her: " One night you will fall into the orchestra and kill yourself—or some of us."

I knew she would fall—and she did. She missed her distance one evening, shot over the footlights and fell in a heap at my feet. I thought she was dead—she lay quite still—but there is only one rule in such circumstances and that is, go on with the show. And so, while frightened almost stiff at what had happened, I went on playing. A few minutes later she came round and disappeared through the orchestra door, much to my relief. Naturally, as soon as possible I left the orchestra and went backstage, prepared to hear the worst. Instead of finding Regine Flory hurt, however, I found her roaring with laughter at the incident, in her dressing-room.

But I noticed that she took very good care not to risk repeating that " joke " during the remainder of the run.

The " lovelies " (what a word!) for whom I have had the pleasure to conduct . . . they present a wonderful display of skill and beauty to the mind's eye. Vesta Tilley (what a perfect " boy " she was), Violet Loraine, Gertie Millar, lovely Vera Pearce, Ada Reeve, who recently came back in a Cochran show after years away in South Africa, Harriet Vernon (what a fine pair of legs—old style—she had, to be sure!), Queenie Leighton, June as a child, the Palace Girls. . . .

The Palace Girls were the forerunners of all these slick, smart, fast, dancing troupes that are taken for granted nowadays. When I first knew them they were " The Manchester Mites." Then they became " The Tiller Girls." And when we first had a troupe at the Palace, I said: " Call them ' The Palace Girls.' "

Undoubtedly, the Palace Girls set a standard for chorus dancing all over the world. They danced in capitals abroad, and then foreign managers tried to recruit similar troupes in their own countries. They failed hopelessly—especially in Paris. England and America are the only countries that breed chorus girls. We catch them young, and when the mothers are too old for the job, the daughters step into their places.

Fearful and wonderful turns came to the Palace during the years I was conductor there. Take, for instance, the Strange

Case of the Whirling Dervish. The dervish arrived, swathed in flowing Oriental robes; even his face was always hidden by a veil. Since, it was explained, this was his national costume and he had never worn any other, the dervish went about the streets in his remarkable robes, while adults threw surprised glances at him, and small boys stood and stared in open-mouthed amazement.

It was difficult to rehearse with the whirling dervish, as he shook his head blankly whatever you said to him, or replied with a stream of guttural syllables which were to us completely meaningless. At rehearsals the dervish was accompanied on to the stage by his manager. The dervish would blurt out some pleasant little sentence such as, " Waougouraheeguhottah," and the manager would then turn to us with : " He says, etc."

At the performance the dervish simply turned round and round until a bored audience coughed and fidgeted; this turning turn was not a great success, in fact, and was put on at the beginning of the programme. While it was on, I played some weird music he had brought me.

However, shortly after the whirling dervish had made his last appearance on the Saturday night, his manager came to me, and said : " The dervish wants you to come across to Kettner's to have a drink with him."

" Can't we have one in the theatre ? " I asked.

" No, do come round to Kettner's ; he particularly wanted to meet you there," said the manager.

" But is he going to be wearing all these robes and veils in Kettner's ? " I asked somewhat nervously.

" Oh, that will be modified a little to-night," said the manager.

" All right," I replied, " I will try to slip across for a few minutes."

I walked into Kettner's and looked round. There was the dervish's manager, but no sign of the whirling dervish : only a normal-looking young man in a lounge suit, leaning against the bar.

" Hello," I said, " where's the dervish ? "

" Why," answered the manager, very surprised, " this is him,

Don't you know him?"—and he pointed to the young man in the lounge suit!

Then the "dervish" himself, with a good Cockney twang, said, "I took a fancy to you at the beginning of the week, and you've no idea how hard it's been to keep on pulling the wool over your eyes. So I wanted you to have a drink with me, and call it all square!"

The Hypnotised Lady also led to a curious incident. This woman was supposed to be placed under hypnotic influence while on the stage, and then to be able to do anything she was asked by a member of the audience.

Actually, she had three or four confederates who, from the auditorium, called out the names of dances which she thereupon danced. Not merely were these dances, apparently done on the spur of the moment, rehearsed, but I had actually had some twenty extra band parts done, as the woman had not sufficient! Despite the rehearsing—or because of it—the turn was not a success, because the audience saw that the "hypnotism" was trickery. Realising that it was not going too well, the woman said to me: "Do you think we could do something quicker and livelier on the last night?"

"Certainly," I replied, "I suggest a tarantella. But you have given me so little notice that it will be difficult to arrange it."

I sent a message down to the Follies, to a friend of mine named Alfred H. West, who wrote so many successful songs for Albert Chevalier and was his accompanist for many years. Alfred was then playing the piano for the Follies, and I asked: "Can you come to the Palace and play your famous 'Tarantella in F' for us?"

West found that he would not be wanted for the Follies just at the time I wanted him, so he saw Péllisier, and Péllisier agreed to him coming to the Palace.

So far so good; but only so far. West was a man who was very wrapped up in his music, so much so that when I sent a message asking him to play his "Tarantella in F," it did not occur to him that he was wanted to play in connection with someone else. He thought he was wanted to play a pianoforte solo to fill a gap in the programme. Even when he was hustled on to the stage he was not disillusioned. He was so intent on what he was doing that he did not hear a voice from the audience call out: "Tarantella in F"; he did not even see the "hypnotised" woman on the stage. He simply sat down at the grand piano and began to play. And how he played. His fingers flashed and thundered up and down the keyboard. It was as though you had rolled Paderewski and Mark Hambourg into one, and were driving the result with a million watt dynamo.

As the tumultuous stream of sound poured from the grand piano, the Hypnotised Lady began to realise that she had asked for some wild music to dance to, and she was getting it. Added to that, the "Tarantella" was a very long piece. The girl danced and danced . . . her legs ached and her wind nearly gave out . . . her head swam round, but still the music went on. At last the girl could not dance another step; she fell in a heap on the stage.

Now that should have been enough to stop any pianist. But not Alfred the Great Pianist. He had not even seen the girl. The torrent of tarantella continued in full flood . . . until I pressed the bell and the curtain came swishing down.

But perhaps the most fearful and wonderful thing the staff at the Palace ever saw was the length to which carefulness could be taken by a famous—in fact, a very famous—Scottish comedian. Some time after he appeared at the Palace, this comedian was on tour, and he asked my friend, Tommy Best, to play the piano for him for a week. Tommy agreed. At the end of the week, the comedian had made £1200, and he said to Tommy and two other men: "Well, boys, will ye ha' a drink wi' me."—"Thank you," they replied in chorus. "Waiter," called the comedian, "one double Scotch and three small ones." Interval for drinking. Then Tommy said: "And now will you have a drink with me?"—"Thank ye, I will," replied the comedian. So Tommy called to the waiter: "Three large whiskies and one small one!"

R. A. Roberts, a man famous for his quick changes, came to the Palace to do a playlet called *Dick Turpin*, in which he himself acted all the roles—an old hag; a young bride; Dick Turpin himself; a Bow Street runner; and other characters. Then, at the end of his show he would take a call in evening dress.

This man was afterwards invited to do *Dick Turpin* with the new revolving stage at the Coliseum; appropriate scenes were to be set in the various compartments of the revolving stage.

At the first performance at the Coliseum his ability as a quick change artist was neutralised by the fact that the revolving stage was not working as it was expected to do. The result was to give the impression that the unhappy " Dick Turpin " was the slowest quick-change artist ever seen.

The climax of his playlet was the line: " I'll ride to York. By God, I'll ride to York," and then he climbed on to a horse and rode away.

I saw him after the first performance and, while we were talking, a note was brought round from Sir Oswald Stoll, congratulating him on his performance, but saying that he could not allow any swearing or blasphemy on the stage.

After his next performance I saw " Dick Turpin " almost in a state of nervous collapse.

" Why, what's the matter? " I asked.

" Oh," he groaned, " everything went wrong with the show. And then, at the end, I suddenly remembered I had to alter the last line. . . . But I couldn't think . . . I hadn't time to think out what I ought to say. I shouted, ' *By Christ*, I'll ride to York.' Oh, dear ! "

Gus Elen was very impressed with the size of the orchestra when he first appeared at the Palace—he had never sung to such a large one. One day, after a rehearsal, he said to me: " Thank you, very much, Mr. Finck. I would stand you all a drink—if the orchestra was not such a big one."

If I missed a little hospitality that day, I received some unexpectedly from the Man Who Was Going Round the World. He rushed up to me as I was making my way to join two friends for a drink while the acrobats were on, and thanked me enthusiastically for having played " Melodious Memories." He declared that he would take it round the world in his head; then he seized my hand warmly—and dashed off to Euston or Waterloo. When I opened the hand he had seized so warmly I found a golden sovereign in it.

Both my friends were very angry. " Never heard of anything more insulting," they declared.

" Oh, well, I'm not going round the world to give it back," I said, " so let us have a bottle of wine out of it." In those not-so-dear days beyond recall, a bottle of champagne cost twelve shillings and sixpence at the Palace. (My two friends at once agreed that the " insulting " traveller was a jolly good fellow.)

Later, seriously thinking the matter over, I felt that the orchestra deserved to share in the sovereign, and in a generous

---

"The Palace Theatre is the most comfortable and well-appointed house, and the entertainment is always of the highest class."—*Times*.

THE PALACE THEATRE.

"There is no stall floor which can show a braver array of well-dressed folk, and there is a decided 'tone' about the Palace.—*Daily Telegraph*.

Week Commencing MONDAY, OCTOBER 25th, 1909.

The Furore of Paris.

M. SILVESTRE as "BEBERT."

"MA GOSSE"

Mlle. MOLLON as "LA GOSSELENE."

THE KRATONS,
In their Hoop Rolling Novelty.
"HOOPLAND."

INTRODUCING THE FAMOUS
"LA DANSE NOIRE."
BY FRANZ LEHAR

THE PESHKOFF TROUPE.
Russian Dancers.

FIRST APPEARANCE IN ENGLAND

SYDNEY JAMES & Co.
Old English Pastoral Pot-Pourri.

THE SOUSLOFFS,
Whirlwind Dancers.

Mlle. Hortense Laugier.   M. Gustave Ricaux.
Mlle Fernande Cookin.   M. Albert Aveline.

RAY FORD,
Comedienne.

JACK LORIMER,
Scotch Comedian.

PREMIERE DANCERS
DIRECT FROM THE
GRAND OPERA, PARIS,
WILL PRESENT

JULIETTES' SEA LIONS.

BERT MARSDEN,
Mimetic Comedian.

DOLLY DENTON,
Comedienne.

I. Adagio Classique.   III. Danse Hongroise.
II. Variations Classique. IV. Czardas.

MALCOLM SCOTT,
"*The Woman who Knows.*"

"**KINEMACOLOR**"
(Animated Scenes in the Actual Tints of Nature.)
Zoological Gardens.

Arranged by M. Staats, Maître de Ballet de l'Opera, Paris.

"**URBANORA**" **BIOSCOPE.**
Aviation at Blackpool and Doncaster

SPECIAL ENGAGEMENT AND FIRST APPEARANCE IN VAUDEVILLE.

Mr. BEN DAVIES

IN SELECTIONS FROM HIS REPERTOIRE.

THE PALACE ORCHESTRA   CONDUCTOR—Mr. HERMAN FINCK.

PRICES.—RESERVED: Boxes, £1 1s. to £3 3s. ; Stalls, 7/6 & 5/- ; Royal Circle, 5/-.
UNRESERVED: Royal Circle, 3/- ; First Circle, 2/- ; Amphitheatre, 1/- ; Doors 7.45, commence at 8.

Matinee every Saturday, at 2 p.m.   Full Programme.   Reduced Prices.

ONE OF MY INNUMERABLE PALACE PROGRAMMES

moment I said they must have ten shillings of the money to spend in the bar. Still later it dawned on me that instead of profiting to the extent of a sovereign I lost half a crown on the deal!

I cannot, of course, name a tenth of all the artistes for whom I played at the Palace. To give you some idea of their number, I need only say that when I was looking out papers for use in writing this book, my wife produced a large cabin trunk packed tight with programmes from the Palace. In fact some day I might write another book from them!

Many artistes made successes and came time after time; some—George Alexander, then tremendously successful at the St. James's Theatre, for one—were failures; some almost failures.

Marie Lloyd was as nearly as possible a failure at the Palace. She was desperately keen to appear there, but when she did, the audiences did not like her songs. Marie was determined not to be beaten if she could help it; every night she tried something different, and one night she did the trick with a song (founded on a melody called "Narcissus," by the popular American composer Nevin) called, "There They Are":

> There they are,
>   The pair of them on their own;
> There they are,
>   Alone, alone, alone;
> They gave me half a crown
>   To go away and play—
> But umpty iddle-y, umpty-iddle-y,
>   Umpty-iddle-y-ay.

So successful was that song with the Palace audience that from that night Marie Lloyd could do what she liked and sing what she liked. She was a remarkable woman and a remarkable artiste, and, by the way, made all her own stage dresses. She wore some very elaborate ones, too.

One of my ideas was that in the programmes of a theatre of varieties, there should be included portions of operas or operettas, and when I suggested this to Sir Alfred Butt, he completely agreed with me. We did a potted version of *The Geisha* with some of the original cast in it; and other operatic things.

It was at that time that I first met Sir Alexander Mackenzie, and he referred to the matter in *A Musician's Narrative*, in which he said :

"In February of 1905 an attempt was made to stimulate an interest in operetta on the music-hall stage. *The Knights of the Road* (by Henry A. Lytton)—an unpretentious piece of the tuneful English type once in vogue—had the advantage of a cast including Walter Hyde (now one of the most distinguished operatic tenors), Leslie Stiles, Cairns James, with the invaluable assistance of my friend Herman Finck and his admirably trained orchestra, and ran for a month. If the venture did nothing else it induced King Edward and other members of the Royal Family successively to visit the Palace Theatre for the first time since ' Variety ' had replaced ' Opera.' "

We failed to create a permanent vogue for potted opera or operetta on the Music Hall stage, though there should have been plenty of demand for good new operettas as curtain-raisers. All shows started with a curtain-raiser at that time, and there was a splendid field for work in that line. Basil Hood and Walter Slaughter, for instance, were brought into prominence by the one-act plays, suitable for curtain-raisers, which they did together. One play which they wrote, *The French Maid*, ran for a year or more. Hood was amazingly successful as a very good imitator of Gilbert.

Looking back over my Palace days and nights, a number of animals come into my mind. First there was the smooth-haired terrier which belonged to Blake, the stage-door keeper. He was a wonderful dog; he would ask for pennies and go to the cat's meat stall by the side of the Shaftesbury Theatre. He never crossed Shaftesbury Avenue without looking both ways at the traffic, and he always brought his meat back intact to the Theatre. But it killed him in the end, poor chap; he no doubt had too much to eat, and he also developed copper poisoning from carrying so many pennies in his mouth.

Then there were the snakes. A dark-skinned girl danced with

these snakes twisted round her neck and body—a sight that gave me the shudders. When talking to her manager, an American, one day I asked: "How do you feed the snakes?"

"Only once a month," he replied. "You must come and see them fed."

I did not like the idea of seeing the snakes fed, but everyone else decided to go to see it, so they finally persuaded me to go with them. We met outside the Palace one Sunday morning. When the American arrived, he looked distrait and uncomfortable, and eventually said: "Say, I'm awful sorry to bring you all here for nothing, boys. But I can't feed those fellows to-day; live chickens are much too dear. They'll have to wait another month!"

A performing crocodile wanted to join my orchestra. A French naturalist brought a number of crocodiles in tanks, as a turn. They arrived on a Sunday and as their glass tank was broken they had to be kept in the green-room till Monday. Someone should write a poem starting: "A malodorous beast is the crocodile."

At the first performance the Frenchman got into his tank, by this time repaired, and waded about among the creatures, giving them smart raps on their noses to keep them in order and make them do his bidding, but presently one of them clambered out of the tank and began to shamble down-stage towards me. True I had a baton with which I might have hit it on the nose and put up a defence of myself, but, being unused to crocodiles, I was taking no risks, and I am not ashamed to say that what I did was to whistle down my tube for the curtain to be brought down. There was no *Nil(e) Desperandum* about me that evening, I can tell you!

An American came to the Palace with a performing dog, but without the right kind of music to fit the act. He was told that the music he had would not do, and that he must get something more appropriate, with the result that I went to talk things over with him at his hotel. We discussed some music which he asked me to arrange for him, and I was just going when he said: "Say, how much is it going to cost me?"

"My fee will be ten guineas," I said.

"Ten guineas!" exclaimed the American in horror. "Say, *maestro*, that's more than I paid for the dog!"

A monkey whose business was supposed to be to ride a bicycle started well, going round the stage on his little cycle, but when he reached a point in front of me he hopped off, jumped on to the wires in front of the footlights, and proceeded to leap and climb round the edge of the dress circle. People in the audience thought it was part of the act, but, of course, it was not, though the monkey repeated the same performance the next night. It was dangerous, naturally, and as the man who was running the show could not stop the monkey doing it, it was decided, after a consultation, that the chief electrician was the man to deal with the situation.

The electrician was asked to electrify the wire from which the monkey took off, and this was a success . . . the first time. The creature leapt back off the wire when he touched it and went back to his bicycle. But the following evening, such is the cunning of monkeys, he went to the very corner of the stage, took good care to dodge the hot wire, and sprang up to one of the stage boxes and so on to his favourite round of the dress circle. That turn was not re-booked after its first engagement.

Then there was the elephant who wanted a night out. He was the offspring of two of "Lockhart's Elephants" (old-time Music Hall goers will remember them), and it was his duty to accompany his parents and assist them on the stage in return for his home and his keep. When "Lockhart's Elephants" were on at the Palace, they were stabled close at hand, and every night they marched up through the back streets for their turn. But one night, when the father and mother elephants arrived at the stage door, Lockhart, who was waiting for them according to his custom, discovered that there was an elephant missing.

Now, you can't very well lose an elephant, and there was at once a great hue-and-cry and search. People ran in all directions to look for the wanderer and eventually the young fellow was found taking a walk along Wardour Street all by himself, gazing at life and people and things and terrifying the denizens of that

PÉLISSIER PLAYS

PÉLISSIER OFF DUTY

part of the world. They say that elephants never forget. But that elephant did forget that night—forgot his duty to his public.

Arrangements were made for me to go one Good Friday morning to Little Missenden, near Great Missenden (presumably mother and daughter), to see a collection of valuable violins. There were four in our party, including Jimmy Dunn and a solicitor, and we arrived at a beautiful old house in Little Missenden. We were shown in and then the butler said : " Mr. So-and-So is very busy just now, but he wishes me to ask you what you will have to drink."

It was then nearly midday, and a raw cold morning, so we all said we should like bottles of Bass.

The butler looked aghast. We had obviously committed a *faux pas ;* we hurriedly changed our minds and said we should like whisky and soda.

After we had been sipping whisky and soda and chatting for quite half an hour the door opened and into the room came a man with a thick mass of hair brushed smoothly back from his forehead, carpet slippers on his feet, and a face which looked as though someone had thrown a pot of strawberry jam at it.

Under each arm was a bottle of Bass and in his hands he held a corkscrew and a large glass. Apparently the butler had been aghast when we asked for Bass because his employer drank nothing else, and the man was in continual fear of a shortage.

Our host showed us all over his grounds, and very fine grounds they were ; but the most remarkable thing was a camouflaged gate, neatly set in a bush . . . as soon as you stepped through this gate you found you were well on your way to a public house. So we went in to have a drink, and found the slowest-witted publican I have ever seen.

I ordered, " Two Bass . . . one sherry . . . one gin-and-bitters . . . one whisky and soda."

" Steady . . . steady," said the publican, " I can't remember all that. Let's take it one at a time. . . . Now what was it ? "

At last we were served with our drinks, and then the publican turned to me and said : " How much ? "

"You must tell me that," I replied, "I don't even know how much you charge for things."

"Well, I can't count," said the publican in a voice of despair, and it was only after long cross-examination of the man that we found out how much we owed him.

Back we went into the baronial-hall-looking dining-room for lunch, which was followed by a game of cricket, early in the year though it was. Hour after hour went by without any sign of the fiddles, so after dinner I said: "What about the violins?" and was taken into a drawing-room where there was a case containing four or five violins of great value.

"I suppose you keep one in another case to play," I said—but he didn't. He said: "We must play something together." He picked up one of the violins worth at least £1000 and I sat down to the piano and eagerly awaited events. I expected a first-class rendering of something classical and was thankful for the knowledge of musical classics my father had given me, when, in answer to the question: "What are you going to play?" my host replied: "Oh, you know . . . you'll be able to follow."

But as soon as he took up his violin I could see that there was something wrong; he did not know how to hold it. And then—what an anti-climax in that setting and with that violin! —he started to play, none too surely, the then popular "Pas de Quatre," by Meyer Lutz, and followed it with one or two other light popular tunes.

At last I said I must be going.

"Would you like to take one of the violins?" asked my host.

"No, thank you," I replied.

"Any time you want to borrow them let me know," he said in parting—and I did. He lent them for a special performance by my violinists at the Palace.

Most of the big people of the theatre professed to despise "the Music Halls" in those days, but many of them were eventually lured to the Palace by the salaries paid. Beerbohm Tree finally came there in the short Kipling play *The Man Who Was*, in which he appeared as a kind of Caliban-like old Indian officer. For this sketch I conducted at the side of the stage, standing on a beer box, and Tree, who had an enormous sense of humour, tried to make me laugh at every show. He had to make his entrance leaning, as if three-parts dead, on the shoulders of two stalwart "soldiers." One of his jokes, unseen by the audience, was to raise himself to his full height—he stood over six feet—and balance himself on the shoulders of his two "soldier-supers" while waiting to make his entrance.

One general election night when all the audience was waiting to hear the results, I told the flunkeys who changed the item numbers at the side of the stage not to push the cards right in. The result was that the audience was surprised to see "ELECTION BY THE ORCHESTRA"—the "s" was hidden.

Talking of elections reminds me of a good story which was told by Col. Stanley Bell, his stage manager, of Beerbohm Tree and Lena Ashwell. It was in the days of the militant suffragettes and Miss Ashwell was very keen on the movement. Tree said to her one day: "But my dear lady, what is it that you women want?"

"We want respect," she said.

"Yes, but if you knock our hats off, how can we show you respect?" inquired Tree.

I frequently used the word "beer" as a generic term to describe liquid refreshment of any kind. When Tree finished his engagement at the Palace he gave me a glass and silver drinking vessel. "There, my dear Finck," he said, "is a little thing for refreshment purposes, for wine, or—as you would call it—beer."

"Ah," he went on as he handed me the tankard, "to what bass uses may we come."

Then came the revues. The first one at the Palace was called *The Palace Review*, for which George R. Sims wrote the words and I wrote the music. A newspaper was printed—more or less—on the stage at each performance. At the end, "newsboys" ran down the gangways with copies of this paper into which the latest news had been stamped.

No theatre has ever had a series of more brilliant revues than those staged at the Palace during the War years. I am sure that those who remember the two *Passing Shows* and *Bric-à-Brac* will agree with me.

When Arthur Playfair left a part in *The Passing Show of* 1914, the rôle was taken by the popular George Tully. Tully has a very good baritone voice but he never could be persuaded to sing on the stage. In this part, however, there was a duet called " The Optimist and the Pessimist." They were both in sentry boxes on opposite sides of the stage and in uniforms, including busbies. Nelson Keys sang the Pessimist.

Tully was afraid of singing with the orchestra, but I told him it was bound to be all right. At the beginning of the piece was a kind of " military murmur " which could be shortened or prolonged at will, so I said to George : " You start when you like. If you come in at the wrong place, I'll follow you." And we had to leave it at that until the performance.

The curtain went up. There stood the two " soldiers " in their busbies. I played the military murmur. Tully did not start. I went on playing the military murmur. Still he did not start. As the opening bars of the song were thus being turned into a serial, I realised there was something really wrong. Had he forgotten the words ? I tried to catch his eye ; that failed.

" He must be nervous," I thought. " He needs something to jog him out of that."

So, very distinctly, I called out : " *Now ! George !* "—and off he went at a tremendous pace !

It was curious that one of the most popular songs I ever composed (Arthur Wimperis wrote the words), " On Sunday I Walk Out with a Soldier," was prophetic—it was sung five months before War broke out. Gwennie Brogden was the singer, and it was extraordinary how the words fell in for recruiting purposes :

> On Sunday I walk with a soldier,
>   On Monday I'm taken by a Tar.
> On Tuesday I'm out with a baby boy scout,
>   On Wednesday a hussar.
> On Thursday I gang out wi' a Scottie,
>   On Friday, the captain of the crew—
> And on Saturday I'm willing,
>   If you'll only take the shilling,
> To make a man of every one of you.

Talking of the War reminds me of a discussion that was

going on one day about the German "Hymn of Hate." Someone turned to me and said: "What do you think, Herman?"

"Oh, I *am* Him of Eight," I replied. And so I was, for on the door of my room at the Palace was painted: "Mr. Finck. No. 8."

Those Palace revue nights were wonderful nights, and wonderful people were in the companies—Arthur Playfair, Nelson Keys (some people could not get on with "Bunch," but he and I were always friends), Elsie Janis and Basil Hallam. Later, when Sir Gerald du Maurier was producing *Pamela*, Owen Nares appeared. He had to sing with the chorus, and at one rehearsal I stopped the band and called out: "Louder! I can't hear a word."

Owen Nares looked distressed and came down and said insistently to me: "Herman, I am giving you the best I can. My singing voice is only a little one, you know."

I laughed. "My dear Owen," I said, "I wasn't talking to you. It's the chorus I can't hear!"

But to return to poor Basil Hallam: when he joined up he went into the balloon service, and on his first leave home from France he came to see me.

"I've come to say good-bye, Herman," he said.

"Good-bye till your next leave," I told him.

"No, good-bye," he said. "You will never see me again."

He had a premonition, poor chap.

When Elgar was having some of his music played at a charity matinée at the Palace, he appeared to doubt whether the orchestra would do it justice. He demanded two rehearsals. "I think you will find that the orchestra will do anything you want in one rehearsal," I said, "and a second one would have to be paid for specially."

They had one rehearsal; Elgar found his fears were not justified, and after the performance he wrote to me:

"I send you many thanks for arranging everything so pleasantly for me at the Theatre, and I shall be very grateful if you will convey to the gentlemen of the orchestra my warmest thanks for their very kind help yesterday; the playing was beautiful."

After that Elgar and I became very friendly, and one of the last letters he wrote, to Mackenzie, related that he had met me outside the Langham Hotel—and I had made him laugh.

At another charity matinée, a work by J. M. Barrie—*Reconstructing the Crime*—was given. A piece of perfect Barrie humour was in the conception of *Case V*. I reproduce an extract from the programme:

The STAGE *v.* SOCIETY

"No *Matinée* being complete nowadays without a performance by gifted society ladies, the following consented to appear and show how their titled sisters grace the stage:

> The DUCHESS D'ETHEL LEVEY
> The LADY VIOLET LORAINE
> The LADY GINA PALERME
> The LADY GWENDOLINE BROGDEN
> The LADY MADGE SAUNDERS
> The Hon. DOROTHY MINTO
> The Hon. PHYLLIS MONKMAN
> The Hon. MARIE BLANCHE

"The LADY MABEL RUSSELL has not been invited, but hopes to appear."

On the very next page was a dazzling list of titled women who were "lending their aid" by selling programmes!

When the late Will Rogers paid one of his occasional visits to London he met Nelson Keys and was eager to hear all the theatrical news of the town. "Bunch" began a recital and presently he said: "Oh, and Herman Finck, of the Palace, has gone to Drury Lane."

"*Of* the Palace?" said Will Rogers, "why he *was* the Palace."

One of Rogers's exaggerations, of course—but it is a fact that I went to the Palace Theatre when it was first opened in 1892 and that, as sub-conductor and conductor, I was there for thirty years.

If ever there was such a thing as a unique variety theatre, it was the Palace. It differed from the Empire and the Alhambra because people went there to see the show, not to promenade and it was totally different in character from the other great Music Halls of its day—the Tivoli, the Oxford and the Pavilion. It had a standing no other place had; to appear at the Palace set the seal on an artist's reputation.

Innumerable letters I have received, and still receive, show how the Palace was loved—yet, as a variety theatre, it was destroyed. Why?

CHAPTER IV

COMEDIANS AND COMEDIENNES

WHEN Morris Harvey first appeared on the stage—it was at the Palace—I " showed him the ropes " as he found everything strange in the theatre world. We soon became great friends and one day he said to me : " Isn't it funny that the first friend I make in my new business is the Musical Director, though I don't use any music in my performance ? "

" That's why ! " I replied.

Still, music-using or not, I have counted many comedians among my friends. Some can show humour on the stage ; some off the stage too ; and some (not among my friends) neither.

Morris Harvey likes a joke any time. He reminded me, when we met a few days ago, of one I cracked at his expense in his early days in the theatre. Morris started his career as a comedian by doing imitations of the popular actors of the day—men like Beerbohm Tree, Wyndham and so on. One day, apparently through some flaw in the organisation of the Palace programme, he had to follow immediately after another mimic—a woman mimic. He was standing on the side of the stage in order to be ready to make his appearance as soon as the woman mimic had finished her turn when the stage manager ordered him off the stage, because the woman objected to a rival mimic watching her performance.

A few moments after this had occurred, I happened to go back-stage, and Morris—feeling guilty of having unwittingly committed a breach of stage etiquette—came to tell me all about his troubles. I laughed. " Don't worry about her," I said. " I don't like any mimics, but at least you have seen some of the artistes you imitate."

One day I went to a funeral with Morris. As we entered the cemetery, Tom Miller said : " What a beautiful place, it looks like a park."

The occasion was solemn, but the temptation was too strong for me. " Yes, Hearse Park," I replied.

I remember the first time I saw Tom Miller at the Palace Theatre. He had left a firm of wine merchants to take the post of Secretary at the Palace, and when he arrived I was with the famous and inimitable Blake, the stage-door keeper. Blake, who had a curious high-pitched voice and always referred to me as " Ower Musical *Di*-rectorr," said to Tom Miller, " Meet, Mr. Finck, ower Musical *Di*-rectorr," and to me he said : " This is Mr. Miller, the new treasurer."

" Oh, the Miller of the L. S. Dee," I remarked. But Tom did not see the joke, and I was told recently that he still had not found anything to laugh at in my statement. Some day, I hope, he will come across that well-known song, " The Miller of the Dee," and then all will be clear.

Blake always had a serious grouse against something or somebody. The London County Council ranked high among his list of abominations; but, in solitary glory, far ahead of anything else, came the telephone system. He demanded a very high standard of service from the telephone service, and when he thought he was not receiving it, he expressed his opinion with some force. " What do you think I pay taxes for ? " I have heard him shout into the telephone. You would have thought he had to pay all the theatre's telephone subscription out of his own pocket !

Finally, there was a crisis ; the Post Office rebelled, and said very politely, but quite firmly : " If you don't take that man away from the telephone, we shall take the telephone away from the theatre." Since it would have been decidedly inconvenient for the Palace to have had its telephones cut off, the business of answering even occasional calls was removed from the list of Blake's duties.

Poor old Blake really had something to grumble about when the Palace was turned into a cinema, for the artistes had " looked after" him well in return for the hundred and one little things he could do for them. I went in to have a chat with him one morning after the change-over, and asked him how things were going. "Oh, not like the old days, Mr. Finck," he said mournfully.

"No," I replied, "all the people who used to give you tips are brought in in tins now!"

Blake was a great friend of mine; he would do anything for me. When a man who, in Blake's opinion, looked rather seedy, presented himself at the stage door and asked for me, Blake dealt with him firmly. "Go aw*ay*," he called out, "we don't want none of the likes of you coming round 'ere bothering ower musical *di*-rectorr. . . ."

The seedy-looking man had come to pay me £10 he had borrowed, and which I had long since considered to be a bad debt.

As saith the ancient proverb: "If God will protect me from my friends, I can protect myself from mine enemies."

Arthur Roberts was always my choice for a "Number One" comedian. If anyone objects that he belonged to days gone by and would not be a hit now, I will say that he was the "father" of many comedians who are, and have been, popular since him. I could—but I won't—mention the names of a dozen comedians who took him as their model. He knew it all. He could act, he could mime, he could sing, he could dance, he could gag—he had cracked the gag before you saw it coming—and he had the superlative quality of being able to hold the stage by himself.

Arthur Roberts talked fast and blinked his eyes as he talked, and I could go on for a very long time with stories about him. One of the quickest things he said was when *The Gay Lord Quex* was at the height of its great success, with John Hare in the leading part. It was suggested that Roberts should do a burlesque of it.

"Change my name from Roberts to Rabbits and imitate Hare, I suppose," he said.

Another very quick flash of his was when he was asked to do something at a charity affair during the Boer War.

"How about me selling photographs?" he suggested.

"Whose photographs?" someone asked.

"Lord Roberts' . . . signed by myself," he said.

One night a man who had not seen him for many years noticed Roberts among a group of people in a club. He walked up to him and exclaimed: "Good God! Arthur Roberts! You must be eighty."

"No, I mustn't," Arthur replied.

Arthur Roberts was the originator of the gag about the man who fell out of the gallery into the stalls one night.

"A terrible thing," said the theatre manager who was telling the story.

"Did he pay for his transfer ticket?" asked Arthur.

On December 10th each year we had an "Anniversary Night" at the Palace to commemorate its opening as a Music Hall. One of the people asked to perform (I didn't ask him) was Professor Cross the phrenologist from the Royal Aquarium, Westminster. Arthur Roberts was the star turn, and as he was not going on for some time he said he would go into the auditorium to watch the show.

"Cross will ask for people to come on to the stage for him to read their 'bumps,'" I said. "When he does, you come on. No one will recognise you in that big fur coat."

So when Cross asked for members of the audience for his demonstration, Arthur Roberts, his vast collar turned up round his face so that he was unrecognisable, came on with them. Cross duly demonstrated with several people, and then he came to Roberts.

Roberts sat down, opened his mouth, thrust his finger into it, and then, as though talking to a dentist, said: "It's this one . . . this one here . . . that's the one that hurts. Take it out."

The roar of laughter was so great that I had to ring for the curtain to be brought down.

Arthur was a past-master in the art of speaking spoof French. This art consists of pouring out a torrent of completely meaningless sounds; among the senseless syllables are a few names of French towns or odd French words, and the completed product is made to sound like rapidly spoken French. Arthur Roberts was doing this at a party one night, when the then Russian Ambassador heard him. The Ambassador listened for a few minutes, and then was heard to remark: "He is a wonderful linguist, Mr. Roberts. He speaks French with such facility ... but he talks so fast ... I cannot understand what he is saying."

The coolness with which Arthur would turn on his spoof French in front of even a Frenchman was amazing. I remember he tried it on M. Leopold Wenzel, then conductor at the Empire, who, after spending some twenty years in England spoke only a few words of English. Wenzel became more and more puzzled, and finally burst out: "Mistaire Roberts, it is extraordinary. You speek French so fluently, but I cannot hear a seengle word of what you say."

I wrote the music, and Arthur Binstead wrote the words for *The Cruise of the "Saucy Puss"*—a "new nautical protean absurdity" at the Empire, for which the programme announced:

CHARACTERS:

Skinyer (*a Steward*)	Mr. Arthur Roberts
The Uproarious Mrs. Hanquerry (*a Person*)	Mr. A Roberts
Baron Otto Von Seidlitzpowder, Limited (*a Natural Water Subject*)	Mr. Roberts
Mrs. Maggie McGlew (*a Sticker*)	Mr. Arthur Roberts
Mr. Twickenham Green (*an Ower*)	Mr. A. Roberts
Captain Kyd of the S.S. *Saucy Puss*	Mr. Roberts.

Chorus of Sailors, Syrens, Syphons, etc.

Willie Edouin was a comedian who could turn his hand to anything. He produced the play *Our Flat* which ran for more than a thousand nights and is still played. But that was nothing. He was equally ready to write a play—or paint the scenery, and he did all these things most skilfully. He could do everything.

One of the first big comedians I ever knew well was G. P. Huntley. Huntley was a Irishman with a very small mouth, who came of a clever theatrical family and had no idea of being a comedian in his younger days. He began as a character actor.

He and I came to know each other as youths, and we set about writing a comic song together. We received a guinea for it and all was very friendly until I found out that, behind my back, he was writing extra topical verses for our song and being paid half-crowns for them. When I taxed him with this he said: " Yes, but look what you make by doing the band parts of your music."

What I actually did receive was five shillings for an extra set of band parts.

Still, that little incident did not interrupt my lifelong friendship with this amazingly clever man. The " silly ass " voice which George Huntley used in some of his most successful musical comedy parts was entirely put on, and altogether he was a funny chap. When he went on tour in *The Circus Girl* he bought a couple of horses and took them round with him. " I suppose I ought to ride a horse in a piece about a circus," he said. But he never did ride one. All he did was to take his horses for rides.

Dan Leno and Alfred Lester were both rather sad-looking comedians. Each was brilliantly funny in his work and each had in him that streak of melancholy pathos—Chaplin has it too, and James Welch had it—which made you a little sorry for him.

Leno's elastic face and his antics always amused me, as did his sense of nonsense. At one Drury Lane pantomime he turned up with a mock love song called : " The Wasp and the Hard Boiled Egg," which he sang as if his heart were breaking. One verse of the song ran :

> But not one word said the hard-boiled egg,
>   The hard-boiled egg,
>   The hard-boiled egg,
> And what a silly insect was the wasp to beg,
> For you can't get any sense out of a hard-boiled egg.

Leno began as a clog dancer and became a number ten comedian (the star place in his days). In fact there was no one to touch him on the Music Hall stage, or at Drury Lane pantomime.

Alfred Lester was discovered by accident for the West End stage. When dear old Charles Morton was managing the Palace Theatre he had on his staff a tall gentleman named Fitzroy-Gardner whose jobs were many and various and who was short-sighted in one eye. One evening Morton told him to go to a South London Music Hall and to report upon some Japanese acrobats who were performing there. Whether Fitzroy-Gardner missed the turn or could not see it properly with his short-sighted eye, I do not know, but I do know that he came back and said that the Japanese acrobats were no good but that he had found a good comic. He was right; he had.

A queer fellow, Alfred Lester. . . . I liked him well. He had the smallest motor-car I have ever seen; it was constantly in danger of being trodden on by pedestrians who were crossing the road. It was so small that I could never accept his kind invitation to go for a ride because there was not room for the two of us in it. I christened it a " one-seater."

For some time he lived next door to a monastery. Once, when I called to see him there, he was looking very solemn and miserable and reading *The Era*. He liked reading and was always asking me to recommend him books. When I told him that he should read Compton Mackenzie's then " latest," *Poor Relations*, he lugubriously said: " Oh, something *sordid*, I suppose." Actually, I was recommending it to him because I thought it was so funny it might cheer him up.

George Graves, with his snuff and his stories, is one of the champion raconteurs among comedians of my acquaintance. He can always gather a crowd round him to listen to his " have-you-heard-this-one," and once when he was reeling them off in a club I tried to give him breathing space by telling one of my stories. I could see that he was not interested in a mere musician daring to be funny. He was thinking what his next one should be and so I said: " As I already know this story, and you are not listening to it, there is no need for me to tell it." But I did tell it, and—I know George Graves will forgive me—when I went into the same club next morning there he was, telling my story to a multitude which he had assembled to listen—and I had to listen as well!

It was George Graves who, talking to me about someone we both knew, remarked: " Although the man is rich, I think his methods are fishy."

" Yes, the Compleat Wangler," I replied.

I now want to tell two stories about actors who must be nameless. A man I knew once asked me if I could introduce him to a certain comedian whom he particularly wanted to meet. The meeting turned out badly, and when the comedian left us—without a smile—the man who had wanted to be introduced to him said, rather accusingly as if I were to blame: " I don't think he's very funny off the stage."

" He isn't very funny on it if it comes to that," I replied.

The second story is about a man who is a very good turn on the stage, but off the stage almost his sole topic of conversation is himself. He was at a variety theatre when I was conducting there, and he was so amusing on the stage that E. V. Lucas, Maurice Baring and one or two others who were in a box thought they would like to meet him. I received a note asking me if I would take him to the box they were in. I did so, and presently, out of the corner of my eye from my place in the orchestra, I saw that he had turned his chair round so that he was sitting with his back to the house, and was holding forth with all his power. I felt sorry for his victims, but equally sorry for myself when, as the evening had worn on, I was brought a note from the box begging me " for heaven's sake come and take away this bore you've brought us."

I wonder why so many people will persist in everlastingly talking about themselves ? To me, the art and charm of conversation is to talk about other people. A brilliant example of this understanding is to be found in Sir Seymour Hicks. Seymour is a great talker, but he never bores you; his mind is not centred upon himself—and he is a great comedian. Just as I rank Arthur Roberts as the finest comedian of his type, so do I rank Seymour Hicks as the finest of his. He is a spontaneous comedian.

Another is Leslie Henson; I should put him very high among comedians I have known, and I do not agree with the idea that he must always have a quantity of hats or stage props or someone on the stage to feed him if he is to be funny. I saw him once —I think it was in *Kissing Time* at the Winter Garden Theatre— sit on a cabin trunk by himself in the middle of the stage and sing a song that I thought was one of the most amusing things of its kind I have ever seen and heard. I should like to see how many comedians could be funny if they had to sit on a trunk.

Arthur Riscoe—who, by the way, is a very good amateur cartoonist, but can never get my moustache right—recently took a holiday on the Riviera, and while he was there penetrated to Monte Carlo's holy of holies—the baccarat room. A short time afterwards, while play was going on in a silence redolent of reverent concentration, a curious sound was heard in that august room. It was small to start with, something like a stormy sea beating a far-away beach; it swelled to the sound of a fleet of lorries rumbling along a rough road; then the air quivered, as with thunder. . . . The noise died away; then started again. Arthur's friends looked up in horror; then wished they were somewhere else. For Arthur, an expression of the utmost satisfaction on his features, was sitting in a chair with his head thrown well back, sleeping the sleep of the just-got-to-bed-by-breakfast-time.

In the days when Arthur Riscoe was being spanked for making other boys laugh at school, there had already appeared on the Music Hall stage a comedian named Du Calion known as " The Loquacious Laddy on the Ladder." Mounting his ladder and moving it about the stage—otherwise he would have lost his balance and fallen into the Orchestra—Du Calion would crack his topical jokes.

When the Palace was opened as a cinema, the management soon found that the attendances at films were nothing like so good as they had hoped they would be; they decided to intersperse the films with variety turns. As Du Calion had been very successful at the Palace when it was a Music Hall, he was engaged by the cinema management to do his turn. One afternoon, the attendance was even sparser than usual. Looking down from the height of his ladder at the stalls—not, in any case, the most popular seats when the Palace was a cinema—Du Calion could see only one man in the audience. He changed his usual style of address from " Ladies and Gentlemen " to " Dear Sir ! "

It would be very ungallant of me to write a chapter on comedians without speaking of the comediennes I have seen and known; even though I have already broken the rule of " ladies first." The first comediennes I saw on the stage were Mrs. John Wood, an enormous but very funny woman of the Marie Dresler type; and Fanny Brough, aunt of the brilliant Mary Brough who died not long ago. Nellie Wallace, of much later memory, has always amused me immensely.

It is surprising how many of our comediennes—as well as a few comedians—have started their careers in non-farcical parts. Ellis Jeffreys, when I first knew her, was a winsome and whimsical young actress in straight parts at the Haymarket; Muriel George was a lovely soprano who could sing all types of songs, serious and otherwise; Vera Pearce was a Principal Boy when I first met her in Glasgow. Connie Ediss and Sidney Fairbrother developed into comediennes after some time on the stage. Cicely Courtneidge was a graceful young person playing opposite her husband Jack Hulbert in plays produced by her father, Robert Courtneidge, at the Shaftesbury when I first knew her. (Among actors to whom the same thing has happened—besides Jack Hulbert, whom I have just mentioned —is Stanley Holloway : he used to take the part of an amorous baritone). Morris Harvey, when on the Stock Exchange, was an amateur actor of serious parts—but I know him too well to say any more about him.

The greatest comedienne of her time was Lottie Venne, who began her stage career as one of the " Sisters Lottie and Topsy Venne."

When Marie Dresler was appearing at the Palace I made, for her burlesque dances, one long tune of all the waltzes which were best known at that time, a medley which very much amused her. Although heavy, Marie was surprisingly agile; she would grab one of the rings on the edge of the moving curtain when she had to take her call, and would give the impression that she was being swung about in the air by the curtain. Audiences always loved that.

One day I went to the old Strand Theatre, which stood on the site of the present Aldwych tube station, with Milly Lindon, who afterwards married Sir Edward Hulton. It was during the run of *The Chinese Honeymoon* in which Louie Freer was the leading comedienne. Louie sometimes became very excited and then was liable not to notice what she was doing. That day was one of those occasions. She came on to the stage and sang her song with great gusto—to the backcloth! As she stood singing away with her back to the audience, everyone roared with laughter, naturally thinking it was part of the programme. I heard one man near me say, between guffaws: " Whatever will these theatrical people be up to next ? "

Violet Loraine sang in a piece called *Round the Map*, for which I wrote the music, at the Alhambra; she was especially good in a song named " Here Comes Tootsie " in that show.

I had a friend who looked just like Mr. Pickwick complete with bald head; he was a planter from Jamaica, but spent a considerable amount of his time in London. One night he came up to my room at the Palace when Vi Loraine was there. She was very anxious to know how old my friend was, but every time she asked him he replied in his curious hesitating way: " Eight-y, dear-ie."

At last he said: " If you will give me a kiss, I'll tell you how old I am."

Vi Loraine kissed him, and then asked: " *Now*, how old are you ? "

" Eight-y, dear-ie," he replied—and everyone laughed. Actually I think he was about sixty-four at that time. He was wont to remark of himself: " Wal-ter Loves the Bran-dy " with such a curious rhythm that I went to the piano and played the famous " Il Bacio " waltz which exactly fitted the rhythm of the sentence.

Bobby Howes was in *Song of the Drum* which I wrote with Vivian Ellis, and I conducted a piece called *Mary* in which Ralph Lynn and Evelyn Laye appeared; Stanley Lupino and Elsie Janis were in *Hello America* at the Palace, but of these I have more to say later.

Joe Coyne, who made such an amazing success in the *Merry Widow* with lovely and equally successful Lily Elsie, was at a party given by Anthony Prinsep at his Regent's Park home, to welcome Edmund Gwenn's return from America. I was one of the guests. Arthur Wimperis and Leslie Henson were both there. After supper we went upstairs to the drawing-room and someone started a gramophone. There was a parquet floor and Joe Coyne, lithe, active and ever young, began to dance, holding an imaginary Lily Elsie in his arms as he floated round the floor. I noticed some " bones " on the top of the piano; after a time when the gramophone began to play a Spanish tango, Joe picked these up and used them as castanets, and most skilfully. He had learned to use the " bones " as a young man when he was in a " nigger minstrel " troupe in America and can still play them perfectly.

George Robey, Billy Merson, Lupino Lane, Nelson Keys, Péllisier, and so many more of my friends . . . a procession of comedians pass in front of my mind.

Robey—now there is a great and generous man. Think of his charity in the War years and at other times. I remember at one charity performance the stage manager said to him : " When would you like to go on, Mr. Robey ? " The reply was characteristic of the man : " Oh, put me on when you like—I'm here for the evening." And that from a man who can command almost any money in reason that he likes to ask. . . .

I remember once conducting at a charity show at which he was one of the stars and the auctioneer, from the stage, of all manner of things to be sold for charity. It was growing very late, and members of the orchestra were beginning to slip out, one by one, to catch trains. I had visions of having no one left to play " The King," and so, to hurry things up, I " jumped " a bid from a few guineas up to " eighty-five pounds " for a picture which no one seemed to want. No particular harm was done—I was not called upon for the eighty-five pounds—and we got the curtain down in time.

My chief experience with Jack Hulbert was when we did a show in Paris in which he appeared with Regine Flory, Leon Morton, the French comedian who was in several C. B. Cochran shows with Delysia and others.

Jack, then not quite so important as he is now, had a top-hat dance to rehearse, but every time he tried to do it someone else got in front of him to do their bit. For hour after hour he kept on trying to slip his dance in, asking me: "I say, can I rehearse my dance now?" till at last I said to him: "Only if we get away from here and go to the Café de Paris."

Stanley Lupino came to the Palace in *Hello America*. He came on in the first scene to sing "Percy of Peckham," but once on the stage he could not remember the words. I made the band play as loud as possible, the chorus sang their hearts out and Lupino did one of his dancing or Leap-ino turns—so no one in the audience realised that there was anything wrong with the scene.

It may sound silly for a man to forget a thing which he has rehearsed until he apparently knows it inside out. But actually no man ever knows when he may not forget the words in front of an audience. W. S. Penley, who played in *Charlie's Aunt*, took the lead in *The Private Secretary*, an enormously successful piece—it is still played to delighted audiences in various parts of the country—which was adapted from a German original by Charles Hawtrey. After playing the part of the curate for a thousand nights, Penley arrived at the theatre on the thousand and first night to find that he had forgotten the words!

Harry Tate tells a story I like very much. It is this. A man walking along the street ran into a friend who owed him £5. There was no chance for the debtor to pretend he had not seen the other man. So he said: "My dear boy, I owe you five pounds and an apology. Please accept the apology now." Exit, hurriedly.

One Sunday, when I was at Brighton, Harry Tate came round to the Bedford Hotel, where I was staying, and announced that

I must let him drive me to his cottage at Kemp Town, not far away. Harry then went away to fetch his motor-car, and did not return. After a long wait I went to find him. He was in the roadway, in the middle of a crowd, and when I penetrated the throng I found him and several assistants, with bits of motor-car lying about, doing a real-life version of his famous sketch *Motoring*—watched by the inevitable boy! I am sure some of the people watching must have thought that Harry was giving a performance in the street (for reasons unknown). The real thing was too much like the imitation to be true.

However, at last the car started and we drove to Harry's home He was soon telling me how much he enjoyed fishing in the neighbourhood.

" Yes," I said, " you talk about fishing, but what do you ever catch ? "

" Oh, all sorts of things," he replied. " Why take this morning. At first we thought we had caught a shark; then we were sure it must be whale—and finally it turned out to be a door off a yacht that had been wrecked.

" If only I'd caught a yacht I would have put a door on it myself."

Harry Randall, the comic singer who died some two years ago, lost his nerve when his wife died and could not go on the stage. It was when he was still in a highly nervous state, that the great Silvertown explosion—it was like an earthquake—occurred. Randall was having lunch with Harry Tate. He dropped his knife and grabbed a chair in one hand and a fork in the other—and rushed out of the restaurant into the street.

Harry Tate, very bewildered, followed him. " What on earth are you standing there for, holding a chair in one hand and a fork in the other ? " Tate asked.

" Oh, am I ? " exclaimed Randall, putting down the chair and looking rather foolish. " I had no idea I had picked them up."

A curious thing about comedies is that nobody ever knows who wrote the music or the words. This subject cropped up in a conversation with a friend, during the run of *The Merry*

Widow at Daly's, as we were on our way to lunch at what was then the Cavour Restaurant.

"You don't know who wrote the music of *The Merry Widow*," I said, "and practically no one else does. As we pass through Leicester Square near to Daly's I'll stop fifty people and ask them, and none of them will know."

Just then we passed the stage door of Daly's and a man I knew to be an official of the theatre was standing outside. I went up to him and said: "The name of the man who wrote the music to *The Merry Widow* has slipped my memory . . . what on earth is it?"

There was a long pause . . . the man looked very uncomfortable, coughed and then said: "I'm afraid I can't call it to mind."

The play had then been running for eighteen months.

As we walked away I said to my companion: "Since the man who works in the theatre doesn't know who wrote the play, I don't think I need bother to question the other forty-nine people I said I would ask!"

CHAPTER V

TEN YEARS AT DRURY LANE

THE whirligig of time plays strange pranks. When I was a boy of about sixteen I played in the orchestra at Drury Lane and forty or so years afterwards I returned there as conductor of the orchestra. It was when Sir Alfred Butt took over Drury Lane and largely rebuilt it; he took practically the whole of the staff he had had at the Palace to Drury Lane with him, and some of them are still working there. Before going to Drury Lane, however, we had had a season at the Queen's Theatre with that very tuneful American play called *Mary*.

Evelyn Laye was in *Mary* with Ralph Lynn, whose spontaneous humour I have always very much admired. During one scene he sat on a garden seat and made love to Evelyn Laye. When he was just going to sit down one night he pretended to catch his finger between the bars of the back of the seat (there was actually room for him to put his fist through if he wanted to). The audience was vastly amused by Lynn's contortions before he "freed" himself to go on with the love scene, and next night I watched particularly for that moment. To my great surprise he did not repeat it, and afterwards I said to him: "Why didn't you do the garden seat gag again?"

"Garden seat gag?"

"Yes, when you pretended to catch your finger in the woodwork."

Lynn took out his monocle and put it back again.

"Really? Really? Did I do that? I don't remember it." After that he did it at every performance.

Which is, I think, a very good proof of how spontaneous Lynn's humour is.

The show *Mary* was financed by a man named Morgan who persisted in having drinks in the bar upstairs instead of the usual one. He constantly sent messages to me asking me to go to see him in this upstairs bar after the first act. By the time I had climbed up all those stairs I had to turn round and come down for the opening of the second act. So at last when one of Morgan's messages arrived, I replied: "No, no. I can't go up all those stairs. That bar's too Morgan-attic."

I had nearly ten years "in the chair" at the Lane, and, in some ways, they were the most interesting in my Melodious Memories. After all, there is no theatre in England quite like Drury Lane, with its history and its tradition, and with *Rose Marie*, *The Desert Song*, *Decameron Nights*, *Show Boat*, a Pantomime and a very fine *A Midsummer Night's Dream* production coming into my years there they were bound to be memorable.

I wrote a "blues" number ("Indigo Blues" I called it), and also a waltz for a play called *London Life*, by Arnold Bennett and E. Knoblock—which reminds me of a story. I don't know if it is against me or against my wife. When we reached home after the first performance, she said: "I liked that waltz you played in the *entr'acte*."

"You mean this one," I said, going to the piano and playing it.

"Yes," she agreed. "It's very good . . . who wrote it?"

"I did," I said, inwardly flattered.

"Oh," she remarked disappointedly, and promptly let the matter drop. Just like a wife. . . .

Solly Joel, the famous financier and race-horse owner, was the chief shareholder at Drury Lane when I was there, and a replica of the bathing-pool at his country house formed the scenery for the first scene of *Good Luck*, which was produced by Arthur Collins, and written by Seymour Hicks and Ian Hay.

Good Luck was a very elaborate production, with all the old ingredients of a spectacular play. There was a shipwreck; there was a fire in a prison, complete with escape of convicts; and, above all, there was the big scene at the Derby. The stage in this part of the play was a representation of the paddock at Epsom. Then, at a signal, up went the curtain to reveal, at the back of the stage, the race being run. This was a most sensational spectacle as real horses were actually running, but they were running on rollers so they did not hurtle from one side of the theatre to the other in a split second.

On one occasion the employee whose duty it was to see to the matter, rang the wrong bell. So instead of the big Derby scene being disclosed, the front curtain came down. Rollers went round as the horses ran over them; we could hear the " crowd " shouting in excitement as the climax of the race was reached—but we could see nothing !

By the law of natural cussedness, three hundred people had come all the way from Scotland, especially to see the Derby scene, that day.

Talking of *Good Luck* reminds me of my only appearance on a racecourse. A friend, a great racing man, arrived at my house with his wife—and a motor-car—one morning about 9.30, and said to my wife and elder daughter: " Would you like to go to Ascot to-day ? "

I was sitting peacefully in my study, hard at work, but it was decided that I must go to Ascot too. I tried to start a rebellion, but my friends and the family joined forces to crush it mercilessly, and I received orders to array myself suitably and sally forth. Defeated, though unbroken in spirit, I climbed into clothes proper for the occasion, still thinking rebelliously of the peace of my study.

My friend had lunch and champagne in his motor-car, and we had a pleasant meal on the way, arriving at Ascot in time for the first race, which was about 1.30.

We were given race-cards, which seemed puzzling things to me, and my friend said : " What would you like to back, Mrs. Finck ? "

My wife studied the race-card, and then said : " I've got a horse."

" What would you like to have on it ? " asked our host.

" Oh, five shillings."

" And which horse is it ? "

" Copyright."

Our host looked serious. "Excuse me, Mrs. Finck," he said, "but I know something about racing, and I really think you would be throwing your money away...."

Still my wife persisted in her choice, and my friend said to me: "You go and put the money on."

"Where?" I asked.

"With that bookie."

I took one look at the book-maker—a horrible face and roaring voice, a brass plate and a bag attached to his huge carcass—and decided I didn't like the idea of doing business with him. I struck; so my friend put the money on—and Copyright won!

Our host, rather shaken, said: "Tell me, Mrs. Finck, why did you back that horse?"

"Oh, my husband being a writer of music has had such a lot to do with questions of copyright, I felt sure it would win," my wife replied.

Shortly after this, we saw a friend of mine named Purfoy (a great authority in the racing world), a charming man, and my host suggested I should ask him for some advice. I started a conversation with Purfoy, and soon he said: "Well, what do you think of things to-day?"

As I had by this time lost my race-card, I did not even know the names of any of the horses, so I replied:

"Well, what do you think?"

He told me the name of a horse—I have forgotten what it was—and I reported to my host what Purfoy advised. And, sure enough, the horse won.

Before long I was so tired of the racing that I went to listen to a band which was playing a short distance away, and after that I read a book which I had wisely brought down with me.

I was then conducting at the Queen's Theatre, and I said I should have to be going back to town, but I left my wife and daughter to return later with our friends.

As I was walking away, I met Frank Curzon, the famous and popular racehorse owner and producer of many successful plays. "Hello, Herman old boy. Come and have a drink," he said, and led me into his box.

Then one of those terrifying technical conversations started. " What do you think of it ? " I was asked. " It " was the last race, and there were only about four horses running.

" Oh, I don't know," I replied cautiously, and hoping that I sounded as though I was weighing my judgment carefully.

" Well, that's the one that's going to win," said Curzon indicating a name on his race-card.

All his friends in the box decided to put " fivers " on the horse, but I kept my bet down to a pound—unfortunately for me, as it turned out, for the horse we backed won.

Then I was driven back to town, and I was in the theatre in time. My family were very surprised to find that I had backed another winner when they thought I was in the train coming back to London.

My host that day was, like me, a member of the Constitutional Club, and on one big racing day he walked into the lounge of the club, took one look at me and turned round and ran out of the room, apparently aghast at the sight of me. Before long he was back again, and said : " I must give some explanation for the extraordinary way I behaved. All the morning I had been trying to make up my mind what to back, but I could not decide. Then I saw you, and I thought : ' Herman . . . funny stories . . . Humorist.' " So I popped out to send a wire (he always betted by telegram) putting something on."

And Humorist won !

One of my favourite racing stories was in a Charlot revue sketch played by Nelson Keys. The Clerk of the Course at Ascot was back in London the day after the meeting ended. He was sitting in his chair, taking things easy, and feeling he deserved a little peace and quiet, when his telephone bell rang.

" Is that the Clerk of the Course at Ascot ? " asked a slightly thick voice.

" Yes, it is."

" Do you mind telling me when the next meeting at Ascot will be ? "

" There isn't another one until next year."

" Oh, I see."

And the unknown stranger rang off.

A little later, the telephone bell rang again.

" Ish that the Clerk of the Coursh at Ashcot ? " asked the same voice as before, only now it was a little thicker.

" Yes, it is."

" D'you mind telling me when the next meeting at Ashcot will be ? "

" There isn't another one until next year."

" Oh, I shee."

Another interval. Then for the third time the telephone bell rang. Wearily the Clerk of the Course stretched out his hand and lifted the receiver.

The familiar voice drawled : " Ish that the (hic) Clerk of the Coursh at Ashcot ? "

" Yes, it is."

" D'you mind (hic) telling me (hic) when the . . . the nexsht meeting at Ashcot will be ? "

" There isn't another one until next year."

" Oh, I shee . . ."

" And do you mind telling me why you keep on ringing up to ask when the next meeting at Ascot will be ? "

" 'Cos I'm locked in the bar ! "

In *Good Luck* at Drury Lane they originally cast Teddy Gwenn for a Hebrew bookmaker. He is, of course, one of the best and most versatile actors we have, but he jibbed.

" I have never played a Jew, and I can't play one," he insisted. So he was allowed to play the part as a Cockney. (Incidentally Teddy may have played Shylock—but then Shylock was not a bookmaker.)

Apropos of this : Maurice Moscovitch, the great Jewish actor who played the lead in *Angelo*—which preceded *Good Luck* at Drury Lane—was one of the nicest and most generous men I have ever come across in the theatre. Arthur Collins and I went to Berlin to see the play (nearly every London manager had turned it down before we saw it) and Moscovitch met us at the great Adlon Hotel—" Grand Hotel " of Vicki Baum's best seller, I believe.

He wanted to spend his money right and left on us, and when I expostulated, he gave an odd reason for wishing to spend so lavishly. " I am generous because I am poor, you see," he said.

Angelo was, I think, the most difficult piece I have ever had to conduct. The orchestra was hidden away under the stage and it was part of my job to press all sorts of electric bells at certain music cues and so produce effects on the stage. At one cue I had to press three bells simultaneously, while conducting with the other hand. I could never see what was happening, and I never could see the audience. Neither could anyone else, for that matter: *Angelo*—to use the technical theatrical expression invented by Rutland Barrington after he had produced *Brantringham Hall,* one of Gilbert's few failures—" failed to attract," and there was hardly ever any audience for it. But I must say I was very conscientious as a bell-pusher.

When Dennis King was in *The Three Musketeers* he and other actors with leading rôles used to fight with tremendous vigour the battles of the seventeenth-century swashbucklers. In fact they put more energy into it than the swords were made to stand. One night a sword broke, and the end of it whizzed over my head and landed in the lap of a lady sitting in the stalls.

She did not give it back, and for days we thought she was preserving it as evidence in an action for damages—though she was not hurt, it was feared she might rake up some grounds for action like shock preventing her from working or necessitating medical treatment.

Eventually, however, we found that we had gravely misjudged the lady, for she wrote a very good-humoured letter, saying that she would like to keep the broken sword as a memento, if nobody minded.

Another night, one of the swords broke, and a piece fell into the orchestra. I used it as a pipe-cleaner.

Decameron Nights, for which I wrote the music, was a lovely production, with a particularly beautiful organ effect in it. The organ was played in a supposed monastery, and for the organist we employed a man on the staff at Drury Lane. He was a fine player, and a most sober and efficient person in every way.

Imagine my horror, then, when one night I heard the most terrible sounds coming from the organ—dreadful noises that began to make the audience titter. There was only one thing to be done—and I did it. I drowned the organ by the orchestra. Still, I was very angry, and as soon as I possibly could I left my conductor's "chair" and went round to the back. There I found our organist looking in a terrible state of contrition and trying to explain things.

"How dare you behave like this?" I demanded. "You ruined the whole scene with those disgusting sounds. Are you drunk, or what is the matter with you?"

When he could get a word in, the organist explained: "Please, it wasn't me."

Somehow, talking with someone, he had missed his cue, and a stage hand, seeing that there was no one to play the organ, had jumped into the breach and tried his hand at it. This stage hand was an ambitious musician who had a harmonium at home and was fond of playing it to his wife on Sunday afternoons. But vaulting ambition o'er-pedalled itself at Drury Lane that night.

Margaret ("Bunny") Bannerman played the heroine in *Decameron Nights*, and I think it is now long enough ago to tell that in the scene in which she was supposed to have been washed up on the shore from a shipwreck she wore no clothes at all—no tights, no nothing. The scene was dimly lit, and the whole stage was cleared for it, no one being allowed in the wings or at the back during it. The only other person allowed on the stage was a very aged man, whose job it was to "rescue" Miss Bannerman, wrapping her up and carrying her off.

One of those sound experienced old actors who can play anything, and play it well—he had been in America for many years—had a minor part (in fact two minor parts) in *Decameron Nights*. He was over seventy at the time, but only died recently. This man appeared in the first scene, and then did not come on again until the last scene, some three hours later, when he played a different character.

As soon as the first scene finished, he would take off all his make-up and go out to meet his friends in the neighbouring hostelries. He would return to the theatre later, put on a most elaborate make-up and costume, and appear in the last scene as an Eastern potentate. He had a long speech to make, and sometimes when he had had a particularly strenuous evening with his friends it was a surprise to me that he went through his speech. But he always did so, without the slightest slip.

Basil Dean's production of *A Midsummer Night's Dream* was a great one. It showed how people will flock to see Shakespeare if it is done in a grand, attractive manner. We used Mendelssohn's music, and Fokine, the famous Russian dancer and choreographer, and I had a great argument about the tempo of one of the dances—that is, the scherzo arranged as a dance of fairies. He said that I took it too quickly and that he could not fit in his steps; I said that I had known it since I was a boy and that he would have to speed up his dancing. Finally, we got a metronome to decide which of us was right. The metronome was on my side, and metronomes (unlike photographs) never lie.

(Incidentally, I am often appalled at the way in which the finest classical music is carved up, speeded up or slowed down for dances on the stage. It seems disgraceful to me, and were the composers alive it would never be permitted.) In my experience of ballet, of which I conducted so much at the Palace, it is always a question of changing the music, changing the scenery, but never changing the steps.

More Mendelssohn. In one scene the famous Nocturne went on for seven or eight minutes, during which time Edith Evans, Athene Seyler, Frank Vosper and Ian Hunter had to remain huddled on the stage. It was an ordeal for them, and they used to wriggle about and do their best to try to prevent themselves from laughing. They all tried to make me shorten the music, but I said: "No, Mendelssohn must not be cut." I am surprised that some of them did not cut me.

When the run of *A Midsummer Night's Dream* finished, Basil Dean wrote to me:

"I have been saving up for myself the great pleasure of chatting with you after the last night of our joint production of *The Dream*, of having a drink or two, and building castles in the air for the future. That, alas! is not to be and, as I have to leave for America on Wednesday, I cannot refrain from thanking you once more for your invaluable help, for the many delightful times we had together in the work of rehearsal; in fact for an altogether delightful experience."

The great show of my time at the Lane was, of course, *Rose Marie*. It ran for so long that for two years there was no pantomime; both the *Desert Song* and *Good Luck* also ran over a pantomime season, for there was no object in taking off a successful play to put on a pantomime which, in any case, would only run for a short time.

On the opening night of *Rose Marie* Oscar Hammerstein II, descendant of the man who built the Stoll Opera House in Kingsway, who was the composer of the play, sent me a telegram: "If you are as good a conductor as you are a comic, this play will run two years." It did; it ran two years and one week.

I have very happy memories of *Rose Marie*. Edith Day was one of the most delightful people I have ever worked with, and Billy Merson used to amuse me immensely as "hard-boiled Herman." He was—and so was I, sometimes.

We had one very big laugh during the rehearsals. Felix Edwardes, who produced the piece for London, never would take off his hat. He wore it for weeks, and all of the company (who did not know) wondered if he had a mane under it, or no hair at all. One day he wanted to show Derek Oldham how he thought that he—Oldham, that is—should take off his hat to a lady. He demonstrated, and in the demonstration off came his hat for the first and only time. He was completely bald. The whole company burst into roars of laughter. They had been waiting for that laugh.

Edith Day has a wonderful range of notes, both soprano and contralto quality, is a first-class dancer and actress, and a very delightful person. When I arrived home one day recently, my wife told me that Edith Day had rung me up about one or two of my songs she was singing at the B.B.C., and would be ringing up again. A few minutes later the telephone bell rang. I went to answer it; it was not Edith Day; I returned to the drawing-room. Within the next half-hour the telephone bell rang four times and each time I walked from the drawing-room to my study thinking that it was the expected call. No sooner had I settled down to my tea again than the telephone bell rang once more. "Oh, dear," I said, "I am having an Edith Day."

Derek Oldham, a Lancastrian, had a saying that I have always remembered. When he could not get something quite right at a rehearsal he remarked: "I know it's wrong—and if you know it's wrong it must be wrong." Which is pretty good philosophy, I think.

Only two people connected with *Rose Marie* went through every performance of it. One was a male chorister, and the other was my drummer, Jackson.

Jackson, who is very versatile—he can draw caricatures, build or paint scenery—is an exceptionally good-looking man. He was always very well dressed too, and, as drummer, was the only person in the orchestra who stood up in view of the audience—except the conductor. I used to tell Jackson that his appearance was so Savile Row that he made me dress better than I should otherwise have done. Recently Jackson was with me in *Merrie England* at the Prince's Theatre; time has been kind to his appearance—I told him not long ago that he looked younger than his own son.

Although he was so well dressed, there was nothing foppish about Jackson; he just had natural good taste with clothes, and unconsciously wore them well. In that he differed from a number of people I have met. One was a conductor who thought more about clothes than about music. I was at his theatre one night when he came towards me, looking a "deuce of a swell," in a new suit of tails and with seals dangling at his waist.

"What you think of the cut of this coat?" he asked.

"A perfect fit," I replied. "By the way, are those *performing* seals?"

One day I had had lunch with a double-bass player who, though he did not earn a large salary, was always extremely well dressed. He had evidently been hoping that I should make some complimentary remark about his clothes, but I did not do so, and eventually he said: "You may have noticed that I have a new suit on . . . what do you think of it?"

"Oh, quite a good fit," I said.

"I will walk ahead," he went on, "and then you can look at the cut of the shoulders."

That was too much for me, and as he stalked on in front I slipped across the road, and went into a shop. From there I watched him swanking self-consciously along, waiting for me to rejoin him and tell him how magnificent the shoulders of his coat were. As I did not rejoin him, he swung round—and found I was not there. It made him look such an ass that he never forgave me.

This handsome double-bass player was rather like the young man who, in the days when men habitually wore rings, had just obtained his first. He was dining out that night, and was completely preoccupied with his new ring; he thought everyone must be, or ought to be, admiring his ring, and hoped they would pass complimentary remarks. He went on hoping all through the dinner, but however much he flashed the ring about, no one took the slightest notice. Eventually, leaning his elbow on the table, and holding up the finger with the ring on it, he remarked: "Ah-h-h . . . surprising the *warmth* there is in a ring!"

The late Mr. Bradley, of Pope and Bradley, the tailors, was a very serious-minded man, and wrote books and plays. One of his plays was produced at the Royalty, and a number of the daily paper critics were somewhat outspoken about its defects. I met Mr. Bradley shortly afterwards and found him very disappointed about the reception which the critics had given to his play. "Ah, well," I said, "I shouldn't worry about the things that were said in such papers as *The Times* and the *Daily Telegraph*. . . . I am sure you will have good notices in the Trouser Press!"

Another day someone referring to Mr. Bradley said to me: "Do you know he's a spiritualist?"

"Yes," I replied, "a be-spook tailor."

However, back to Drury Lane. The successor to *Rose Marie* was *The Desert Song*. It was composed by Sigmund Romberg, and his idea was to have two harps in the orchestra. Nothing else mattered so much to him as the two harps, and he pestered our lives out about them—harped on the subject, in fact. Harpists are expensive, and when I asked him why he was so keen to have two harps in the orchestra, he replied: "Well, they look so nice." The harpists were the only women in the orchestra.

Still, Romberg's two harps did make more music than did Cedric Hardwicke's violin in *Show Boat*. Hardwicke is no violinist, and in that play all he did was to go through the motions of playing a violin on the stage, while someone else played the instrument off stage. The danger about faking of this sort is that the person who is pretending to play may not synchronise his movements with the music. In this case it was done splendidly by Cedric Hardwicke. But then, he is a splendid actor.

At the dress rehearsal of *Show Boat*, Sir Alfred Butt said: "We are not going to stop for anything. We must go straight through with it, whatever happens."

The opening chorus started, but within a few minutes something had gone wrong, and a voice shouted, "Stop," and then, "Peter!" But the man called Peter had to play another part later in the play and had gone off to change. There was a delay while he put on his original costume and hurried back on to the stage so that the faulty passage could be gone through again. As soon as he had finished his appearance he began to change again. Once more something went wrong, and there was a cry of "Peter"—for it was impossible to rehearse this scene without him. A new delay—and the same thing happened all over again. In fact, it happened four times. At the fourth shout of "Peter!" I turned to the people near to me and said: "Peter? They ought to call him repeater." There was a burst of laughter, and the people who were farther away from us crowded down to find out what the joke was. They had to be told; they laughed—and the confusion was worse than ever. Altogether, twenty minutes was lost—and we were supposed to be " stopping for nothing."

When Paul Robeson was singing " Ole Man River " in *Show Boat*, I suggested to Sir Alfred Butt that we were not making the use of his talents that we might, and that it would be a good idea to give afternoon concerts of his songs. This was done—and was an enormous success, Robeson singing sad spirituals very well indeed, of course.

During the first Robeson concert an old lady sitting in the front row of the stalls came over, tapped me on the shoulder, and said, " Do you mind asking him to sing ' Poor Old Joe ' ? "

" No, I'm afraid we cannot change the programme," I replied.

That afternoon we played Dvorak's famous symphony, " The New World," which is partially founded on tunes the composer heard in America, and Coleridge Taylor's " Danse Nègre."

A little later the old lady from the front-row stall again tapped me on the shoulder and said : " Do you think he would sing ' Swanee River ' ? " Again I told her that I regretted that we could not change the programme for her; but twice after that she came to me with requests.

I told Robeson about the old lady and her requests afterwards, and he said, " I will sing the four songs she wants at my next concerts."

So I arranged them for the orchestra, and Robeson sang two at the next matinée and two at the one after that. But we never saw the old lady again !

Several years after this, Robeson came up to me in the Café Royal one night and said : " Well, Mr. Finck, now I do so many recitals I want to thank you for suggesting my first one."

If I had been an agent I should have collected ten per cent !

During the run of *Show Boat* I used to hear a tremendous amount from Robeson about " my boy." Robeson was very wrapped up in his little son and one day the lad came up to the theatre, and was duly brought in to see me—Robeson's room at Drury Lane was then next to mine.

Soon after I had gone down to the orchestra Robeson came through to me on the telephone in a terrible state of distress. " O, where's my boy ? " he said, in his drawling rather plaintive voice. " I've lost my boy . . . I've lost my boy."

" The last time I saw him he was walking towards the door of your room," I said. " Wait a minute and I'll come up to you."

I left the orchestra and went up to my room. As I was looking round wondering where on earth the child could be, I heard a slight rustling sound as of someone moving. It seemed to come from under the table : I looked—and there was young Robeson in the waste-paper basket !

During the run of *Show Boat*, I took Charles La Trobe, of the Theatre Royal, Haymarket, into the orchestra with me, as there was no room in front. Why, I don't know, but the orchestra thought that a distinguished musician was in their midst. Those nearest rose and bowed. La Trobe bowed and was offered a seat (complete with cushion) by the leader of the orchestra, on my right hand. La Trobe alleges that I hit him over the head more than once with my baton during the act. We adjourned to my room for the interval, and the bowing was repeated when we entered the orchestra for Act 2. I was most puzzled, and asked the leader of the orchestra what was the reason for all the bowing.

" The distinguished guest," he murmured.

" Ah," I said impressively.

" What's his name ? " whispered the leader of the orchestra.

" He would rather remain incognito," I whispered back.

So the orchestra never knew who the " distinguished musician " was.

Talking of La Trobe of the Haymarket reminds me of a curious thing that happened there a few years ago. It was during Basil Dean's production of *Pickwick* for which Norman O'Neil wrote the music. Unknown to O'Neill, some loud-speakers had been installed in the auditorium with a microphone in a room at the back of the stage, for amplifying effects. The distant coach horn from the approaching Pickwickian coach was also played in this room, but by some mistake the microphone was switched on when the horn cue came. The result was that an awful blast resounded in the theatre. Norman flew out of the orchestra and into the room where the horn player was, and told him in good round terms what he thought of him. Norman did not know that the microphone was carrying his vigorous language straight to the audience!

One of my many memories of *New Moon* concerns a " battle " which was shown taking place at sea. The decks of the ship on the stage were filled with spick-and-span sailors; and although the fighting was supposed to be terrific, and the din was tremendous, what I could never get over was the fact that, at the end of the strife, the spick-and-span sailors were as spick-and-span as when it began. I suspect that audiences do notice little things like that....

This " battle " created so much noise that it interfered with the play going on at the little Fortune Theatre, which faces the side of Drury Lane. During its progress, people at the Fortune could not properly hear the play going on there.

Vera Pearce was in *New Moon*, and danced a hornpipe among other things. It was, of course, in that play that such a delightful rendering of " Lover, Come Back to Me " was given by Evelyn Laye, whom I have known since she was a tiny child and was known as " Boo "—her father gave her the name because she used to say " Boo " if she were not pleased about anything. When she was a little girl she developed the habit of calling me " Daddy Two," and she still did so all those years later at Drury Lane.

When you enter Drury Lane you must either go upstairs or downstairs to reach your seat. One evening, at the height of the crush to get into the theatre, an old lady went up to the box-office and explained to the man behind the wicket—in the most long-winded way she could—that she was suffering from rheumatism and so she wanted a seat which she could go to without having to negotiate a staircase.

"Well, Madam," replied the box-office manager, "you can either have a stall which you will reach by going downstairs and then upstairs, or a seat in the circle which you can only reach by going upstairs and then downstairs."

The line of people behind the old lady had meanwhile been growing longer and longer. People were becoming more and more impatient, and only the restraints of civilisation prevented them from obeying their primal impulse to massacre the obstructionist old lady and buy tickets over her body.

Still, she was completely unconscious of the fact that she was disorganising the theatre, and making large numbers of people run the risk of missing the beginning of the play. She went on discussing the matter, until she eventually decided to take a stall.

Herbert Darran, a most efficient man at his job and a genial and patient one withal, in spite of the irritation of that life, was in the box-office.

"Thank goodness, that's got rid of her," he thought, and began to serve the other people waiting for tickets.

About a minute and a half later there was a swirl and an eddy in the crowd near the box-office. The old lady was back again, resolutely pushing her way through the mass of people. Finally she reached the box-office, pushed her head close to the grille, and said: "Young man, I told you wrong when I said that I was suffering from rheumatism. It's sciatica I have."

A box-office keeper is always blamed for anything by the public. For instance, Bill Leverton of the Haymarket, genial doyen of London's box-office keepers—his high collars are famous throughout the theatre world—received this amusing letter, during the run of *Touch Wood*, from a man who had booked seats in the gallery:

"Did you know when you sold me these 2 tickets that I would have a bar across my eyes to behead every actor and actress on your stage? I think you must have done, because with the great number of years you have been at the Haymarket, you must be conversant with that brassy piece of execution. If the play had been poor I could have forgiven you, but no right-minded person could be content to have the lovely features of Miss Marie Ney, and Miss Dorothy Hyson scarred by a dull piece of metal.

"I ducked and I craned, but for all my contortions someone was decapitated. It was too bad. It was too hot, too, but the heat did not hide a lovely actress nor distract attention from the play's charm. I would like you to sit up there in those very seats, with your high collar; your sufferings would have been even more acute than mine. That sentence seems a little hard, especially as the play was far too good for me to wish anyone to suffer because of its playing. I read your book a year or so ago. Unfortunately the pleasure and esteem its reading gave me were both left on the wretched perch you allotted me last night.

"Your phrase 'So much for booking 'em' was delicious. It wasn't so delicious to say 'Off with his head' every time Mr. Ian Hunter or Mr. Arundell moved up or down stage. Just give this a thought, and then you might pardon me for writing this letter."

The lights at Drury Lane were always turned out at midnight, a fact that was due to D. B. Wyndham Lewis, for the arrangement was made after the fireman had revealed that "a friend of Mr. Finck (none other than D. B. W. L.) had been in Mr. Finck's room with him till a quarter-past one."

I did not particularly notice this "lights out" business until Leslie Sarony, the comedian and writer of so many comic songs, came to the theatre for *Show Boat*. For that play we wanted a comedian who was funny (very rare) and who could do tap dancing. I heard, saw, and played for a number of applicants who failed to qualify; then someone came into the theatre and said: "I've found him—at the Victoria Palace. His name's Sarony." So Leslie Sarony was engaged, and very well he played the part.

Sarony was accustomed to working in variety, and when he came to the theatre he felt rather strange and lonely. But apparently he felt that he at least knew me well enough to have

TEN YEARS AT DRURY LANE

some companionship, for, after the show, when it was nearly midnight, he asked for me.

He was told where my room was, with the added advice: "You'll have to go up quickly for it's 'lights out' at midnight, and it's nearly midnight now."

I had already put my hat and coat on when I heard a knock at the door of my room, and I opened it to find Sarony outside—with two outsize candles in one hand and a ukelele in the other.

The lights went out, but as he had candles, Sarony was completely unperturbed by that. "Have a drink," I said, "but don't play that thing at me."

"What? Not play my ukelele?" he said, very hurt. "Oh, you must let me play just one tune."

"All right," I replied, "if you must...."

Thereupon, he sat down, a ghostly sight, with a candle burning on each side of him, and began to play; he played the instrument very well.

"That tune's familiar, but I can't think what it is or where I have heard it," I said when he finished.

"Well, that's curious, because you wrote it. It's in *My Lady Frayle*," said Sarony.

One of the most agonising afternoons I spent at Drury Lane was during the *Sleeping Beauty*. Two brothers were sitting near to me in the front row of the stalls. G. S. Melvin rushed on to the stage, and I heard behind me: "He gave him a good old wallop on the ear...."

"Eh?"

"HE ... GAVE ... HIM ... A ... GOOD ... OLD ... WALLOP ... ON ... THE ... EAR."

"Oh, yes ... yes."

Then Melvin said something.

"What did he say?"

"He said he was just going downstairs to sing a song."

"Eh?"

"HE ... SAID ... HE ... WAS ... JUST ... GOING ... DOWNSTAIRS ... TO ... SING ... A ... SONG."

At this point the terrible realisation came to me that this awful interpreting and shouting business for the benefit of the deaf but terribly inquisitive man was going on throughout the afternoon. I prayed for music and music only, or ballet, or anything where there were no words so that we might have a few moments rest, the poor tortured question-answering brother and I. But even a time when no words were being spoken on the stage did not always guarantee us from that merciless deaf man. We had interludes like this: "What are they saying now?"

"They're not saying anything, they're starting a dance."

"Eh?"

"THEY'RE ... NOT ... SAYING ... ANYTHING. ... THEY'RE ... STARTING ... A ... DANCE."

"Oh, well, tell me when they begin to talk again."

A more amusing happening with people in the front row of the stalls was when a woman came to me, leaning over, and saying: "Do any guns go off, or are there any explosions during the play?"

"Yes, there is one in the last act," I replied.

"Oh, dear," said the woman, "my little grandson here is so nervous. I'm terribly afraid it will upset him for days when the explosion occurs."

I thought no more of this conversation until the firing actually took place in the last act. Then I turned round to see the small grandson on his feet, applauding wildly. He caught my eye, and called out: "Can't they do that again!"

Another front-row-of-the-stalls playgoer I remember at Drury Lane was a manufacturer of turtle soup. He also made soap, and, at the end of the show, would present me with a stick of shaving soap. "Turtle soap" I called it.

Finally, there was an impatient man who, at the end of the performance, was apparently in such a hurry to leave the theatre that he was annoyed at having to listen to fourteen bars of the National Anthem.

"By what right do you play the whole of 'God Save the King?'" he asked.

"We have no right to do otherwise," I replied.

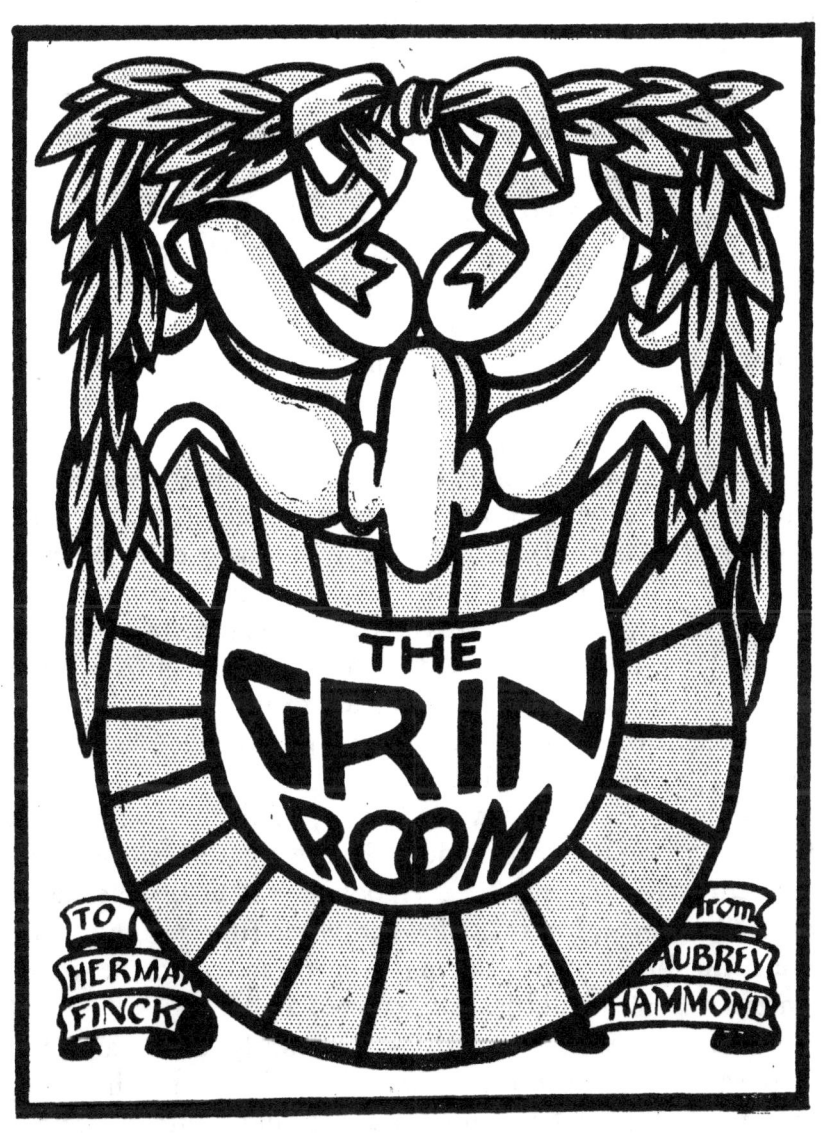

SIGN FROM MY DOOR AT DRURY LANE

My room at the Lane became a sort of club during the nine or ten years I was there. All kinds of people got into the habit of dropping in there during the evening. I called it " The Grin Room," and Aubrey Hammond drew a symbolic laughing mask which I hung on the door. If I had kept a record of all the gags which were invented and said in " The Grin Room," they would make a book at least as big, and much funnier than, Joe Miller's volume of first aid for funny men.

George Orrell, who was leading violinist of the orchestra when I was at Drury Lane, was in London during part of the War and although he was a serving member of the Forces, he found his evenings free. As his income of a shilling a day had reduced him almost to teetotalism, he obtained a job playing the violin at a small South London cinema, where an orchestra of four or five played each evening.

After he had been there a little time the manager told him a strange story about the orchestra's predecessor; it was this: " We used to have a ladies quartette to play here, and they were excellent. But, you may have noticed, there is a very cold draught during these wintry days when the exit doors are open; as the doors are at either end of the orchestra pit the ladies complained strongly that they suffered from cold hands. So I installed an electric fire in the orchestra pit itself, and the players grouped themselves round it.

" All went well for a week or two, until the 'cellist had a brain wave. About ten minutes before the tea interval—the quartette played during the afternoon as well as the evening—the 'cellist fastened her C string across the front of the electric fire, with four kippers hanging from it, and soon the whole cinema was filled with the smell of cooking kippers.

" The smell was so appetising that nearly all the audience trooped out, asking for ' pass-out checks ' because, they said, they wanted to go home for tea and would return to see the remainder of the show during the evening."

Orrell was a close friend of the manager of a little cinema near Victoria station. At this cinema they had only a trio of ladies playing the piano, violin and 'cello. Consequently, it was necessary to hire extra help when the manager booked the *Four Horsemen of the Apocalypse*, the big film of the time; for there were bombardment scenes which made it essential to have a man in the orchestra doing nothing but "effects."

Just before the arrival of the film, a young man called to see the manager, and said he was a drummer; not only that, he explained, he had invented a chemical "gun" which would give off a tremendous bang whenever there was an explosion on the screen.

The manager was so pleased at having the great film of the day, and at having arranged such special "effects," that he asked Orrell to go to the first performance. The two of them stood at the back of the hall, listening to the drummer give an occasional tap, and waiting for the beginning of the battle. As the fight became thicker, the drummer crashed away more and more loudly.

Then the audience saw an ammunition dump blown up—and at that moment there was a tremendous crash, and a little streak of smoke, from the chemical gun in the orchestra.

A smile of satisfaction covered the manager's face—then it turned to alarm. Not a sound was coming from the orchestra. Orrell and the manager hurried to the orchestra pit. They found the three women prostrate on the floor, and the drummer huddled over his drums—all gassed.

They recovered, but the cinema manager was satisfied with less ambitious "effects" for the rest of the film's run.

Orrell was bandmaster of the *Carpathia*, the ship which went to the help of the *Titanic* when she struck an iceberg and sank. More than seven hundred people were saved by those on board the *Carpathia*; Orrell received a medal and a gratuity of two months' salary. From the survivors he received the story of how the *Titanic's* band, with such wonderful courage, played "Nearer, my God, to Thee" as the ship sank.

"The ship's band in any emergency," he relates, "is expected to play to calm the passengers. After the *Titanic* struck the iceberg the band began to play bright music, dance music, comic songs—anything that would prevent the passengers from becoming panic-stricken. The ship was so badly holed that it was soon obvious that disaster was ahead. Then various awe-stricken passengers began to think of the death that faced them, and asked the bandmaster to play hymns. The one which appealed to all was 'Nearer, my God, to Thee.' And soon the liner broke in two and sank, with fourteen hundred people on board; among them were the eight gallant musicians."

There was an earthquake at Monte Carlo during a play called *A Million of Money* at Drury Lane. At the beginning of the play the son of the ancient and noble family is being ejected from the ancestral mansion. He is parting sadly from the old place when what he thinks is another broker turns out to be a solicitor, who walks up to the young man and says: " You have come into a million of money." Whereto the hero replies: " Here am I with a million of money; what am I to do with it?" Curtain falls; end of Act 1.

By Act 2 the young millionaire has reached Monte Carlo, a place where plenty of people are willing to help him solve his problem. In this act there was an earthquake. The hotel collapsed and there was a wonderful realistic cascade of bricks as the building crumpled up.

One night the bricks cascaded off the stage into the orchestra and the audience. It was an alarming moment, but as the bricks were really soft cloth things like hassocks, painted to look like bricks, no one was the worse for being hit by them.

I have had so many experiences of crocodiles, cycles, swords, performing eagles, dancers and bucking mules falling into the orchestra that I have naturally become wary when there is anything on the stage which might crash. The potential orchestra-crasher I looked at most askance was a coach drawn by two horses which drove on to the stage in splendid style in a play called *Ned Kean*, at the Lane. Happily the coach always stayed on the stage.

The Hanlon-Lees pantomime troupe, I remember, drove on to the stage in a comic ballet called *Voyage en Suisse*, and their coach apparently crashed over and threw everyone off. Actually it was nothing to those acrobats to jump off a coach without hurting themselves, and the coach did not really crash on to the stage—it was held off by spikes invisible to the audience.

W. S. Percy, the brilliant little comedian, author and artist who played Gilbert and Sullivan all round Australia and wrote and illustrated *Strolling Through Scotland*, and other books, saved a nasty situation when we were on tour together at Oxford, with *Merrie England*.

There was a scene in Windsor Forest. Percy was standing in the wings when he saw one of the small part players make what he thought was an impressive exit, and bump into the book-wing in the prompt corner which had not been braced properly. It started to wobble and then fell slowly backwards, knocking over all the wings and showing the bare walls of the theatre.

Electric light cables and battens—several bulbs fixed together —were revealed. The public is always liable to panic at the slightest suggestion of the possibility of fire, and from my conductor's " chair " I could already hear a vague murmur of alarm running round the theatre.

W. S. Percy thought that if he could hold the audience by turning the whole thing into a joke, it would be better than having to lower the curtain—not to mention the prevention of the possibility of a panic in the house.

He rushed on to the stage, pointed to the mingled mass of scenery, and said : " This is what we call ' Bringing the house down.' " He held up one of the " trees " in Windsor Forest and kept on gagging with whatever came into his mind. The biggest laugh came when he was struggling with a huge electric light batten, and said : " We make light of this sort of thing."

During all this time there was no sign of any stage hands, and it was found out later that they were all enjoying a pint in the " pub " next door. When order was restored, Percy's final gag was : " We will now go back to Elizabethan times ! " And on we went with the play.

The popular saying is : " Worse things happen at sea." I think it would be truer to life if it were : " Worse things happen on tour." The great menace is, of course, the "supers" recruited locally to fill small parts. You will judge what a crowd of supers can do from this sample :

"The king has passed this way."

Supers : "We will, we will."

"He must have gone the other way."

Supers : "Hooray ! "

Another time supers were told to say " Allah " and bow, but nothing on earth would prevent them, every time they were supposed to address the Moslem deity, from shouting out a cheery " 'Allo ! ' "

The comfort, and even the safety, of conductors, is an unconsidered trifle in the provincial theatres. During the tour on which, as I have related, W. S. Percy " saved the situation " at Oxford, I found that in many of the theatres the seats for the orchestral players were all that could be desired. But invariably I was expected to stand on an old box to conduct. On more than one occasion I was given a superannuated box in such a state of decay that I had to protest that it was not safe for me to stand upon it, and to demand that proper provision should be made for me.

It was a strict rule at Drury Lane that no stranger should be allowed to be present at the final dress rehearsal. But when I arrived for one dress rehearsal I was amazed to find the theatre packed. The audience, I was soon informed, consisted of Alfred Butt's constituents from Balham !

We all tried to lend our support during his election campaigns and I went down to his committee rooms one day. As soon as he saw me, Butt exclaimed : " Hello, Finck, have you brought the band down with you ? "

" Oh, yes," I replied, " I've brought it down for you. They're going to play ' Rule Buttania.' "

In a cupboard in my room at Drury Lane was kept a bottle of brandy, for use in case of illness. It seemed to me, however, that a number of my friends must have been having sudden attacks of illness when I was not in the room, for—although I did not drink brandy myself—the quantity in the bottle steadily

diminished. So I said to Morris Benjamin, the manager:
" Have you been drinking my brandy ? "

" No," he replied. " Why ? "

" Well," I said, " I never drink it, but what happens when I'm not in the room, I don't know. Anyway, it's vanishing."

" In that case the mystery can soon be cleared up," laughed the manager. " I want you to meet a party of detectives. They're from Scotland Yard and they're entertaining Pinkerton, the famous American detective."

" I hope he'll be able to tell us who stole the brandy ? " I remarked.

" Soon afterwards Pinkerton arrived—a delightful man— and I told him the whole story of the brandy (he had a glass of what remained himself, by the way : thorough, these detectives).

" I'll fix you up a gadget so that if anyone touches your brandy a bell will ring for twenty-four hours," he said.

He sent along a burglar alarm, something like an alarm clock ; it had been wound up with a key, and was duly installed and screwed down to guard the cupboard.

Besides the bottle of brandy I kept coats and other things in my cupboard, and just before the matinée was due to begin I went to the cupboard to take a coat out, completely forgetting the burglar alarm. As soon as I touched the door I jumped backwards, my ears tingling with a noise like a fire-alarm, so loud that it could be heard in every part of the theatre. And then I remembered Pinkerton's boast : " The bell will ring for twenty-four hours. . . ."

Above the din I bellowed a telephone message to the Manager : " The key . . . bring the key quickly . . . we can't turn it off without the key."

The answer to that was that the Manager could not find the key. Unless it *were* found it would be impossible to give a performance that afternoon, for the din would drown everyone on the stage. So I was left, worried beyond belief, shut up in my room with that beastly alarm which by this time had a nasty defiant note, and was obviously taking a pleasure in the disaster it was causing.

At last the Manager came tumbling excitedly into the room with the key—found, thank goodness. So we turned the machine off. The man who first said " Silence is golden," must have had trouble with a burglar alarm.

Still, the brandy continued to disappear. We put secret marks on the bottle to make sure that it really was going.

" I feel sure that somebody regularly in the theatre must be taking it," I said. " We must find out. I can't go on paying for brandy which I never drink."

We arranged for a man employed in the theatre, a gigantic ex-guardsman, to stay in my room all night; he crammed himself into a cupboard next to the one containing the brandy and, by a superhuman effort of will, remained in that horribly uncomfortable position all night.

A good many glasses had been put on the table to lure on the thief if such a person turned up, and about eight o'clock in the morning the door opened, a woman entered, saw the glasses, and said: " Oh, the boys must have been enjoying themselves last night.... Now I'm going to drink their health."

And she produced a key, opened the cupboard and poured herself out a good stiff glass of brandy.

The stage manager at Drury Lane was named Bax, and one morning he was attending a dress parade—a kind of rehearsal at which all the costumes of the cast are inspected to make certain they are ship-shape and Bristol fashion. It was for a show which was being produced by Felix Edwardes, who had made himself a reputation for a very brusque manner. A row of girls lined up in front of Edwardes and he looked at their dresses and found them all in order, at any rate the front part which he could see.

At that moment Edwardes decided he wanted to speak to the stage manager.

" Bax ! " he shouted.

And, to his amazement, the row of girls in front of him made a neat about-turn and showed him their backs !

From time to time gala performances were given at Drury Lane to help various charities. King George and Queen Mary attended these charity performances on a number of occasions and, when they did, there was always a chance that the King might send for someone connected with the show and knight him. When this happened in the case of Sir Frank Benson the theatre was caught napping: there was not a sword in the place. The most terrible hurry-scurry took place to find one; sword-snatchers were despatched pell-mell into Covent Garden and other resorts of theatrical costumiers. To prevent any repetition of such an unfortunate and unseemly contretemps I took the precaution of having half a dozen " property " swords in " The Grin Room."

One of these charity matinées was devoted to a one-day revival of Neil Lyons' play, *London Pride*. All the parts, including the small ones, were played by famous actors and actresses—which on these occasions means that nobody really remembers a line of the play.

That afternoon people kept coming into my room to have a drink—Lawrence (" Jack ") Anderson, the actor-nephew of beautiful Mary Anderson, had a part in the play, and was my " barman " in his spare time.

I had put a number of wooden property swords on the settee, and when anyone asked: " What are these for?" I replied: " For emergency knighthoods."

However, there was no call for a sword wanted from the royal box. So when it was all over, thinking that I must do something to make up for certain disappointments, I took up one of the property swords and solemnly said: " Kneel Lyons."

CHAPTER VI

MY PANTOMIME DAYS

I REMEMBER as a very small boy being taken to see my first Drury Lane pantomime by my father. He was leader of the orchestra there for seven years before I entered it as an extremely young player, and though I forget what that first pantomime of mine was, I do recall that I was put into a corner of the orchestra pit and told that I might laugh but that I must not applaud. If I had clapped, people would have thought that I had been put there as a claque—and that would never have done!

Those were the days, I remember, when "stage-door johnnies" with bouquets would wait in the hope that the principal girl would let them take her out to supper—and champagne. They were the days of Principal Girls and Unprincipled Boys, as a newspaper editor recently remarked when I wrote an article on pantomime for him.

In one of the first pantomimes I ever saw was a duet which still amuses me. It was sung by two people who came on as hard-up working men, and the words were:

> We're 'orny 'anded sons of toil
> And our fate is wery sad.
> We ain't 'ad no work this winter,
> And we wouldn't 'a done it if we 'ad.

Looking back as far as I can, it is amazing how pantomime has developed and developed until to-day it is not pantomime at all. For "pantomime" refers to the harlequinade which in bygone days came at the end of the performance; everything else was supposed simply to lead up to this harlequinade and whatever came before it was called "the opening." However, the "opening" grew longer and longer—a couple of hours was quite normal. In the end the "opening" overgrew itself to such an extent that it led to the harlequinade—which really *was* the pantomime—being left out, as it always is to-day.

Julian Wylie was so determined to be King of *Pantomime* that he decided one year that he must have a harlequinade somewhere, so he put it in the *middle* of the show!

The length some of the pantomimes reached on the first night—they always had to be drastically cut down afterwards—was fantastic. It was a terrible test of endurance for the audience. People would slip off to sleep in their seats, and wake hours later, to find that the show was still remorselessly going on. Men who arrived at the theatre with that smooth shaving-soap-advertisement look crept out with a thick, black stubble rasping against the remains of their white ties, and slunk shiftily home, expecting their disreputable appearance would lead to their arrest at any moment. Girls who entered the theatre in the first bloom of young womanhood were on the threshold of middle age—or at any rate all their make-up had come off—by the time the yawning, snoring audience rubbed the sleep out of its eyes and stood up wearily for the National Anthem.

But the people who produced these pantomimes never would cut them until the first night was over, though every year the most pathetic pleas not to subject the audience to such a dreadful ordeal were made to them.

One Boxing Night I took my wife round to Drury Lane for the first night of the pantomime, watched the opening scene, and then went off to the Palace, where we started our programmes at a civilised time. Some three hours later, after our programme at the Palace had finished, I went back to Drury Lane to fetch my wife. The pantomime was by then just about getting into its stride, and I watched it move from scene to scene for at least another hour. When the final scenes had been grimly glared at by an audience wearied to death by the immense length of the performance, but horribly determined to have their money's worth or die of old age in the attempt (especially the dead-heads, who always stay to the bitter end and long to boo the author), and we were leaving the theatre, my wife said to me (between yawns): "What time is it?"

"You mean what *day* is it?" I replied.

There was a loud laugh just behind me, and a stranger said: "Thank you, sir. That's the first joke I have heard this evening!"

"... This morning," I added.

Sometimes when they had two performances in a day at the beginning of a run of a pantomime, the last scenes of the first performance would still be in progress after the second performance should have started.

A curious incident happened at one of those Boxing-Day pantomime openings. One of a family of talented brothers—he did theatrical drawings to go with the notices of a well-known dramatic critic—was, to use an expression common in theatrical circles, "addicted." He started celebrations of Boxing Day among his friends in Chelsea; then he had a sleep which partially counteracted the effect of these celebrations; celebrated some more—and, in a fumbling and uncertain way, clambered into his evening dress and went to Drury Lane.

The pantomime had already begun when he arrived; he saw his partner, the dramatic critic, was there; but was either unable to find his own seat, or else did not want to find it. In any case, he walked into the bar and ordered a whisky and soda.

"I'm sorry, I can't serve you," said the girl behind the bar.

"Why not?" demanded the artist. "I may have had a few drinks during the course of the day, but if you think I'm drunk you're very much mistaken."

"Well, go and look at yourself in the mirror," replied the girl.

The artist did—and understood. He was wearing a dozen collars! In his fuddled and hurried state when dressing he had picked up a collar and put it round his neck, without realising that it was one of a packet of twelve, all neatly tied up with pale blue ribbon; and he had gone to the theatre, wearing his complete supply of new collars.

The first clown I saw at Drury Lane was Fred Evans—father of Will Evans, the famous comedian who became the writer of a famous Aldwych farce. There were Harry Payne and Harry

MY PANTOMIME DAYS

Paulo, a very good clown; Whimsical Walker, though he was more a circus clown than a stage clown; and Charles Lauri. " What about Grimaldi ? " you may say. Well, he was a little before my time !

Arthur Sturgess and J. Hickory Wood were the most successful and prolific writers of pantomimes of the past generation, though others who made their mark in that type of work were E. L. Blanchard, once a journalist; Harry Nicholls, Cecil Raleigh, George R. Sims and F. C. Burnand, a famous editor of *Punch*.

The music was always an assortment of everybody else's music; it was arranged, not written, by the man who was responsible for it. And that is, after all, very reasonable, for you can hardly expect a man to write a whole pantomime of original music when he knows perfectly well before he starts that the most it can do is to stagger along as far as Easter.

Among the great pantomime families the Vokes are too well known in theatrical history for me to need say much about them. The position they occupied in pantomime during my boyhood was really amazing. They could—and often did—provide a complete cast, for one or other member of the family could do everything. Take, for instance, *Bluebeard*, produced in the 1879–1880 season. The cast for that was :

Fatima, Miss Victoria Vokes; Selim, Miss Jessie Vokes; Bluebeard, Mr. Fred Vokes; Shacabac, Mr. Fawdon Vokes; Sister Anne, Mrs. Fred Vokes.

That *Bluebeard* was, by the way, Augustus Harris's first pantomime, and was by E. L. Blanchard, who also wrote *The White Cat*, produced two seasons earlier, with this cast :

Prince Natty, Miss Victoria Vokes; Prince Nectar, Miss Jessie Vokes; Prince Tremor, Mr. Fred Vokes; King Gnome, Mr. Fawdon Vokes.

Another famous family were the Girards; they were all very tall and wore black tights and red wigs, their faces being made up very white in contrast. They would dash about the stage and slide across long tables and do all kinds of other acrobatic tricks—a fact which brought me into horrible disgrace.

They were in a pantomime at Covent Garden which I was taken to see when I was a very small boy; I suppose that I should be about seven years old at the time. After watching the Girards for a few minutes I was in such a state of enthusiastic excitement that I shouted out: " How-a-devil-do-a-do-it ? "

Everyone was most shocked to hear such dreadful (for those days) language used in public, and by such a little boy. The question of the hour was: " Wherever can he have heard that terrible expression ? "

Drury Lane pantomime in my boyhood days was run by an imperious, not too musical man named F. B. Chatterton, and the conductor was a large German called Karl Meyder. This story about them was told me by my father: It was the morning of a first " band call," and after about an hour's sawing and blaring, the rehearsal was suddenly called to a halt by Chatterton, who informed all and sundry (including the unfortunate composer of the music) that he did not like it. " What we want is a march that the gallery boys can whistle," he said.

Meyder, the aforesaid large German, thereupon flew into a passion and shouted: " So—vell, I vill myself write a march mid so many tunes in it dat dey von't know vich one to vistle."

A real King of Pantomime was Oscar Barrett the elder, who (as I have said) is still fit and well at the age of eighty-nine. He produced pantomimes at the Crystal Palace many years ago, as well as being conductor at Drury Lane. (Before that he was at one of the oldest theatres in London, the Grecian Theatre, which became the Grand Theatre, at Islington; it was for years the great place for pantomime.)

Besides the pantomimes, Oscar Barrett was employed as a conductor at the Crystal Palace for the daily concerts, and I am afraid the players in the orchestra there disliked the pantomime heartily, for they regarded it as an imposition to have to play for it on top of their ordinary work.

I went to one pantomime matinée there to play as a deputy (the " villain " of the orchestra). There must have been a great many deputies that day, or else the members of the orchestra were not taking the interest they should have done in what they were playing. The orchestra began to wobble instead of playing with the necessary precision. This irritated Oscar, a man of great ability and enthusiasm, and as the orchestra did not seem to follow the movements of his baton properly, he began to count the beats of four-time. . . . " One . . . two . . . three . . . four. . . . One . . . two . . . three . . . four. . . ." Somebody in the orchestra took this up when Oscar reached a four, and went on, " Five . . . six . . . seven . . . eight. . . ." The counting spread from one player to another—not loud enough to be heard above the music, of course—until, eventually, the whole orchestra were solemnly saying : " Eighty-eight . . . eighty-nine . . . ninety . . . ninety-one. . . ." They did not stop until they had reached about a hundred.

Sir Augustus Harris, who had rolling eyes, like those of my dear friend, Tommy Beecham, rolled down to Drury Lane as if he were rolling down to Rio. He followed Chatterton (not the boy poet) as manager of the Lane in 1886, and under him came a great array of stars—Dan Leno, Herbert Campbell, Marie Lloyd, Arthur Roberts, Harry Nicholls, Letty Lind, James Fawn and a lovely woman and lovely singer—and my first love, worshipped dumbly from afar—Miss Wadman.

Arthur Roberts was never paid more than £40 a week at Drury Lane, but there was never a greater comedian there. He had the supreme faculty of being able to hold the stage by himself.

Dan Leno was found by " Gus " Harris at the Surrey Theatre, in Blackfriars Road, a house then run by George Conquest. They had a notice in the pit there, " No bottles allowed," for beer was sold in the theatre and they objected to anyone spoiling the trade by bringing in their own. I recollect that one night when I was there, a merry chap brought in a four and a half gallons' cask of beer and kept on saying : " This isn't a bottle," whenever an attendant with beer on a tray looked askance at him.

I do not know what Harris paid Dan Leno at the start, but I do know that he did eventually pay him £250 a week—and £250 a week was £250 a week in those days. It makes some of those Hollywood salaries—the real ones revealed by the United States income tax authorities, and not the fairy-tale ones "revealed" by the high-powered publicity men attached to the various studios—look somewhat stupid. And—still in the days when a pound was a pound—George Graves once received £350 a week in pantomime at Drury Lane. He was so proud of his first cheque that he had it photographed and framed.

In that pantomime George Graves had a song to sing, the words of which he could never remember. I suggested to him that he should have them typed and put inside his hat, and read them off from there. But he preferred to have prompters hidden in the wings and behind pieces of scenery, and very busy indeed those prompters were at every performance. In fact, they were so busy that I said to George: "You should bring them all on to bow at the end"—which they did! And it amused the audience vastly.

George Graves and Wilkie Bard once appeared in the same pantomime; and the authors and producer had the tricky job of arranging that throughout the whole performance they should never have to appear on the stage at the same time.

Another brilliant pantomime comedian was G. S. Melvin, who was in *The Sleeping Beauty* which I conducted—a pleasurable job in spite of the length of the piece—with the assistance of Simpson's-in-the-Strand. Years before he appeared in pantomime I had conducted for Melvin when he was a first-turn comedian at the Palace.

Before *The Sleeping Beauty* he had never been on the stage at Drury Lane, but as soon as he appeared as a dame, my daughter Marjorie exclaimed: "Oh, he is going to be good!"—and he was.

Just before I go on from "Gus" Harris to his successor, Arthur Collins, I must tell a story of how he once unknowingly awarded me a prize of £25. An advertising firm offered the prize for music to be set to certain words, and I was persuaded to go in for it. There was no sort of collusion—the entries were numbered and bore no names—and, to my surprise, I won the prize by the expedient of setting in polka time a set of words that everyone else fell into the obvious trap of setting to waltz time. When the nearest numbers were correlated by the scrutineers—a horrible word and I'm not sure how to spell it—and Harris discovered that I was the winner, he was rather upset. In the theatre, later, he said to me: "I wouldn't have given you the prize on any account if I had known it was you." He, of course, didn't mean it.

I eventually made my prize-winning tune into a polka which was played at the Covent Garden balls which were so famous in those days, and at which I sometimes conducted during my Palace years. At one of them, many years later—a costume ball—I remember, between dances, seeing Arnold Bennett in a magnificent eighteenth-century costume standing alone on a staircase leading to the dance floor. He was extremely fond of dancing and, as I approached him to have a few moments' chat, his whole attitude seemed to say pathetically: "I am Arnold Bennett . . . and I have no one to dance with me." Another gap between greatness and happiness.

Arthur Collins was the best manager I ever worked for; his reign was the best that Drury Lane ever knew, and if he had not been a martyr to gout—by a curious coincidence he always had a seizure of gout during the rehearsals of the show—he would have been even greater than he was. He had an enormous flair for the business of entertainment and he rose from the ranks—he began in the paint-room. And so, by the way, did Aubrey Hammond, in the same theatre.

Collins had two failings: he told the longest stories I have ever had to try to listen to (they went on for about two hours) and his idea that whisky and soda was good for his gout was difficult to cope with. He hardly ever ate anything, but there was one day on which he demolished two big rump steaks. We were rehearsing a play and, at the break for lunch, he said to me: "Where are you going, Herman?"

I said: "I am going to Romano's in the Strand, to have a steak and a bottle of Bass."

"I'll come with you and have the same," replied Arthur Collins.

Hours later, when rehearsal was at last finished for that day and I was weary and famished, Collins came to me and said—as if he had just thought of an entirely new and original idea : " Herman, let's go to the Roman's and have a rump steak and a bottle of Bass." He did . . . and—being so unused to a beefsteak and Bass diet—was ill for a week afterwards.

I have at home a crayon drawing of Arthur Collins, done by Seymour Lucas. Before it was framed, E. V. Lucas happened to see it and wrote on it : " Seymour Hicks and I did this together."

Julian Wylie, who had a profound knowledge of the history of pantomime, was another Drury Lane producer for whom I worked. I liked him very much, but, somehow, I always wanted to pull his leg. He had such a serious mind that you could hardly ever persuade him to have a drink. He had, however, a passion for eating ice cream at all hours of the day and night.

Poor chap, he also had periodical attacks of vertigo. They would come on suddenly during rehearsals and Julian would put his head in his hands and not know where he was or what he was doing for the time being. I am afraid that on one of those occasions I was guilty of a gag that did not amuse him. It was his first pantomime at Drury Lane and he had got a big publicity drive in full swing. (Generally, my experience of theatre publicity men is that they are " sup-Press " men, but this time the papers were full of Julian Wylie and his show.) Well, he had one of his attacks in the theatre and said : " I can't go on—this vertigo. . . ."

" You mean this advert-ego, don't you," I could not help saying.

At three o'clock on the night, or rather morning, of a dress rehearsal, a troupe of little children who should have tripped on in a certain scene were not on the stage at the appointed time.

" Where are the kids ? " asked Julian Wylie. " Aren't they down yet ? "

" They should not be up yet," I replied.

Give me men to deal with in pantomime—or in any other kind of theatrical production. Most women are far more difficult.

Savage Club
76th Annual Dinner
DECEMBER 2nd 1933

Set in the keys F and G.

In the Chair — HERMAN FINCK
Guest of the Club — SIR EDWARD GERMAN

I remember when we had the late Lilian Davies, a fine singer, and Eve Grey, not such a good singer—as she herself knew and admitted—in one pantomine at the Lane. They had to rehearse a duet in my room, and it became so fierce between them that finally I said in despair: " Ladies, this is a duet, not a competition. I am going to leave you to it. . . ."

I did leave them to it—but when, at last, I ventured back I found them firm friends, and toasting each other in port wine—my port. Oh, well, any port in a storm. . . . Two dear girls.

So much for Drury Lane. I would be most unfair, however, not to mention the delightful pantomimes produced at the Lyceum. It is true that they are not so spectacular as the elaborate productions at the Lane, but they certainly have a more intimate atmosphere, and the authors and producers always bear in mind the tastes of the large number of children who will be taken to see the show. Long live the Melvilles !

The most unfortunate pantomime with which I was ever connected was produced many years ago at His (Her) Majesty's Theatre in the Haymarket. There were nearly as many composers as in a present-day revue—Edward Solomon (who conducted), Alfred Cellier, George Jacobi (of the old Alhambra ; I have talked of him elsewhere), Edward Jones (" Pantomime Rehearsal ") and J. L. Molloy (" Love's Old Sweet Song ") were among them, and I played in the orchestra.

Despite all this glittering array of talent and a strong company, the whole thing was a dreadful fiasco. After it had been running about a week I arrived at the theatre for the matinée and found that there would be no performance, and that no one would be admitted to the theatre. The official receiver had stepped in and received everything, including my violin. . . .

Alfred Cellier, very ill at the time, had written most of his music in bed. I went to see him three or four times, in quest of further music for rehearsal, and on one visit I went into his bedroom and inquired after his health. He looked wearily at me and, through his long, bedraggled moustache, muttered: " Young man, I'm sorry, but I'm unfit for publication."

CHAPTER VII

THOSE PLAY PRODUCERS

WHEN W. S. Gilbert produced an opera he worked out all the situations with dolls on a model theatre, and the production as he arranged it with the dolls had to be adhered to when the piece was played. People since the time of Gilbert have freely criticised his methods on the ground that they resulted in woodenness. It is true that there may have been a tendency that way—especially when the method was employed by someone other than the master himself—latent in the meticulous ordering of details which was part and parcel of his system. But consider how far to the other extreme many have gone since his time—consider the sloppy half-produced work we have so often seen; consider, for instance, the number of plays in which actors walk about the stage without the slightest idea of what to do with their hands except fill their pockets with them. A first-class producer should never have allowed slovenly work on the actor's part—and on his own part, for he should have told the player—to rob the acting of so much of its effect. The sight of an actor committing obvious gaucheries with his all-too-conspicuous hands has more than once irritated me so much that I have thought he needed a rap over the knuckles with a good big cane to remind him of one of the important elements in the art of acting.

In these most recent years we have seen producers who produce very badly (don't misunderstand me: they are not all bad; some are brilliant); and producers unable to do their job properly after they have seen the piece played, and played well, abroad. I remember one man who was making such a mess of producing a show which he had seen *seventeen* times in another country, that assistance had to be brought in to sort things out. Not *producers*, but *reproducers*, I call them in cases like this—even if they do the job properly. (Some are also non-producers: it took me a good eight weeks to make one man produce a cheque for the £15 he owed me.)

Then, too, we have seen the big-business producer, a new kind of person who does not produce shows—could not, I suppose, but employs other men to do the real work of producing under his ægis.

The late Mr. Jimmy White, the one-time millionaire financier who committed suicide, took Daly's Theatre, and, after watching other men produce shows which he was providing with financial backing, he came to the conclusion that he could produce plays himself (Oscar Asche at one time produced for White; they had a play called *Cleopatra* which White invariably pronounced " Cleopatr-i-a "; he was like that.)

Later, White persuaded Seymour Hicks to produce for him, and he wanted Seymour and myself to write a new and elaborate finale for the play, instead of the short one it originally had.

White, though a noisy, bullying type of man, was amusing in a way. He invited Hicks and myself to have lunch with him—and I found, much to my surprise, that this meant lunch in his office at Daly's. We sat down among all the business papers and ate salmon and beef—all through the meal I was trying to find out, without success, whether the food was supposed to be hot or cold; it was actually neither—which we washed down with bottles of lager: altogether, it was far from my idea of what a meal ought to be.

After a time White pressed a bell. An enormous man appeared in the office doorway.

" What time's bluddy 'orse to-day? " asked White in his thick North-country voice.

" Two o'clock, sir," replied the enormous employee.

" Going to have a bit on? " said White, turning to Hicks and myself.

" I'm afraid I don't know anything about racing," I began, but White stopped me with an " Aw, that's awl right. . . . What about a fiver? "

So Hicks and I said we would put a fiver each on the horse—whatever it was.

About twenty past two, White picked up his telephone mouthpiece and said: " What about bluddy 'orse ? "—and a voice replied: " It's won."

White said to me: " You must coom 'un see bluddy play."

" No, I'm afraid I can't," I said, " I shall be busy with my own work."

" Well, you must write finale. If ye can't coom to performance because y're conducting at tother theatre, I'll call a rehearsal to-morrow morning, if that'll soot ye."

We arranged that I should have a postcard by the first post the next morning, telling me what time White was going to have the rehearsal. But it never arrived; instead, I received a cheque for £18—my winnings on the horse! And that was the finale, too. I never saw Jimmy White again.

However, let us consider some of the producers I remember who could produce. The first two names that jump into your consciousness (after Gilbert) are, of course, Henry Irving and Beerbohm Tree. Still, I think enough torrents of ink and furlongs of typewriter ribbon have already flowed in their homage. In any case, although I once played in his orchestra, I never had any experience of Irving at rehearsals.

H. B. Farnie was the great power in the world of comic opera for years and years. He translated and adapted much French comic opera and had tremendous success with his productions. He certainly knew his job, but he was a strange man in appearance, as you may gather from the description of him given by his great friend, M. Charles Alias, the theatrical costumier:

" . . . A monstrous creature. He always wore the smallest ' billy-cock ' his head would carry, and an exceedingly short reefer-coat. An eccentric collar and tie completed his grotesque appearance—people used to turn round and stare at him as he walked along; and he always politely declared they were guying me! He believed himself a tremendous success with women, but that side of his character it is not edifying to discuss.

"Farnie's libretti were the butt of the critics, who were never weary of chaffing his inane rhymes and banal sentiment. But he was impervious. The fact is that Farnie did not depend for success on any literary skill, but on business acumen. He could in an instant judge of the possibilities of a French production here. We would go to Paris together, and at once close a deal. *Madame Favart* was at the outset a failure there, but coined money here. It established Florence St. John in popular favour, and Herbert Tree made one of his first successes as the Marquis de Pontsable on tour. Once, I recall, Farnie scribbled a complete translation of a 'book' on our way home from Paris. It was of *Belle Lurette*, I think."

Robert Courtneidge, the Scottish boy who was so determined to go on the stage that he ran away from home to do so and had to "rough it" well and truly, first made his mark as a producer in Manchester. He there produced a *Cinderella* that made everyone who thought they knew something about pantomime sit up in surprise. Since that far-off day his successes have been historic: *Madame Sans Gene* ... *Tom Jones* ... *The Dairymaids* ... *The Blue Moon* ... *The Arcadians*, which had a run of two years and six months at the Shaftesbury. The most extraordinary thing about the career of Robert Courtneidge is that he has acted in and produced Shakespeare, and acted in and produced pantomime. I do not know anyone else who has done that.

Courtneidge is a somewhat restless man; as soon as he leaves his work he wants to go back to it. To me it was rather trying, when lunching with him, to find that, while I was still hungry, he had bolted his snack and was saying, watch in hand: "Now, my boy, come along. Time we both got back to work, you know. Can't dilly-dally about here all day."

At last this grew altogether too much for me. Before lunching with Courtneidge I roped in the prospective table-companion, and we two had a hearty lunch before meeting Courtneidge.

Then I could carry off my part with the necessary aplomb : " What will I have to eat ? Oh, I don't know. Perhaps a chicken sandwich ... or perhaps a little Gruyere and biscuits ... and then a white coffee...."

On this, Courtneidge would comment delightedly : " That's right, my boy. That's the sort of lunch to have. I don't believe in these heavy meals in the middle of the day. Prevents a man from working properly in the afternoon."

It was for Courtneidge that I wrote most of the music in *My Lady Frayle*, by Max Pemberton and Arthur Wimperis. It is, in my opinion, a wonderful play and has something that is extremely rare in a musical play—a really dramatic plot.

The B.B.C. broadcast *My Lady Frayle* last April, and on the day of the broadcast, which was from St. George's Hall, near to Broadcasting House, I rang up and said that I would look in before going on to conduct elsewhere.

" That's fine ; I'll get you some seats in the listeners' room." said my friend at the other end of the telephone.

" Listeners' room! " I exclaimed. " Why the listeners' room ? I was coming into the theatre."

" Oh, no, that's impossible. Absolutely impossible. Even God couldn't come into the theatre while the broadcast is on."

" Perhaps so," I replied, " but God didn't write the music for *My Lady Frayle*."

Granville Barker was connected with the Shaw plays when they first appeared. He once produced a remarkable *Midsummer Night's Dream*. None of the Mendelssohn music was used, and I think that Shakespeare would have had even more shocks than usual had he seen that version of his work. Gold spangles were the really outstanding thing about it.

A production of the *Midsummer Night's Dream* which I liked much better was done by Basil Dean. It was magifincent. Basil Dean also produced *London Life*, both of which I have written about in my chapter on Drury Lane.

Augustus Harris, who was christened " Druriolanus " by F. C. Burnand of *Punch*, was—besides being one of the greatest producers of drama and pantomime at Drury Lane—an actor, author, sheriff—and *almost* a Lord Mayor.

Harris had an unusually hearty appetite—and also the habit of taking a nap in any odd moment he might find to do so. One night he went into the Green Room Club and ordered a chop. As that was bound to take at least ten minutes to grill he went to sleep. A few minutes later another member came in, sat down near to the sleeping Harris, and also ordered a chop. After a short interval a waiter arrived with the chop Harris had ordered. But the other member, seeing that Harris was sound asleep, insisted that the waiter should give him the chop. When he had finished the chop he pushed the empty plate across the table towards Harris—and a moment later Harris woke up.

" Where's my chop ? " he demanded.

" Why, you've eaten it," was the reply.

" Of course ! So I did," said Harris looking at the empty plate. " And a very good chop it was, too ! "

At Kettner's one day a stilton was standing on one side of a buffet and a bowl of strawberries and cream on the other side. Harris helped himself to alternate mouthfuls of cheese and strawberries and cream. Cheese and strawberries —before lunch !

Another doughty theatrical trencherman is Alan (Tony) Ainsworth, the good-looking actor who has been the *jeune premier* in so many successful plays, and has recently been in *Tovarich* with Cedric Hardwicke and Eugenie Leontovich at the Lyric. I have been told that one night Tony ate two dinners and then went on to act at the Haymarket. The play, aptly enough, was Somerset Maugham's *The Circle !*

Whenever I think of Oscar Asche I think of burglars. Not that he was a burglar in his spare time, or anything like that, but because he was once mistaken for a burglar at my house.

The drawing-room of the house in which I was then living in Hampstead had a large semicircular bay facing on to the garden, and the top of this bay made a small flat roof along the side of the house and level with the first floor—it was a favourite playground for my daughters when they were children; they could climb along the roof into various windows, a none too safe pastime in which they then took great pleasure.

Some six or seven years ago my daughter Marjorie was sleeping in a bedroom facing directly on to this small flat roof. In the early hours of one morning she was awakened by a strong light shining through the window. For a moment or two she thought—naturally she was still half asleep—that it was brilliant sunshine and that morning had arrived (actually it was only about 3 a.m.). Then she realised that the light was the beam of an electric torch, and a man's face (pretty villainous-looking, I gathered) glowered through the window. Marjorie jumped up and switched on the light in the room. This frightened the man, who must have thought that the bedroom was empty, otherwise he would not have shone his torch through the window into it, and he escaped. Marjorie rushed into our room, and told us all about what had happened. Then I telephoned to the police.

Platoons of police on bicycles soon arrived, and explored every inch of the garden, shining torches hither and thither, and obtaining some very pretty stage lighting effects. I immediately christened the whole proceedings "The Policemen's Ballet." Still, as the burglar was by that time at home sitting comfortably over a cup of hot cocoa and bread and dripping (I always imagine that to be standard diet in burglar circles), and thinking, " Even if I didn't get anything, at least I wasn't caught," all the searching was in vain, so I suggested to the police that they should call it a night, and come inside to have something to keep out the cold.

When the police departed, I hoped we should be able to go to sleep again (actually we did not get any more sleep that night). Marjorie refused to go back to her room, and she and her mother sent me to sleep there. I have never been able to find out whether the theory behind this was that I was born burglar-proof, or that I don't matter anyway!

After that I told the maids that when anyone came to the door and asked for me they were in no circumstances to let them in unless they were assured that it was all right to do so. I said: "You must ask, 'Have you an appointment with Mr. Finck?' and if the answer is 'No,' you must say, 'Please write or telephone him to fix up an appointment. He cannot see anyone while he is working.'" (Incidentally I still have this rule; I consider it is essential for anyone who works in his own home. The hours between 9 a.m. and midday are sacred to me.)

Just about at the same time as the burglar (the day before, I believe), Oscar Asche had asked me to write the music for his play, *The Good Old Days*, and said, "I must read it to you...." (I agreed to this, although I dread being read to; I like to have a thing before me in black and white so that I can digest it at my leisure).

On the Sunday morning following the burglar, I and the family went out for a walk together. While we were gone the front door-bell was rung. The maid peeped through the window and saw an enormous man standing at the door and holding by the hand an extremely small child. She then timidly opened the door.

"Good morning," said the enormous man amiably, "I am a friend of Mr. Finck and ..."

But he was cut short by having the door slammed in his face. The maid was convinced this terrifying bulk of a man was only trying to gain admission to the house on some pretext or other in order to rob it; she thought the tiny child was a "lure."

When I returned from the walk and heard about this I exclaimed: "Why, it must have been Oscar Asche!" So I rang him up and explained the whole situation. Fortunately he was a good-tempered man and I found him ready to have a good laugh about the incident.

Dr. Jackson Lang, who was at that time my neighbour, and was an enthusiastic member of the National Sporting Club, found a burglar in his kitchen one night.

"What are you doing here?" he demanded.

The man did not answer, and in fact the situation was too obvious for any reply to be needed.

"Now look here," said the doctor, "I am going to be fair

to you. You're younger than me (Dr. Lang was then nearly seventy). You're taller than me, and you're heavier than me. So put up your fists and see whether you can defend yourself."

Both of them set to right heartily, but the burglar found from the start that he was no match for the sporting doctor. The doctor gave him a terrible hiding, thrashing him all round the kitchen.

Then the bruised and crestfallen burglar was given a drink and a sandwich and sent on his way, and the following day, as a warning to other would-be malefactors the doctor put up a notice in his back-yard giving a highly terrifying account of the affair. It ran something like this:

" The last burglar we had here went away with two black eyes, four teeth missing, very little hair and a bump as big as a goose's egg on his forehead.

" So keep away."

Even the fighting doctor was less severe than one of Harry Tate's friends. This man was so enraged when he found a burglar who had broken into his house just when he was going out that he took a length of rope, tied the burglar securely to a tree in the garden—and left him there until his return twelve hours later.

But to return to Asche and the maid who mistook him for a robber. It must be admitted that Oscar's bulk was alarming. It was so great that when, in his later years, he went to the Duchess Theatre to produce a revue, he found that he was unable to go through the pass-door from the auditorium to the stage. Whenever he wanted to go from the stalls to the stage, he had to go outside the theatre and walk round to the stage door!

Oscar weighed well over twenty stone; he was a remarkable trencherman and intensely interested in the finer points of cooking; he was very proud of the fact that he had designed a special cooker. In his reminiscences he recorded that: " I sold a good many privately and gave demonstrations. I could not, however, find anyone to put in capital for mass production. The utility of the stove was never questioned.

"I fried a two-pound trout in butter and grilled a two-pound steak and steamed onions in my car going at fifty miles an hour, with no windscreen. One Sunday in the summer a party of ten descended. José Collins, Bobbie Evett, Lord Innes Kerr, Spencer Trevor, Teddy Gwenn and others. And I cooked their lunch for them on my cooker on the lawn—a dozen trout straight out of the water, and a fourteen-pound sirloin, with vegetables."

Oscar often asked me to go to his farm in Gloucestershire, but I was never able to do so. It would have been better for Oscar if he had never heard of Gloucestershire, for the farm proved terribly expensive. "It was money going out all the time and nothing coming in," he said. "I was always spending money on improvements and, in all, over ninety friends and members of the Green Room Club came down and helped me to pass cheery week-ends."

Before he reached the stage of being able to buy a farm, Oscar had passed through many hard times. He was born in Australia, of Norwegian descent, and when he won £80 he decided to run away from home—his twin ambitions were to be an actor and to possess a greyhound. Eventually his wanderings ended in London and he went to a boarding-house in Guilford Street, Bloomsbury, where the charge was thirty shillings a week. But after he had been in the place only a day, the landlady asked him to leave because he asked for a second helping of curried rabbit. At one time he was so hard up that he spent nights on the Embankment and was glad to earn a little by calling cabs for people.

Someone gave him a letter of introduction to Sir Henry Irving. Irving told him to go away and study; but Oscar persuaded F. R. Benson to give him Shakespearean roles. When they first met, Benson asked him to recite; then he said: "Can you keep wicket?" "Yes," said Oscar—so Benson gave him a job.

It was while in Benson's company that he met—and at once

fell in love with—Lily Brayton, and their courtship must have been somewhat tempestuous, to judge from this story that he told:

"I remember once I was rehearsing her in Juliet, and she disagreed with one of my readings. We quarrelled, and she put my shoes on the fire. I replied by putting her silver brushes on the fire."

They had financial ups and downs, too, as you can judge from this passage in a letter which he wrote to me:

". . . I have had no salary for four weeks. Neither has Harding, Miss Brayton, nor Basil Holloway. By the end of the week we shall be about £1500 to the bad. We are going to Streatham and Golders Green on the chance of getting something back."

What he did make money from was *Chu Chin Chow*, which he wrote and produced and which was the most successful musical play in the history of the English stage. It took the fancy of the soldiers home on leave and of the war-time public generally and ran from August 31, 1916, to July 22, 1921—a total run of 2,238 performances. Oscar made some £200,000 from that play . . . but he died a poor man. The income-tax authorities demanded £40,000 from him and he said that his farm cost him, altogether, £100,000.

Success as astounding as that of Oscar Asche—but not, fortunately, followed by losses so terrible—was that of Harry Gabriel Pélissier, Pélissier of the Follies. Pélissier started life by working in an office and also in the jewel-dealing business of his father. He did not, however, as stated by Arthur Wimperis on inadequate documentary evidence, go to sea. Nor did he consequently have the experience attributed to him by the same distinguished theatre-programme historian, that:

"On his return from his first voyage he was cheered by an enormous crowd, with whom he gratefully shook hands. His coolness in action was remarkable. On one occasion, under the very guns of Sevastopol, he absorbed several of the enemy's lagers, and then, placing his blind eye to the speaking-trumpet, exclaimed: 'I cannot see the signals!'" At the end of the action he turned to Captain Keir Hardie, commanding the Zulu levies, and said, 'Kiss me, Hardie.' Eye-witnesses attest that he bore the operation without flinching."

Pélissier's guiding idea in his earlier years as proprietor of the Follies was to revive the art of burlesque, and he burlesqued grand opera, musical comedy, and wordless plays. At the beginning of 1904, he brought the Follies to the Palace where, during a fog that broke records even for London fogs, they opened with *Bill Bailey*, a skit of the normal Christmas pantomime (though not so long as the pantomimes of those days, thank goodness!). Later, at the Palace, the Follies burlesqued *Hamlet*, and they appeared there altogether six times in five years—although, strangely enough, Charles Morton had feared that they would not be popular with the Palace audiences.

Max Beerbohm wrote, with justice, of Pélissier:

"He is a comedian of a really high order. He does not make fun, fun makes itself in him, and bubbles gaily up and forth, even when he is not doing anything in particular. Pélissier's humour is pre-eminently one of curves . . . he has the good fortune to be a very large and rotund man . . . his face is a mirror in which myriads of expressions, broad and subtle, are reflected in bewitching succession."

This verdict goes to support a view I have held for many years—that a capable actor makes a good producer; he knows what he is doing. Consider, besides Pélissier, Gerald du Maurier, Noel Coward, Seymour Hicks and Leslie Henson. Authors, too, I maintain, produce well—when anyone gives them a chance: so many producers think that their first task is to obliterate the author.

Dion Boucicault, Charles Wyndham, Charles Hawtrey. . . . I have seen so many brilliant productions by all of them. Max Reinhardt, when he had made such an enormous success of the Cochran show, *The Miracle*, came to the Palace. He produced a mime by Vollmoeller called *A Venetian Night*, for which a complete German company was brought over. I have somewhat blurred recollections of a maze of gutteral sound from which emerged occasionally comprehensible words such as " Herr von Finck. . . . . Musik . . ." but I found all those Germans a little overwhelming at rehearsals. *A Venetian Night* was beautifully produced, but it was not a success.

Stanley Bell, who was assistant stage manager for Tree when Cecil King was stage manager, and who has since produced Shakespeare for Sir Oswald Stoll; Auriol Lee, one of our few women producers, and a very good one; Ralph Reader at Drury Lane; George Black at the Palladium; Ayliff, who produced *Yellow Sands* and *The Farmer's Wife* which Barry Jackson had the sense and courage to keep on even when it was not an immediate success; Lewis Casson and Maxwell Wray, who produced so many pieces for Sidney Carroll and did the very difficult job of producing *The Streets of London;* Bourchier; Robert Atkins, a true Shakespearian—he has produced Shakespeare at the Old Vic and at the open-air theatre in Regent's Park; Leon M. Lion, who has done very good work with his Galsworthy seasons, and his more recent Ibsen season at the Criterion; Frank Parker, who started as a call-boy at Drury Lane. . . . I could extend the list on and on . . .

Atkins went with Forbes Robertson on his first farewell tour of America, but with the beginning of the War he came back to England to join up. Before the Army would have him, however, he had to undergo a slight operation with a three months' convalescence. Fisher White suggested that he should fill in his time by helping Lilian Baylis at the Old Vic. He saw her and arranged to help by stage managing. It was then that Atkins first met Sir Phillip Ben Greet. Atkins made it a condition that he should appear in the roles of Richard III and Cassius.

" By all means . . . you have such a villainous forehead," Greet replied.

Of Julian Wylie and Willie Edouin I have spoken elsewhere. But I must not forget my old friend William Mollison, son of the great William Mollison, the Scottish actor, and brother of Clifford Mollison, the comedian; frequently chairman of the Stage Golfing Society—and an authority on brown sherry. William Mollison is the producer of *No, no, Nanette* and many present-day musical comedies.

The late W. H. C. Nation, an old and very rich man, wrote plays and " songs adapted from the French," and would have them produced for his private amusement, even if there was no one else in the theatre, like Ludwig II of Bavaria, who would have performances of Wagner—with real rain—for himself alone.

Bobby (I beg his pardon, *Robert*) Evett, who created many parts in Gilbert and Sullivan operas, was one of the speakers at a dinner I attended. When I left the dinner to go to the theatre and conduct he was making a speech . . . and when I returned to the dinner after the end of our programme, he was *still* speaking. When he sat down I was asked to make a speech, but all I said was : " I should like to call Mr. Evett's attention to the fact that one of the most famous songs he ever sang was called : ' A Tenor Can't Do Himself Justice.' " He had that night!

(This song, incidentally, was in *Utopia (Limited)*, and was written specially for Bobby.)

Evett gave up being a singer to become a producer at Daly's —which, I suppose, accounts for the phrase " Voice Production."

Teddy Royce is the brilliant son of the famous Royce of the old Gaiety. He was brought up in the theatre and was efficient as assistant stage manager, as a dancer—had, in fact, all the necessary mental equipment, unlike so many producers, who have no knowledge of the theatre. He produced *Bric-à-Brac* at the Palace so well that it was decided that he should be the permanent producer of the succeeding revues, and his engagement should start on January 1. In the meantime he took a trip to America to produce a show there . . . and I did not see him again for nineteen years.

The dress rehearsal of *Bric-à-Brac* lasted until three o'clock in the morning—the show went without a hitch on the first night—and I remember walking up and down the Haymarket with Alfred Butt, discussing it. I was optimistic, but he said: "This will never last any time." It ran for over a year.

William J. Wilson, who died in America only a few weeks ago, produced the comic opera *Merrie England*, which I conducted, in London recently. He was, I thought, a model producer. He never shouted or used a megaphone. He never swore; his manners were always perfect. He was, in fact, a shining contrast to what we have been and still are used to from producers. Wilson did his work smoothly and efficiently, sitting in the stalls waving a walking-stick. When he could not find his own walking-stick, he borrowed someone else's. And when he could not borrow a walking-stick, he helped himself to my baton!

CHAPTER VIII

COMPOSERS AND CONDUCTORS

WHEN I was fetched from school to see my first rehearsal I sat, delighted and amazed, watching red-bearded Hans Richter conduct. And he was worth watching too; his skill, his dominant presence and a tongue that could often be caustic made an orchestra realise that things had to be done properly when he appeared. When he reached this country he was completely unknown by name to the English patrons of music; yet he soon established himself so firmly that he did more than anyone else to build up Wagner's reputation and to cultivate a love for his music in England. He was undoubtedly the greatest concert and opera conductor of his day.

Richter used to give sixteen concerts a year at one period; later he became the conductor of the Hallé orchestra at Manchester. He was made a Doctor of Music; he was tremendously fêted; he received numerous honours; and his daughter married an Englishman. Yet always his heart loved his Fatherland and not (or at least only second) the country where he had made his career. When the Great War broke out the old man returned all the honours which had been conferred upon him in this country.

Hans Richter persistently wore a wide-brimmed black hat which, from one year's end to another, was never brushed. He arrived at Covent Garden in this hat one day when I went there to see him at rehearsal. As he was very sensitive on the subject of spectators during rehearsals and would refuse to work if there were any strangers in the theatre, I was placed well out of the way in a box; the curtain prevented me from being seen, but my position enabled me to hear perfectly what was going on.

Richter's objection to visitors at rehearsals was the result of an incident which had happened when he had agreed to the request of an offensive little German named Engel to be present at a rehearsal. This man Engel was then music critic on Edmund Yates' paper, *The World*. During the rehearsal Richter had an argument with the flute player who was doing something he did not like—after all, the purpose of rehearsals is to put people right when they do things wrongly—and Engel wrote a highly dramatic account of the incident which was published in *The World*.

When Richter knew who I was he made an exception in my favour. But if he saw me lurking about, as unobtrusively as possible, he would send his assistant stage manager to ask who I was. The assistant stage manager knew perfectly well who I was, and his carrying out of Richter's instructions became like a formal " challenge " by a soldier on sentry-go. When I returned home to lunch after attending one of these rehearsals, my father would examine me on what I had heard; it was a good way of learning.

Although Richter was so emphatic that he would not have unknown visitors in the theatre, the ban had apparently not been extended to cleaners, for one day, years later, as he conducted and rehearsed the company on the stage, a charlady was pushing a vacuum-cleaner to and fro behind him; and the low, irritating whirr-whirr of the mechanism could be heard above the instruments and voices. At last Richter could stand this interrupting but mysterious sound no longer; he stopped the rehearsal, turned to the leader of the orchestra, and said:

" Vot iss this noise? Vere does this funny whirring sound come from ? "

" That's a vacuum-cleaner," replied the leader.

" A vacuum-gleaner? Vot iss that? Vot iss it for ? "

" It's instead of a brush. . . . It fetches dust out by suction."

" Ah, very goot. Gif her my hat ! "

On one occasion Richter went down to Eastbourne to conduct an orchestra consisting of local players with a few imported from London.

COMPOSERS AND CONDUCTORS

The pads in the bassoon player's instrument had worn away, and when he played there was, from time to time, a sharp click.

Richter heard these clicks, but did not realise what caused them, until he had investigated and had the trouble explained to him. Then he said: " Well, now, let us take this once more. And, if you please, more music and less mechanics from the bassoon ! "

Richter's baton was a light flexible piece of cane about two feet long, and when one day I noticed it lying about I was amused to see that on the end of it there was the grip off a bicycle handlebar. Apparently he had seen it somewhere and said: " Thiss iss goot to get holdtt off. . . . It vill be excellent for me to conduct."

It is, incidentally, extraordinary what a variety of batons are used. Some people use funny little sticks ; Henry Wood uses a long thin one ; Beecham a much smaller one. Jazz conductors don't use a baton at all—and it seems to make no difference however much they wave their fingers or bounce about, because once the time of a piece is set it goes on the same until the end is reached ; so there is really nothing to conduct.

Richter, as I said, made his name in this country by conducting Wagner. This bears out the view which I have long held (a view with which my friend Mr. James Agate thoroughly agrees, though we differ so strongly in our opinions of Berlioz) that every conductor must have a pet composer through whom to make himself known. Beecham, for instance, specialises in Mozart and Delius ; Harty in Berlioz ; Weingartner in Beethoven ; Coates in Wagner and Russian music ; and Wood in everything !

For many years my father was leader of the orchestra, at the Gaiety Theatre, to the unsmiling Meyer Lutz whose features never relaxed even at the antics of the funniest comedians.

Although he wrote burlesque, Lutz was really a serious musician. He would leave the Gaiety at midnight on a Saturday, and at eleven o'clock on Sunday morning he would be on the organ stool of Southwark Cathedral ! Sometimes, at festivals, he would have a little band in the Cathedral, a thing not uncommon in churches a generation ago. Members of the Gaiety orchestra would be recruited for this duty—at five shillings a time.

"Praising the Lord for five bob" this was called.

I was with Lutz, after my father died, at the time of that famous burlesque by George R. Sims—*Faust Up-to-date*—in which Florence St. John took the lead, E. L. Lonnen, the comedian, was Mephistopheles, and four girls did the famous "Pas de Quatre."

Lutz went to the theatre every single day, whatever was happening, to rehearse or to write music in his little room under the stage. One morning I went to the theatre to fetch my violin for another engagement. Four understudy dancers were rehearsing the "Pas de Quatre," and Lutz was playing for them. He was a tubby, short man, with a little white pointed beard and thick glasses which stamped him with a Teutonic look; and he was half-standing, lolling against the piano and playing with one hand. As I watched him, he grew tired of remaining in that position; so he rolled over to make his other side rest against the piano, and went on playing the tune with his left hand instead of his right. And if you think it is easy to do that without interrupting the movement—try it!

Lutz always wore a muffler, and a top hat on the back of his head, though how he kept it there in defiance of the law of gravity I do not know.

He was asked, when the Gaiety did not need him for a time one summer, if he would like to go to Scarborough to conduct an open-air band and he agreed to take the Gaiety orchestra to Scarborough.

This was to be what was called a "military" band. If, when one of these "conversions" was carried out, a violin player could play the clarinet, all was well. But my father played only the violin. However, Lutz offered him the drums, and he accepted; so he was at the top of the orchestra in London, but at the bottom in Scarborough.

All the time the band was in Scarborough, all through the boiling August afternoons, the members wore top hats and

THE OLD DINING-ROOM AT THE SAVAGE CLUB

frock coats. Top hats and frock coats—and they called that a military band!

When a season of French plays came to the Gaiety, Lutz was not required as conductor so the Gaiety management "lent" him to the Opéra-Comique. There he, like every other conductor, found himself handicapped by the deputy system. "I do not like these tammed teputies," he would mutter angrily.

In the Opéra-Comique orchestra there was only one drummer, a brother of Edward Solomon, the composer. One Monday this drummer said to Lutz: "Herr Lutz, I want to be away on Wednesday evening. I hope you won't mind if a deputy takes my place."

"No, no. Always these tammed teputies," said Lutz. "You must be here yourself. If you send a teputy he vill not have rehearsed the music; he vill ruin the blaying of the whole orchestra. It is impossible."

"Oh, but Herr Lutz," replied Solomon, "I have already rehearsed the deputy. He's a first-class drummer: I can assure you you won't have anything to complain about . . . and it really is most important for me to be away on Wednesday."

"Vell, vell," said Lutz, "if that is so, perhaps chust this once I will permit a teputy to blay for you; but mind, it is only this once. . . ."

So on Wednesday evening, another figure took the place of the familiar Solomon at the drum. Lutz was so annoyed about the sending of the deputy that he fully expected this unknown drummer to make mistakes and spoil the performance. But as they played he noticed that the drummer did not make mistakes. He seemed to know the music. He came in right to a fraction of a second every time. Solomon must have been as good as his word and rehearsed the stranger thoroughly.

Lutz looked at the man. There was something vaguely familiar about his appearance. He was sure he had seen this unknown drummer who played so well; he was *certain* he had seen him somewhere—but where? That tubby short figure; that little white pointed beard; those thick glasses, the hair, the German look . . . confound it he had seen that man somewhere, seen him often. Lutz stared at his drummer. He *knew* he had seen him; but where? To his last day Lutz never found out where he had seen the drummer whose appearance was so familiar. . . .

He saw him every time he looked in a mirror.

The stubby German hair, the little white pointed beard, the thick glasses . . . they were the hall-mark of Lutz himself. And the man who stood a few yards away from Lutz, playing the drum with the calmest air imaginable, was no stranger, and there was nothing mysterious about the fact that he knew the music so well. It was Solomon! He had had himself disguised as Lutz, and gone back to the orchestra as his own deputy (wig, as usual, by Clarkson). So there were two Lutzes in the orchestra that night.

The joke was a wild one, a crazy one, to play. But it was a typical frolic for a member of the Solomon family. The drummer and his composer brother, Teddy Solomon, could never resist a chance to play a practical joke. Several times I saw them in action, for I was a pupil of Teddy Solomon, who was so brilliant that at one time he threatened to become a serious rival to Sullivan—a name which by the way is said to be a variation on Solomon.

Solomon wrote comic operas, and wrote every note himself —a method of workmanship that contrasts strangely with those of the present day when it apparently takes five people to write one simple tune, and people who can merely strum vaguely on a piano consider themselves composers although they are completely ignorant of harmony, orchestration, or any other of the basic requirements for the writing of music.

Solomon was, in brilliant contrast to these ignorant amateurs, a fine workman, and I always feel that he would have risen to greater reputation and prosperity than he did had it not been for the fact that he had a curious fascination for women, and some woman or other was always running after him. The woman that *he* ran after, and married, was Lilian Russell, a famous beauty and a *real* blonde. It is only two years since she died in America.

For Marie Tempest Solomon wrote *The Red Hussar;* with Burnand, the famous editor of *Punch,* he wrote a playlet founded on an incident in the *Pickwick Papers*, and called *Pickwick*. This playlet dealt with the fact which most people seem to read Pickwick without discovering that Mrs. Bardell, with whom Pickwick was in love, had a lover—a baker. There is very little dialogue, but it includes the moment when Mrs. Bardell, carrying a feather broom, is asked by Mr. Pickwick why she has come back.

" Oh, I am returning to dust," she replies.

" What a funereal expression! " exclaims Mr. Pickwick.

The music for the playlet was a barcarolle, but, since Mrs. Bardell's lover was a baker, I have always insisted on calling it a baker-roll.

Pickwick was produced at the Court Theatre in 1891, with Arthur Cecil as Pickwick, Rutland Barrington as the Baker and Lottie Venne as Mrs. Bardell. Two years later it was given at the Shaftesbury with Little as Pickwick, Charles Hawtrey as the Baker, and Jessie Bond as Mrs. Bardell. I very much like the songs in it, as, for example :

> A bachelor who
> At forty-two
> Has not the fixed intention
> To be merry but wise,
> And contract no ties,
> Is not,
> I wot,
> Among the lot
> Of those I mean to mention.
>
> A bachelor may
> Be blithe and gay,
> And by the fair sex petted,
> And every hour
> From flow'r to flow'r
> He'll pop
> And stop
> To sip each drop,
> Pursued, but never netted.
>
> A bachelor, a bachelor,
> That shall be my degree,
> Notion delectable,
> Who a respectable
> Bachelor would not be,
> My boys,
> Bachelor would not be ?

Then there is " The Pickwick Portmanteau . . ."

> I can't go about
> Any longer without
> A footman or a valet,
> And so I've decided
> To be provided
> With one paid liber*ally* ;
> For whenever I pack
> I've a pain in my back,
> Which does of age remind me,
> And when I've done,
> It's ten to one
> That I've left my boots behind me.
> A list I make
> Of things to take
> To suit our varying climate ;
> White ties, like a waiter's,
> Knee-breeches, and gaiters,
> Quite worthy of the Primate.
> My list is such,
> 'Tis much too much,
> And when packed *tanto quanto*,
> It takes three chaps
> To tug at the straps
> And sit on my portmanteau.

Solomon also wrote *The Nautch Girl*, which was produced at the Savoy by George Dance during one of the quarrels between Gilbert and Sullivan. Some of his works were put on as entertainments at the Chelsea Barracks, where the women's parts were taken by men. In one, naturally without any thought of offence, he burlesqued Sullivan's " Lost Chord " by weaving it into a hornpipe—and this upset Sullivan who begged him not to allow it to be played again. " I wrote that when my brother was dying," he said.

On the occasion which I mentioned of the performance at the Chelsea Barracks there were only four of us in the band. Just near to the band, in the front row of the " stalls," sat the Duke and Duchess of Teck—he was, I well remember, a fine-looking old man—and their daughter whom England has since loved so well as Queen Mary.

However, as I said, all the Solomons had what was, to use the politest word possible, an extravagant sense of humour. To give two examples : When *Nautch Girl* was being produced a great deal of the business communication was done by telegram, and at that time Fred Darrell, a tenor who was a little "beyond it," was acting as Solomon's secretary. One day Solomon, looking as though the matter were of one life and death, said to Fred Darrell, "Oh, Fred, do you mind taking this telegram down the road to the post office.... It's to Mr. D'Oyly Carte and it's very urgent indeed."

"Why, certainly," said Fred, "of course I'll take it for you."

"Here you are then," replied Solomon, handing him a telegram. "And, as I said, it's very urgent, so whatever you do, Fred, don't walk; run, as hard as you possibly can, all the way."

At this point Fred thought there was some reflection on his running powers, so he replied: "Run? Of course I'll run. Why, do you think I'm getting beyond it? If so, you're wrong ... there's many a younger man would be glad to be able to run as well as I can. You just watch me...."

And so, in the old-fashioned frock coat which he always wore, Fred dashed off along the street.

And whirring madly—and vastly to the surprise of all the passers-by—went a child's windmill which the Solomons had cleverly fastened to his back, and of which Fred was gloriously unconscious as he rushed along to the post office determined to show that he could run as well, and better, than any of these young fellows who thought they were so quick on their feet.

Teddy Solomon loved to work at night. I hate it, but in those days I was younger, and in any case I was flattered at being asked to work with such a well-known composer. So late one night we settled down to work in his rooms with a great joint of ribs of beef, and salad and a supply of bottled beer to sustain us through the long watches. One of this small party was John S. Baker, composer of "Up I Came with My Little Lot," writer of comic songs, accompanist, organist—though he made very little money out of any of his activities despite considerable industry—and a remarkably skilful copyist. It was as a copyist that John S. Baker was working for Solomon that night.

When we had fortified ourselves with cold beef and beer against the chill of the midnight hour, we started work. After a time, Baker became tired and said: "Can I have half an hour's rest in front of the fire?"

"Why, certainly you can, old boy," said Teddy Solomon, "you'll feel fine after a nap," and so Baker settled himself in an easy chair by the fireside.

But the occasion struck the Solomons as funny; in fact as one which could not be allowed to pass without a practical joke of some kind. They thought; thought hard. Then they fetched rope—first by careful observation making sure that Baker was well and truly asleep—and ever so delicately, lest he should awake, startled, and spoil their plan, they bound Baker to the easy chair. Still moving as quietly as they could they piled lump after lump of coal on to the fire until eventually it was almost heaped into the chimney. All preparations were complete; the Solomons retired to their seats at the table—to watch.

Baker must have been tired; for as that vast fire grew gradually hotter, as the flames leaped and the glowing coals made the room almost unbearable, he slept on. Perspiration poured down his face; he stirred uneasily, moved slightly from side to side in his sleep; muttered incomprehensibly . . . he must have been having a nightmare, probably thought he was in the nether regions.

The stage was set for the Solomons; they set up a concerted shout: "Fire! Fire! Look out, the house is on fire. Fire! Fire!"

Baker's eyes opened. The cry of "Fire!" was in his ears. His eyes were looking at that vast heap of blazing coal . . . he thought he really was in a burning house. He tried to leap from the chair; he could not; could not move his legs, could not raise his arms. He was far too frightened and bemused to notice the ropes that bound him to the chair, and he let out a dreadful shout: "I'm paralysed!"

Both the Solomons roared with laughter—and released their victim. They thought the joke was enormously funny, but I have never approved of practical jokes; I think that the pain caused to the victim more than outweighs any amusement that may be gained by the perpetrators of the joke or by bystanders. I believe, and always have believed, that if a man cannot be funny verbally (No, I don't mean orally; I want to include the written word) it is much better for himself and others if he does not try to be funny at all. However, as I have said, the Solomons —good-natured though they certainly were—did not see the matter from the same angle as myself.

One of the jokes they devised was to send their dog—it was a French poodle, one of those curious-looking animals which are shaved in patches—out into the street painted in a number of vivid and violently-contrasting colours, a sight which greatly surprised people walking along the streets round their house in Great Queen Street, near Drury Lane.

That neighbourhood was, I recollect with annoyance, a happy hunting ground for street criers. Now I have not the slightest objection to people going along the street and trying to sell their wares from house to house. But what does annoy me is that instead of shouting out something sensible which will tell me that if I want muffins or coal, a man who wants to sell me some is outside, they utter yells and screeches so unintelligible and so weird that anybody making such a din would, I am convinced, be cut dead, or given a very nasty look, by even the strangest inhabitants (green-spotted tigers, two-tailed mongooses—mongeese?—and the like) of an Amazonian jungle. It is impossible to tell whether the street vendor is trying to sell you flowers or coal or strawberries, or to buy from you the broken-down kitchen stove or a pile of empty bottles.

One very weird screecher used to pass the Solomons' home at regular intervals. His cry was beyond them, but they did not like to be beaten. They settled down to make an intensive study of the matter. They invited their friends to be present when the weird cry was due to be heard. They collected, and collated, all the most authoritative opinions they could obtain. And the result of this collection and collation was that the cry undoubtedly was:

"My wife's 'ad it—all 'er life."

The mystery was as bad as ever. What had the street-vendor's wife had? It sounded like a horrible disease. But anyway, why should a man spend his whole life shouting out a thing like that in the streets of London? It was baffling, tantalising. Finally, the tension of this infernal question was clouding their whole lives. The Solomons decided on a desperate move; they would *ask* the man. So they laid in wait until, echoing from house to house, filling the street until it was only a chasm of horrible sound, came the weird cry. The man was waylaid and most politely asked:

" Excuse me, but what *is* it you are shouting? "

He replied: " Fine fresh 'addick all alive, whadjerthink? "

A street cry also for a long time troubled my friend Sir Alexander Mackenzie. . . . It was a diabolical, overwhelming cry; women collapsed when they heard it. Strong men blanched and let wine-glasses fall from their nerveless fingers as they groped blindly for the support of the mantelpiece.

This case was, too, more subtle and insidious than the one that troubled the Solomons, for no one could ever catch the crier, though everyone who had heard him (or her) went through life in trembling apprehension, wondering in their calmer moments whether the screech were meant to advertise fish, watercress or coal.

The mystery remained unsolved until one day, when I was leaving the Mackenzies' house, I heard the terrible cry coming from the distance. I grasped my walking-stick with a determined grip. " Herman," I said to myself, " now is the time for action, the moment to strike, the moment to plumb the depths of this horrible problem. . . . There must be no flinching."

I called a cab. In tones that left no doubt of the gravity of my mission I told the driver to catch up with the street crier. . . . But meanwhile the crier was making good speed away from us, and the cab crawled as only a cab can crawl. Still, little by little we gained. . . . Hurray! The quarry's ahead! There he is, shouting his head off in front of a convalescent home on Primrose Hill . . . fine for the patients, isn't it?

Well, *what's* the fellow selling?

Oh, flowers. . . . They look a bit wilted, too.

Whenever I had lunch with Sir Alexander (of which I shall relate more in my chapter on Clubs) I always tried to steer him away from the hors d'œuvre . . . but my efforts were always in vain, for as hors d'œuvre were one of the things he did not have for lunch at home he always made a point of having them when he lunched in a restaurant. Now my objection to Sir Alexander eating hors d'œuvre was not a dietetic one: it was concerned purely with time. For he was a very widely travelled man, and everything to which he helped himself—a sardine, an anchovy, an olive, a pimento, salami (his favourite), anything else—reminded him of some incident which had happened when he was at the place where olives, sardines, pimentos, salami or anchovies were grown or caught or pickled. And the amount of time it takes a man to help himself to hors d'œuvre if he tells a story with each spoonful is almost beyond belief.

Mackenzie, whose friendship I valued as much as I admired his services to British music, had several stories about himself which I very much liked. One of them was this:

Mackenzie wrote the music for Irving's production of *Coriolanus* at the Lyceum; and Alma Tadema designed the scenery. At the dress rehearsal, Mackenzie heard a weary stage-hand say in a tone of disgust, " Three knights ! " (Irving, Alma Tadema and Mackenzie) " That's about all I'll give it."

The stage-hand's judgment was a little harsher than the public's; the play actually ran for thirty-seven knights (sorry, nights).

During the latter part of his life Mackenzie was so loaded with degrees, honours and distinctions of one sort or another that one of his friends despaired of getting them all on to an envelope. So he addressed it:

" Sir Alexander Mackenzie, A to Z."

A composer named Rawlings was so prolific that he had to write under all kinds of pseudonyms, because if too much stuff is turned out by one man, the public is glutted and his reputation is damaged. Although Petersburg Square was about as near to Russia as Rawlings had been, he wrote a Russian Dance Suite under the name, if I remember rightly, of Ivan Tchakoff. The dances sold so well that his publishers said: " Will you write another of those Russian suites for us ? "—and write another he did.

This also quickly became popular, and a " flood of letters " —as newspapers say of any number above two—was received by the publishers, asking: " Who is this Ivan Tchakoff ? "

The question was awkward, but the publishers enterprisingly replied: " We have had this music by us a long time. No one has heard of M. Tchakoff for a considerable time; he must have been sent to the Siberian salt mines."

But still the admirers of the unknown composer wrote, many of them demanding to see a photograph of him. The publishers held another council of war; then they descended to the packing-room, where dwelt an old old man who had worked for them for many years, and forthwith he was offered £2 if he would allow himself to be photographed in a wig. As £2 was more than the old man's weekly wage, he immediately accepted— and the next day he was so ill recovering from the celebrations that he could not come to work.

However, the third volume of Ivan Tchakoff's Russian dance music had a most artistic-looking man with a mass of tousled hair on the cover . . . and all his admirers agreed that the face was indeed that of a genius.

The sad side of the story concerns the old man from the packing department. For truth to tell, grave moral degradation set in. He would display unholy pride as he showed his companions—baffled and bewildered—in the neighbouring pubs that Ivan Tchakoff was none other than himself. And since the photograph was on the music as proof, none could deny him. Also, alas, he held the knowledge of the true state of affairs over his employer's heads, and did his best to make what he could out of their anxiety to keep the story to themselves.

Sullivan was the first organist of St. Peter's, Cranleigh Gardens, and my old friend Arthur Helmore tells this story of the days when he played there. As a special service, the Bishop was late: so Sullivan played: " I waited for the Lord." The

Bishop, after a further lapse of some minutes, did not appear, so Sullivan played his own lovely ballad: " Will He come ? " At last, when hope had practically been abandoned, the Bishop stalked majestically up the aisle. And Sullivan played: " We that endure to the end . . ."

When Sullivan wrote the incidental music for Irving's production of *Macbeth*, at the Lyceum, I was doing a short spell in the Lyceum orchestra. The music Sullivan had written was most elaborate (for those times), and he wanted to have a private rehearsal at the Savoy, away from all the bustle and possible interruptions which he would have encountered at the Lyceum. So the polite monocled Sullivan began to take the rehearsal at the Savoy; but he soon discovered that the orchestra found his music—especially the overture and the violin parts—extremely difficult. Things were not going at all well, and Sullivan became more and more worried. At last he said: " Gentlemen, gentlemen, if you knew the hours and hours it has taken me to write all these hundreds and thousands of notes I am sure you would bear with me and help me out with this."

This direct human appeal, so obviously made with great emotion, electrified the players; they tackled the music with a new enthusiasm and determination, and in due course they gave a magnificent performance.

Sullivan had a curious habit of conducting at a slant, and it was far from easy to follow the movements of his baton. But I noticed that once Sullivan had developed the habit it spread to François Cellier—father of Frank Cellier, the noted actor, and brother of Alfred Cellier—who conducted for Sullivan at the Savoy, and to the conductor who went with the operas on tour.

François Cellier was, by the way, a strange example of an unimaginative eater. Every evening at six o'clock he would go into Simpson's-in-the-Strand and eat a dinner which consisted of fish pie, saddle of mutton, lemon pudding, and one large whisky and soda. Now for one night that dinner might be excellent (if you can forgive the drinking of whisky and soda with meals); but just think of eating the same dinner every night for weeks, months, years . . .

Alfred Cellier's most famous work was *Dorothy*. This opera started by being a failure; then it caught the public fancy and ran for over a thousand nights. Cellier was not a strong man —he constantly suffered with his chest—and at the time he had left England for a warmer and drier climate which would bring him back to health. So, far away from London, the composer knew nothing of the astounding success of his work—until he received an enormous cheque. Which was proof enough.

Another famous work of Cellier was *The Mountebanks* in which he co-operated with Gilbert.

When John Crook wrote the music for *Peter Pan* he can little have dreamed of the future it had before it. As year after year that eternally popular production has been put on, Crook has conducted his own composition.

The Spanish conductor So decided to do some work on the other side of the Atlantic. He went to the United States and was a tremendous success. Therefore—I nearly said So— Señor So changed his name to Sousa: So-u.s.a.

Jimmy Glover, my predecessor at Drury Lane, was a huge and humorous man, but was not a whale for work. It was usually when he heard that someone important was in the theatre that he would decide to conduct a number himself. Then his vast bulk would barge its way remorselessly through the orchestra, music stands going down before him in all directions. When eventually he arrived at his appointed place and began to conduct—he had often not conducted a note for days previously —he would cheerfully conduct the wrong number; not that the orchestra worried; they played the right one and took no notice! Jimmy didn't mind either, and when opportunity occurred he would turn round most magnificently and wave to his friends in the audience.

A similar habit was that of Luigi Arditi, who used to conduct all the Italian operas at Covent Garden. He always entered the orchestra in very good time, and there would be a vast stamping of feet and rapping of bows on the backs of fiddles, to announce the fact of his arrival, according to the custom of the day (a custom, incidentally, which I would never permit, for I do not think any man should be applauded until he has done something to earn applause). After the first act Luigi would stop in the orchestra and with enormous urbanity would bow to the boxes.

One night (so 'tis said) an actor could not get to sleep. He recited to himself; he counted sheep jumping over stiles ... it was all useless. His insomnia was as bad as ever. After much more turning and twisting and banging the pillow and pulling the eiderdown over himself when it slipped on to the floor, the actor had an idea. "I will count all the Lupinos," he said. So he started ... but long before he had completed the task, a gentle noise—a kind of mixture between shunting engines and a thunderstorm over Mont Blanc—told the world that he was profoundly lost in sleep.

It is the same with the Godfreys. There was old Dan Godfrey, who was bandmaster of the Grenadier Guards. There is Sir Dan Godfrey, who has just retired and still lives in Bournemouth. His son went to Africa and died suddenly there not long ago. There is Herbert Godfrey. There is Arthur Godfrey. Charles Godfrey died a year ago. And the name of the cousins is legion. . . .

The eternally amusing Tommy Beecham took the chair at a Foyle Literary Luncheon to which I went. Sitting opposite to me was Dame Ethel Smyth, and she was apparently fascinated by the sight of the gorgeous toastmaster in uniform which gave you the impression that a Field-Marshal was such small fry that he would say "Thank you," and mean it, when offered a twopenny tip, who from time to time called out: "My lord, ladies and gentlemen. . . ."

When Dame Smyth rose to speak she commented on this. "We keep hearing 'My lord,'" she said, "but is there a lord present? If so will he please stand up so we can have a look at him?"

The opportunity could not be neglected. I rose. "Oh, I see. . . . I beg your pardon . . ." said Dame Smyth, considerably startled to see someone stand up, and evidently not recognising me. We shook hands, with great solemnity, across the table.

And next morning a newspaper headline announced: "Lord Herman Finck."

I was in the orchestra of Edward German for *Richard III*, which he wrote, as long ago as 1888, and we have been fast friends ever since that time. Recently I conducted German's *Merrie England*, an opera I have always very much admired; as, indeed, I do all his work, including the way in which he took in hand the opera *The Emerald Isle*, which Sullivan left incomplete at his death, and finished it. It was, by the way, the manner in which German carried out that task which led to his being taken into the Savoy.

Arthur Nikisch, with his eternally tousled hair and big moustache, was adored by every orchestra he conducted because of his electric personality.

One night I met Nikisch having dinner in Kettner's, and I asked him to come over to the Palace, where the *Passing Show of 1914* was then running.

"You must come over to see some of the show, and you must conduct a number for us," I said.

Fortunately, Nikisch was dressed, as he had been conducting at an early concert; and he willingly came back to the Palace with me. The Palace orchestra, when they saw him, were puzzled to know whether it really was Nikisch or someone who looked like him. Both he and they entered into the fun with a right good spirit, and the number he conducted went off splendidly.

To my mind, Nikisch was an ideal conductor and a most good-natured fellow; he took one of the big orchestras to America for a concert tour and when they returned to this country the players were unanimous in saying that they had had a wonderful time with him—mostly playing poker in trains!

Ivan Caryll—whose real name was Felix Tilkens—conducted *Dorothy* throughout its run and used to write for the Gaiety. He went to America and did very well there, but he was always a very extravagant man. I have never seen anyone travel in such princely style as Ivan Caryll. Everyone was expected to bow to him when he stepped into a boat or a train; he bought their bows, of course, and bought them dear.

Landon Ronald, a very old friend of mine is, at one and the same time, an excellent conductor, a fine song writer, and the head of the Guildhall School of Music. In spite of all his positions and worries he still retains a sense of humour and the ability to be amusing. At a recent dinner of the Musicians' Benevolent Fund he told a story about deputies—which are, as I have said, the bugbear of every conductor. Sir Landon was himself deputising, as an after-dinner speaker for Seymour Hicks, and after some discourse on the curse of deputies, he remarked: "It was the inimitable Sir Thomas Beecham who on one occasion said he had started rehearsing with the London Symphony Orchestra, but finished by conducting the City and Suburban!"

Landon Ronald wrote the music of the song "Down in the Forest," and thereby (to make use of a cliché) hangs a tale. I have often heard debates about the question of the relative importance of words and music in the success of a popular song (of course, I have my own ideas on the subject). One thing, however, which is beyond dispute is the fact that the name of the lyric writer is very seldom known, even to those singers who constantly " feature " the song.

One day my dear friend Harold Simpson, who wrote the words of " Down in the Forest," called on the late Madame Albani, in connection with a book he was writing, and sat talking to her husband, Mr. Gye, while she was giving a singing lesson upstairs.

Suddenly the familiar strains of " Down in the Forest " floated into the room. Simpson immediately sat up and remarked: " Hello, that's my song."

" What do you mean, *your* song ? " asked Mr. Gye, a little scornfully. " It was written by Landon Ronald."

" Yes," replied Simpson humbly, " but I happened to write the words."

Mr. Gye smiled, " I'll bet Emma doesn't know that," he said, " and she's been teaching the song for years."

When Madame Albani came into the room, Mr. Gye asked her: " Who wrote the words of ' Down in the Forest,' Emma ? "

" How should *I* know ? " answered Madame Albani.

Once when Harold Simpson was staying at a hotel in Wynberg, South Africa, he noticed that a man at the next table stared at him all through dinner. He stared so hard, in fact, that Simpson began to feel uncomfortable. At last the man pushed back his chair, rose from the table, walked across to Simpson and said: " Pardon me, but aren't you a member of the musical profession ? "

" How did you guess that ? " Simpson replied.

The stranger took this for an affirmative answer to his question, and he beamed: " Oh, well, I've often heard you sing, *Mr. Kellie !* "

Simpson had been mistaken for Lawrence Kellie, the song writer who sang his own songs, and whom he had never, at that time, met. The resemblance between them was so extraordinary that similar mistakes were made on a number of occasions.

No conductor I know travels so much or so quickly as Henry Wood. One day I met him coming out of the Langham Hotel—where he often stays as it is so handy for him when he is conducting the Promenade Concerts at the Queen's Hall, just opposite. He was wearing a travelling coat and carrying a bag, so I said: " Hello, where are you off to this time ? Is it Siberia ? "

" No," he replied laughing, " only Torpuay. Back to-night or in the morning."

Hamilton Harty is a passionate lover of Berlioz—though I admit that I am among the large number of people whose enthusiasm for the work of Berlioz is kept well within bounds; and who are unimpressed by the fourteen drummers in his *Messe des Morts* (not to be confused with *Messe d'Amour*, i.e. a divorce).

Harty was conducting one of Berlioz's works at Manchester and was about two-thirds of the way through a long sustained movement when, with a terrific crash, the drummer came in about two pages too soon !

COMPOSERS AND CONDUCTORS

PAUL WHITEMAN ALARMED SOME OF THE SERIOUS "BROTHERS"

Harty was a boiling cauldron of wrath inside, though there was nothing for him to do but to go on conducting and pretend nothing wrong had happened. (Anyway the would-be Berlioz fans were admiring the wonderful tympani effect achieved by the master composer, or so they thought. The poor wretches thought that that curious crash meant something; they did not realise that it was an accident.)

After the concert, Harty—still quietly seething—said to the secretary: " I want you to ask that drummer who did his best to wreck the performance to come and speak to me before he goes."

Then all the more distinguished music lovers there pressed around Harty to congratulate him and shake hands with him. Last of all came a most effusive man who said: " Really, sir, I must congratulate you on the wonderful way you conducted to-night. You have no idea what pleasure you gave me."

As soon as this man disappeared through the door, Harty said to the secretary: " Where's the drummer that I asked you to send to me?"

The Secretary looked surprised. " Why you've just been talking to him," he said; " It was the man that went out last. . . ."

Which just shows that cheek will get a man out of any corner!

Paul Whiteman—perhaps I should say *Colonel* Paul Whiteman, for the State of Kentucky has bestowed that rank upon this very capable 22-stone musician, brought his band over from America for a show at the Hippodrome, for which I had written the music. I liked Whiteman very much and his players—then a sensational novelty—were so good that I asked them if they would come round to the Savage Club and play three or four pieces (which alarmed some of the serious " Brothers "). They cheerfully agreed and they thoroughly enjoyed themselves.

I brought a set of papier mâché instruments—the kind you hum through—and after Paul Whiteman's band had played I got a rival team, headed by Mark Hambourg, to come on and play the papier mâché instruments.

Shortly afterwards I was told that Paul Whiteman was asking if I could go to see him in a private room at the Hippodrome.

"I hope there wasn't a misunderstanding about that night at the Savage," I thought. "It will be very awkward if they ask for a fee."

In thinking that I did them a grave injustice, for when I arrived they were all assembled and Paul Whiteman presented me with a large loving cup on which signatures of all the members of the band had been engraved, and on which was inscribed:

> To My Friend
> HERMAN FINCK
> with many thanks for
> a great time
> at the
> Savage Club
> PAUL WHITEMAN
> 7 *April*, 1923.

Mark Hambourg, one of my papier mâché band the night Whiteman and his players were at the Savage, was giving a recital at Brighton one afternoon during the War. He was wearing his usual wide-brimmed hat, and a fur coat, and very much "looking the part" as he went about Brighton.

After the concert Mark Hambourg told me he was going to have dinner with some people he had known many years on and off.

"What is their name?" I asked.

"I don't know," he replied cheerfully.

"Surely that is going to be a little awkward?" I said.

"Oh, I shall be all right. Walk along with me and see, if you have nothing to do for half an hour."

So Mark Hambourg took under his arm a brown paper parcel containing a piece of salmon and off we went. The salmon may appear a little eccentric nowadays, but during the War, if anyone asked you out for a meal, it was only a matter of common decency to do anything your ration coupons allowed to eke out the feast.

When Hambourg eventually rang a door bell, a maid appeared

and he did a nice line of " patter " to hide his ignorance until his hostess appeared and took charge of him.

Afterwards, I asked Mark: " What was their name ? "

" I spent the whole evening trying to find out," he said, " and I *still* don't know."

Next day there was a war meeting at the Brighton Hippodrome, at which Horatio Bottomley was one of the speakers. Almost the first person I saw at the Hippodrome was Ben Tillett, and as we were chatting I heard someone remark : " That's Mark Hambourg."

Ben Tillett was wearing a big hat like Mark Hambourg's. Both wear their hair fairly long and both are men of about the same figure. So I began to introduce Ben Tillett as " Mark Hambourg," and no one to whom I did so suspected that there was anything wrong.

Then we walked along to the Theatre Royal. I was wearing a fur coat—a vast garment which appears only on very rare occasions—and I made Ben Tillett put it on to complete his " disguise."

When people at the theatre saw him at the interval, they were all convinced that they were looking at Mark Hambourg.

For an important concert at the Queen's Hall it was decided to invite a very eminent conductor down from the North of England. It was the first time he had appeared at such a concert and the invitation was, indeed, a great honour.

On arrival in London, he went to stay at a famous hotel, on the opposite side of the road to the Queen's Hall, and from the hotel he walked over to take a three hours' rehearsal. After lunch he rested for a time and then the moment arrived for him to dress and have dinner before going to the concert. So shortly after half-past six he asked the valet to put his clothes out. The valet began to do so, but before long, looking very worried, he came to the eminent one and said : " Please sir, I can't find the trousers."

It was appalling news. There was the *maestro* about to conduct before the most musically *élite* audience London could muster —and without any dress trousers. It was by then too late

THE A.C.M. CLUB

to rush out to a ready-made tailor or to one of those useful establishments where the ill-equipped male is arrayed in borrowed, or rather hired, glory for a wedding, a funeral, a visit to Ascot or an evening out : all the shops were shut.

The conductor cursed his careless packing and thought—hard. Then he sought the advice of the manager of the hotel, whom he knew. They went into conference, as business men say when discussing blondes or horse-racing.

The manager is a man of resource. This situation needed resource : it called in agonised tones for the breadth of vision of a Francis Bacon; for the inventiveness of a Leonardo da Vinci; for the strong swift action of a Napoleon. The manager showed all three. He surveyed all the potential trouser sources; he chose one; he invented the means of obtaining the trousers; and he put his plan into action.

"The only hope," he said to the conductor, "is to find a waiter wearing trousers that will fit you." He looked him up and down and then gave the order : "Send all the small waiters to me."

A body of small waiters arrived. They were lined up in what looked an identification parade—and that is what they feared it was. They were convinced that somebody was going to be given the sack; especially when, from the low-voiced conversation between Musicus and the manager emerged such phrases as : "The third from the left, I think . . . or perhaps that man on the right."

At last a choice was made. A waiter was told to surrender his trousers and change into his ordinary clothes (my mistake; he was told to change into his ordinary clothes and surrender his trousers). Then he was told he could have the evening off.

The concert was a tremendous success. But the glittering audience that applauded Apollo so enthusiastically little thought that their idol had, not feet of clay, but the trousers of a waiter.

I conducted for John MacCormack when he was making a record of the song "Questa o quella"—"Yes, the one is as fair as the other"—from Rigoletto. He had not done any gramophone work, which is a complicated business, before. First it is necessary to rehearse a song with the orchestra; then it must be gone through again to be timed. Finally, it must be sung and played for the recording. It is absolutely essential that the final rendering should be flawless beyond doubt because when the song has been recorded on the wax, you cannot " try it over " to see whether it has been a success. You have to wait until the metal matrix has been made; and then if there is anything wrong the singer, conductor and orchestra must all be brought back and made to go through the whole process again.

MacCormack went through the rehearsing in due form. Then he sang the song for recording. All went well; it would have been a highly successful record. As he finished, MacCormack said loudly: " Well, thank God that damned thing's over! " and prepared to leave.

Everyone laughed. The machine was still recording! MacCormack's comment was duly stuck on the end of the song.

I have always felt annoyed with the gramophone company because they destroyed that unique record.

One evening when Eric Coates and I were waiting to broadcast, he played his new suite " London Again." He began to tell a number of us about this suite and explained that the first part of it was " Oxford Street," which he played.

" Oxford Street ? " I said. " I hope you got the right side."

The " pubs " on one side of Oxford Street were open half an hour longer than those on the other side.

Still, silly though the licensing laws have been in London, they are worse in some other cities. When I was in Glasgow, I arranged to have lunch one Saturday, before the matinée with D. G. Parker, the critic, whom I had met some time before in London.

He arrived at my hotel at about a quarter to one, and we went straight in to lunch.

" What will you have to drink ? " I asked, " A bottle of claret ? "

" Yes, that would be excellent," replied Parker who, I gathered later, scarcely ever drank anything and so did not know the oddities of the local licensing laws.

I called the waiter, asked for the wine list and chose a claret.

" Of course I can serve you, as you are a guest at the hotel, sir," said the waiter, " but your friend can only have ginger beer."

I then found out that the public-houses in Glasgow are not allowed to open until tea time on Saturday. The idea of this is to prevent men from drawing their wages at lunch-time and immediately spending all the money on beer or whisky. I am sure that the actual effect is to stimulate the thirst of many men who, if the public-houses were open at lunch-time, would have only one drink—or perhaps not even one—but who spend all the afternoon thinking about the time when they will be able to buy a drink, and develop a tremendous thirst in the meantime.

But even supposing that the regulation about closing the public-houses were a wise one, what possible justification can there be for preventing a man from giving his guest a drink with a meal in his hotel ?

A conductor never knows when something may go wrong among the orchestra. When orchestral players have time off during the evening—but not long enough to leave the theatre—they usually play cards. One evening at the old Her Majesty's Theatre, when the orchestra returned to play the *entr'acte* music, one player had " cleaned out " another one of all his small change. The winner cupped all the coppers in his hands and held them towards the loser, laughing. The loser was tempted—and fell. He gave the hands full of coppers a sharp rap, and the coins fell clinking and tinkling all over the orchestra.

Coppers played their part in another—and much earlier—theatrical incident I remember. It was at the same theatre. An Italian opera season was brought over ; the chorus was rather old, but all members of the company were thoroughly proficient. Business was terrible. I went to see Beethoven's *Fidelio*, and when the curtain went up for the second act a man came forward to the footlights and said in broken English : " We cannot go on . . . we have not been paid our salaries . . . we are starving."

There was a pause. Then, from the few people in the audience chiefly in the gallery where the true musical enthusiasts are always to be found in numbers—came a shower of pennies on to the stage. The poor singers collected the money—and the opera was continued.

To cheer you up after that pathetic story I must tell you about the sailor and the trombone. Three drunken sailors bought three front row seats in a theatre one night. Two of them soon became bored with the play and went out, but the third man stayed, and during the *entr'acte* he watched the trombone player with a fascinated stare. When the trombone player came back to the orchestra for the last music of the evening he saw, with horror, that his trombone had been taken in two and that half of it was missing. " Ha, ha," said the sailor, "*you've* been trying to get that off all the evening. *I* did it first time ! "

The late Mr. Alfred Rothschild, a bachelor member of the famous family, invited a number of London conductors to a party once a year—and wonderful parties they were, for Alfred Rothschild was a lavish and accomplished host. I remember seeing Melba at one of these parties—there was always the finest musical talent at entertainments given by Rothschild.

He seemed to have a special fondness for conductors, and would send a number of us presents of *pâté de foie gras*; the presents were so lavish that even the most hardened *pâté de foie gras* enthusiasts found it difficult for one household to consume it all before it went bad.

When the famous play without words *L'Enfant Prodigue* was brought over from France one of the characters—an elderly man—was dressed and made-up in exact imitation of Alfred Rothschild.

My grandfather was a well-known conductor in Amsterdam, and on one occasion was asked to conduct a band at a wedding. Just before they were due to start, they were tuning in the vestry of the church when the excitable and excited mother of the bride rushed in and said :

" Oh, Mr. Finck, what are you doing ? "

" We're tuning," said my grandfather.

"Tuning!" exclaimed the bride's mother. "Now? Why, I engaged you three months ago!"

My maternal grandfather was a journalist on the staff of *The World*; an erudite man and, in particular, a great student of Shakespeare; he wore a beard but no moustache, I remember. One night he took a seat in the gallery at Drury Lane for *Hamlet*, and next to him sat a man and a woman with a small child. This man and woman had entered the theatre by mistake; they wanted more sensational entertainment than *Hamlet*, and by the end of the first act they were so bored that they slipped quietly out of the theatre.

When the play finished and the beautiful green baize curtain descended, my grandfather, after being completely absorbed by the play, again took notice of his surroundings, and found a child sound asleep on the seat next to him.

"Nothing to do with me," said the manager when my grandfather told him that he had found this child which had been left alone by its parents.

So my grandfather took the sleeping child under his arm and prepared to leave it at Bow Street police station to be cared for until its parents were found. Meanwhile, after several hours in the theatre, he was extremely thirsty and dropped into a tavern on his way to Bow Street. As he was having a drink, he heard a tremendous amount of noise in an adjoining bar; he pushed open the door, and there were the parents of the child he was carrying.

"Here's your child," he said. "You left him in the theatre."

The father and mother looked at the child and at my grandfather, and then together they exclaimed: "Good gracious. So we did!"

CHAPTER IX

MUSIC—AND MODERNISM

AT a Savage Club Annual Dinner some years ago, the three arts, Drama, Painting and Music were represented by three famous men. A very entertaining and amusing speech on the drama was made by Sir John Martin-Harvey. Painting brought forth an amusing and instructive speech by Augustus John. Perhaps by the time he had finished, "cut the cackle" was in the minds of the members and guests. A young man who was then well known as a modernist in music and manners (and whose name I have forgotten) stood up and in a drawling and half-yawning way said: "I suppose you want me to talk about music."

"Oh, no we don't!" was shouted by several of the members.

That is the position in which I find myself in this chapter. But as I cannot hear your views I propose to say a few hundred (I mean thousand: hard luck) words regarding the great art to which I have been attached since I was a small boy.

I started my musical career as a serious musican and with a thorough education in classical music. By the time I was seventeen I was hard at work, with a brother violinist who wrote the book, composing a grand opera. In the middle of the task my collaborator suddenly became engaged. I decided that I must write a wedding march for him, and with the grandiloquence of youth called it, "A Grand Nuptial March." I am afraid it did not help my romantic friend much, although it was once played on the organ at the Albert Hall, for within a year of his marriage there was a divorce.

As a youth I wrote a fugue, a sonata for violin and piano, and a trio for horn, violin and piano; and I have written fantasias on the works of Chopin, Schubert and Brahms. As a student I orchestrated three of the piano sonatas of Beethoven. In fact

MUSIC—AND MODERNISM

in my student days at the Guildhall School of Music I went right through the curriculum of classical music, and that is why I am glad that I am now a Fellow of the School—a fact I feel that I owe largely to my old friend Landon Ronald, now its head. He and I are not far apart either in age or in views upon music, and hence I greatly appreciated his comments in the *News Chronicle* on the music for *The Streets of London* in 1933, when he wrote:

> "I suppose no name is better known in this country as a composer of light music (which bears the unmistakable stamp of the musician) than that of Herman Finck. He is a man who has written countless revues, ballets, pantomimes and musical sketches, many of which have achieved great popularity. He is such an excellent musican that I have often wondered why he has not attempted something rather more serious. Still, I admire him for being content to do a small thing really well rather than do a big thing poorly.
>
> "These thoughts came into my mind a few days ago when I went to see that extremely amusing satire, *The Streets of London*. The programme aptly states 'Appropriate Music by Herman Finck'; and that is exactly what it is. I do not think there is an original bar during the entire three acts and eleven scenes; and yet how carefully and cleverly every bit of it is chosen and how it helps the atmosphere and enhances the fun of the play!
>
> "Nothing rouses my enthusiasm more than a thing well done; and, indeed, here Herman Finck has arranged 'appropriate music' perfectly."

Apropos of *The Streets of London*, if a little apart from the subject matter of the chapter, is a story about Sam Livesey who played the villain in that piece, and played it perfectly, as well as being splendidly made up. The play, though originally a serious one, struck the audience as funny by the time it was produced in London, and it ran for six months.

Several small parties of people came repeatedly to see it, and eventually knew the piece thoroughly: and they always hissed the villain when he appeared and the green light shone on him.

One night six people, all in evening dress, came round to the stage door and asked: "Has Mr. Livesey gone?"

"No, he's just dressing," replied the door-keeper.

So they waited until a man came in sight. "Is this him?" they asked, for he was unrecognisable without his make-up. "Yes, that's him," replied the door-keeper.

Directly Livesey stepped outside, the waiting party began to hiss him—and they followed him down Charing Cross Road hissing all the time!

A very rich man called Stuart Ogilvie a good many years ago wrote a play called: *The Sin of St. Hulda,* and arranged for it to be produced at the Shaftesbury Theatre. The author wanted serious music, based on old German themes, to accompany the play, and the stage manager and producer (one man) was dispatched in a hansom cab to approach various eminent musicians on the subject. The stage manager interviewed Mackenzie and Frederic Cowen and others, but they all refused to undertake the work, and when he returned to the Shaftesbury he reported: "I haven't fixed up with anyone to write it, but I know the very man for the job. His name's Finck; over the road."

"What do you mean, 'Over the road?'" asked the author.

"At the Palace."

"Oh? A Music Hall . . ."

Undeterred, the stage manager came across the road and fetched me, but when I returned with him I found the wealthy author still "up in the air."

" . . . But you can't write the music for this play," he said. "You are associated with a Music Hall."

To which I replied somewhat brusquely: "Do you think that my father, when it was decided that my career would be in a Variety Theatre, allowed me to do so without a thorough education in classical music? I started as a serious musician, and I will guarantee to write whatever music you want for this play."

So I supplied the music for the play, founding it on various old German tunes. In addition I wrote original vocal and incidental music. The author was so surprised when he found that

MUSIC—AND MODERNISM

I was able to write what was wanted that he did nothing but congratulate me. Even that did not make the play run!

Rehearsals were a little difficult because the chief male character, played by Lewis Waller, was named Herman . . . and we were never sure whether it was him or me that people were talking about or shouting to.

It is because I feel so strongly that a writer of light music must above all things be a competent musician that I particularly like a story about myself told by a writer in *The Era*, some half a dozen years ago:

" When at school (he wrote) I studied piano playing with a scholarly professor of music trained in the austere atmosphere of Leipzig Conservatoire. I am ashamed to say that I was distinctly bored by the minor classics in whom this kind, good man tried to interest me. I was a reluctant pupil; and so that my hour with him might at least terminate pleasantly, he used to devote the last ten minutes of it to playing to me whatever piece of music I wanted. And I invariably chose some ragtime, which in those days was a very raw and blatant affair indeed. I shall never forget the expression on the face of the teacher—he might have been the Court musician in some eighteenth-century German state—as he played me these early hiccupping Broadway 'hits,' while I beat time with my foot.

" Then one day I took him a selection from a musical piece by Mr. Herman Finck. I remember he started rendering it with the usual look of amused contempt on his face. But his expression gradually changed. He turned back a page to look at the composer's name, and continued to play with increasing interest and pleasure. When he reached the end of the selection, he began beamingly to run through it once more! After that I believe that he began to toy with the idea of writing light music himself.

" Musicians, like the gods of old, are always able to recognise each other though the fields in which they practise their art may be wide apart. So my donnish old professor saluted

Mr. Herman Finck, the musical man-of-the-world, and member of that splendid band of composers who after the death of their supreme master and inspiration, Sullivan, continued to provide the English people with gay tripping melodies which could be whistled immediately and treasured for all time."

I need not go through the list of my classical favourites—headed by Beethoven, Bach, Schumann, Brahms, Mendelssohn, Wagner, Tchaikowski, Glazounov, Sibelius, Saint-Saëns, Bizet, Massenet, Delibes, all the rest—except Berlioz—before speaking of the moderns.

There is, for instance, Stravinsky. Edward German had an extension from his wireless set, with a second loud speaker, so that his housekeeper could listen to broadcasts in her own room. One evening she rushed into his room and said: "Oh, Sir Edward, has your wireless gone wrong? Because mine has; it's making the most dreadful noises."

Stravinsky's "Sacre de Printemps" was being played! I must admit that I have considerable sympathy with the housekeeper's view-point. Nor, I feel, should one be too hasty in one's condemnation of the dear old lady who, on seeing a newspaper headline, "Stavisky Shot After Flight From Police," remarked: "Well, I always said something dreadful would happen to him, writing the kind of music he does."

Still, if I don't like Stravinsky, various other people don't—or persuade themselves that they don't—like Beethoven. Some years ago an Anti-Beethoven Society was actually founded in London ("Anything to be Different" should have been its motto).

Norman O'Neill expressed to me one day the peculiar view that he thought that Beethoven was good only for teaching purposes, and on another occasion Philip Page said to me: "I don't think that I like Beethoven, any more than I like Burgundy or beef."

Shortly after that I invited him to lunch. As he arrived I was playing the part of a melodious and very beautiful Beethoven

Sonata. A few minutes later the lunch-gong rang, and when we reached the dining-room there were the roast beef of old England and Burgundy. When Page tackled the beef and Burgundy with evident pleasure and agreed with me about the quality of the music I had been playing, I came to the conclusion that the Anti-Beethoven movement rested on the insecurest of foundations.

Page, Hannen Swaffer, A. C. Mackenzie and myself went one day to the Queen's Hall to hear one of the other modernists, Schomberg; his work was certainly the last thing in strange noises. It would, I am sure, have caused Dr. Johnson to reverse his dictum that he did not like music but thought it was the pleasantest kind of noise anyone could make.

Schomberg, after his first work, was hissed and laughed at—a thing almost unheard of with English audiences. He moved his baton in a curious way, it seemed rather to be dangling from his fingers, than to be used for conducting: then amazing noises issued from the orchestra.

There was a most curious effect with a duet between the double-basses and the piccolo—the two extremes of the orchestra—which I suppose depicted something in the composer's mind, though not in anybody else's. It seemed almost as though he wanted to laugh at the public, but they laughed at him instead.

All through this strange duet, the double-basses made curious grunting noises, like the giant being killed by Jack, and the piccolo responded with noises which sounded like a dying bird. Then the noises ceased, but the conductor went on conducting in his own dangling way for some time after the silence began.

The whole business puzzled us immensely, so at the end I asked a member of the orchestra whom I knew to come across to Verrey's with us to tell us all about it. " What happened when there was that exchange of peculiar noises between the double-bass and the piccolo, and then the conductor went on alone?" I asked.

" Ah," he replied, " that was where we dried up!"

The music and the conducting had so baffled the instrumentalists that they could not play any further!

Pace and noise are the hall-marks of really " modern " music, except perhaps in the dance hall where men in evening dress walk with deadly seriousness about the floor, clutching girls in a preoccupied sort of way. Strangely enough this is called a "fox trot." It's not even an amble. When that has been going on for a considerable time, the band switches over to a waltz which is not a waltz, for though it is in three-four time, it is slower than a minuet and has a dirge-like and dreary movement.

The thing that is incredible to me is that, apart from the words, it takes four or five men to produce one of these jazz horrors. One man " takes it down "; another harmonises it and a third does the orchestration; they have the co-operation, very often of two writers of what they are pleased to call the lyric. In fact, everybody except the composer has a hand in it. Then, too, music is "framed": two bars are taken from one thing and added to two bars of another to make a tune.

One way and another, there is to-day a good deal of justification for the remark I heard not long ago: "Oh, he's a real musician. He can write it down!"

Some six years ago, I expressed myself fairly plainly on the subject of certain aspects of modern music to an interviewer from *The Era*, and as I have found no reason to change my views in the time which has elapsed since then, I will reproduce here what I then said:

"It amazes me that the Americans, who put up so many barriers against the negroes, copy the negroid idiom so freely in their music. The negro talks in his own rhythm, and this is evident in nearly all the light music which comes to us from America. It is all right in moderation and in its own way but we have been having a little too much of it. What I deplore particularly is the habit of certain British composers of imitating the American model. If a man blacks his face, he doesn't become a negro; and however slavishly a British writer may copy American methods in song-writing, he never comes near the real thing. All he succeeds in doing is to produce something in which all the individuality is missing, and without individuality, music is worth nothing at all.

"It is true that numbers of the Americans have been influenced a great deal by the European school of light opera. I don't know if it is due to their mixed population, but several good writers from this side have gone over and been at home there at once. Kerker, the composer of *The Belle of New York*—the first musical comedy from America to take the London stage by storm—was born in Germany; and Ivan Caryll and Rudolf Friml are other Europeans who have done very well. Jerome Kern, perhaps the best of all America's composers of light music, began his career in this country. I have known him for over twenty-five years. I remember orchestrating one of his first songs, ' How'd you like to spoon with me?' Kern is very fond of England. He married an English wife who likes America, so he lives over there. The music he writes is not like the accepted American stuff. He doesn't write the usual monotonous fox-trots; but his tunes may be used for dance purposes. He said to me once: 'I still like the George Edwardes school.'

"The worst fault of much of the American music is that it is all written in one tempo and no colour or light and shade, simply a noise. It reminds me of spring-cleaning—you know—beating the carpet on the lawn. Another name I gave it is that of ' Fun in the Fireplace.' There are no variations. But in the old days we had waltzes, polkas, square dances, lancers, etc. and two-steps. I think we may see a revival of the old type of thing. The other evening at the Green Room Club, I arranged an old Music Hall programme. I went back to the 'sixties for some of the numbers, and you should have heard how they were enjoyed. It was like a riot. . . .

"In pre-War London there was (among the outstanding musical figures) Monckton, who was in the true Sullivan tradition. Then there was poor Paul Rubens whom I knew for years. He gave me a picture of himself signed, ' Yours from infancy, Paul Rubens.' It was stolen from my room at the Palace Theatre. He was a man with a wonderful gift, and his early death was a great loss to the English stage. If he were alive to-day he would help to stem this American tide. He wrote catchy airs which were whistled everywhere. But how often do you hear American tunes whistled in the street? Very rarely, because they are composed at the piano and not in the head; as the fingers and not the brain dictate.

"The modern song-writer can seldom orchestrate or even write down his music. He is not properly equipped. The procedure seems to be: 'Compose music first, and learn it afterwards.' I am told that the publishers do everything in their power to keep their writers of 'hits' from coming under the influence of the professors. They fear they might lose their gift for inventing melodies. Melody is a splendid thing, but you want something else besides. And you can't sing a lot of American music as it is written; and much of it seems to be orchestrated with a view to drowning the singer's voice. In the best musical plays, the music and the lyrics should fit each other perfectly and follow the action of the play in a consistent fashion. To get this effect, the composer and author must be trained in their work."

One of the great regrets of my musical career is that I had a seat for the first night of Richard Strauss's *Rosenkavalier* at Dresden but was unable to go to the performance because it coincided with a first-night at the Palace. My seat was sold for £30!

My first experience of Richard Strauss's work was when I played at afternoon concerts at the Crystal Palace: to us, at that time, it seemed so difficult that we could hardly unravel it. But since Manns, the conductor there, was always enthusiastic for anything new, he made us struggle through it. Fortunately, there was hardly any audience at the concerts so we could do what we liked (musically) without causing too much trouble. And so strange did some of Strauss's music seem to the world of that day, that I very much doubt whether the few listeners could tell whether it was being played rightly or wrongly.

Though I have played and conducted in many places, widely varying in type, I have never been enthusiastic about giving performances out of doors, though I attend and greatly enjoy the performances given at the Open-Air Theatre in Regent's Park. The gardens in which the theatre is situated used to be known as the Botanical Gardens. At the time when Sydney Caroll began to give Shakespeare in the park, I met Marie Burke, that accomplished singer and actress. "Are you going to conduct for Caroll in the gardens?" she asked.

"No," I replied, "I don't think my batonics would go with his Botanics."

Earlier in this chapter, I quoted some remarks by Sir Landon Ronald about the appropriateness of music. But I think the most remarkable case of a really appropriate programme is contained in a strange document which was given to me some years ago, and which I here reproduce:

SPECIAL PROGRAMME FOR THE BRITISH UNDERTAKERS' ASSOCIATION CONFERENCE

1. (a) "Funeral March of an Elephant" . *Guitton.*
   (b) "Funeral March of a Marionette" . *Gounod.*
2. Tone Poem. "Dance Macabre" . *Saint-Saëns.*
3. Song. "The Sailor's Grave" . . *Sullivan.*
4. Variations for Piano and Orchestra on
   "Down Among the Dead Men" . . *Ernest Farrar.*
   BARRS PARTRIDGE
5. (a) "Pavane pour une infante defunte" . *Ravel.*
   (b) Intermezzo "The Last Good-bye" . *Moretti.*
6. A Keltic Lament . . . . *J. H. Foulds.*
   Solo 'Cello: H. M. Calve.
   Solo Harp: Hilda Atkinson.
7. Song. "Tom Bowling" . . *Dibdin.*
8. (a) Entracte for String Orchestra (with mutes)
   "The Death of Asa" (*Peer Gynt*) . *Grieg.*
   (b) Irish Sketch "The Wake" . . *John Ansell.*

One evening I found myself in a club with a crowd of City men. Their conversation was all of the mysteries of high finance and business. They were talking about how so-and-so had been "done"; about the affairs of another man being in a rocky condition.

"And," said one of these super-sharp City men, "if you ask me, I think What's-His-Name's business is unsound."

Disgusted by their talk, I rose to go. "Thank God I belong to a profession that is *sound*," I said as I left them.

Music, besides having charms, can also serve at times as a weapon of sarcasm. To the editor of a paper which produced a weekly column of the most appalling chestnuts, I sent the following bars of music:

It was rather wasted, though, for he did not know music, and wrote asking me what it meant. I had to be cruel enough to reply: "'The Village Blacksmith,' by Longfellow. First line." Then, of course, he remembered: "Under the spreading chestnut tree."

A terrible thing is a joke that fails to "register." A Lancashire friend has not, I am afraid, forgiven me for telling him on return from Blackpool, that I was suffering from a disease known as bah-goomboil.

A musician of the old school whom I remember well was Nicholas Mori, a great friend of my father, who used to lunch with us on alternate Sundays. He played for the Gilbert and Sullivan operas in their early days, the days of the Opéra-Comique Theatre. But, although he recognised how good Sullivan's work was, repetition made him so sick of hearing the same tunes time after time, that he left!

He was fond of sitting at the piano at my home, amusing himself, and I can remember him putting his fingers on Middle C and C Sharp and remarking: "So near and yet so far."

Another time he was playing the song "The screw may twist," from the *Yeoman of the Guard*, which was such an immediate success when sung by Rosina Brandrum. Despite the reminders of my mother that it was time for lunch, he went on playing over and over again the last few bass notes—tonic and dominant. Then, looking at his fingers and the notes, he said: " I respect you because of your age."

One day I was going to hear Benno Moiseiwitsch give a Beethoven recital at the Wigmore Hall when I met " Jack " Anderson, and as I had two tickets I invited him to come with me, which he did. Benno, as well as having a splendid sense of humour, is a superlative pianist, and we both thoroughly enjoyed his perfectly played concert.

After the concert we dropped into a nearby hostelry for refreshment, and on the table were a set of dominoes. We were the only people there and we began to play—although I had not played dominoes since I was a boy—and I won. " Benno's been pounding the dominoes and now we're pushing them about," I said. When we had finished our game, I went on to the Savage and there I found Moiseiwitsch looking amazingly unruffled after the tremendous exertion of a concert like the one he had given.

" Benno," I said, " after what you have done to-day you deserve a drink. I'm going to give you half a bottle of Cliquot."

When he had finished the champagne, Benno went upstairs to the card-room, where some friends were expecting him. It was two or three days later when I next saw him, and he said: " Herman, it was very kind of you to give me that champagne. But the results were disastrous. I didn't know what I was doing with the cards. . . . I lost over £5 ! "

When I was on tour with *Merrie England* in Glasgow, I went upstairs to dress before dinner, and was surprised to hear brilliant pianoforte playing. Someone was playing Chopin, then dropping into the *Midsummer Night's Dream* scherzo. A part of the scherzo would be played so very slowly, then more Chopin would follow.

I was so fascinated by the playing that I began to undress in the corridor, outside my bedroom door, to listen.

" Who is that playing ? " I asked the chambermaid.

" Oh, I can't pronounce his name," she replied.

"Rachmaninoff?" I asked.

"Yes, that's it."

Rachmaninoff was giving a recital in Glasgow that night, but as I stood in the corridor wrestling with a white tie I could not for the life of me think why he should be playing Mendelssohn at that dirge-like tempo.

Months later I heard that Rachmaninoff had prepared an elaborate pianoforte arrangement of the scherzo. So I was the first person to hear it; he had been going through it slowly that night in Glasgow.

The French composer Ravel orchestrated some of the *études* of Chopin for a Nijinski ballet season at the Palace and his orchestrations were sent on to me. I found one was incomplete, and was trying to sort the matter out when Philip Page came into the theatre.

"What are you doing?" he asked.

"Trying to unravel Ravel," I replied.

(So that shows where that much-quoted joke comes from!)

When, in 1901, George Jacobi was about to retire from the Alhambra he was given a Benefit Performance—fifty-six turns on the programme! One of his acquaintances, a chiropodist in the West End, wrote offering any help he could give. Jacobi handed the letter to John Hollingshead, who was in charge of the arrangements.

"But who is the man?" he asked.

"Oh, he's a corn-doctor," answered Jacobi, who spoke with a distinct foreign accent.

Some days later, the proofs of the programme for the Benefit Performance came in, and, looking over it, Jacobi was amazed to find the name of the chiropodist among the honorary conductors.

"What on earth is this man doing in the list?" he asked Hollingshead.

"You told he was a *conductor*," Hollingshead replied.

"I did not," said Jacobi, "I told you he was a *corn-doctor*."

Incidentally, among the honorary "corn-doctors" that day were John Crook, Teddy Jones, Sidney Jones, Ivan Caryll, Jimmy Glover, Maurice Jacobi (George Jacobi's son)—and myself.

One day when I was lunching with Lewis Saville, of Cramer and Co., the Bond Street music publishers, Saville said: "I have always loved your music. I have more of it than you have."

Always ready to improve the shining hour, I said: "Well, I have one piece in my pocket now. Would you like to see it?" I put my hand into my pocket and half pulled out a mass of miscellaneous papers; for a moment I feared he would want to see what I had in my pocket, but I knew I was saved when he replied: "I'll take anything of yours without looking at it."

Next morning I supplied him with "Dancing Stars" which he duly published. The latest thing of mine he has published is the suite "Marie Antoinette" written in the French style.

Publishers, although I have had so many dealings with them to "mutual advantage," as they say in commercial circles I believe, are undoubtedly curious people. Take, for example, the strange story of my "Opera Bouffe."

When *The Gondoliers* was produced Sullivan, presumably because he was too pressed for time, did not write an overture. I, then aged about twenty, contended that when an opera went on tour an overture was needed, and so I wrote an "Opera Bouffe" overture in the French idiom. Then I went to Oliver Hawkes, the famous publisher, and explained my idea to him; he would not look at it.

"Let me play it to you," I said when my explanation failed to convince him that I had something good.

"Ah," he said, "that's the way we deal with composers. . . . We haven't a piano on the premises!" (Things have very much advanced in that firm—Ralph Hawkes, son of Oliver, has in his sumptuous office a magnificent Beckstein grand.)

Still I believed that I had done something worth while, and "Opera Bouffe" was transcribed and played from manuscript at the Palace.

One evening, *after* I had written "In the Shadows," Hawkes and his wife came to have dinner with us. After dinner I said: "I have a work which I have only just finished. It betrays all the *motifs* in an imaginary French opera."

"What a good idea!" Hawkes exclaimed. "Have you got it?"

I fetched the manuscript and said to Hawkes: "That was submitted to you twenty years ago, and you would not look at it. You will see the date it was written on the last sheet."

Anyway, Hawkes published "Opera Bouffe," and it is one of the most popular things I have ever written. I have just written another called "Musical Comedy."

It would be most unfair to write a chapter on music without referring to a body without which we musicians could not live, the body which to-day means the difference between prosperity and starvation to British composers. I mean the Performing Rights Society, of which I am an original member and now a member of the board of directors.

Under the Copyright Act of 1911, authors and composers were given the sole right in the public performance of works they have written. But at first this law was of little benefit to anybody, for the composer seldom knew when or where his works were being performed and even if he did it was difficult for him to enforce the law if the people performing his work were recalcitrant.

At the beginning of 1914, however, the Performing Rights Society was formed to make it possible for composers and authors to receive the livelihood which was due to them by law. Composers, authors and publishers who joined the Society vested in it the control of their performing rights. Three years ago, the Society published a review of twenty years' work in which it was explained that the Performing Rights Society:

"Not only aided the composer in protecting his performing right; it also enabled the user of music for public entertainment to obtain from a central organisation a general permission in respect of a large number of copyright musical works, instead of having to deal separately with individual copyright owners.

". . . The Society came into existence as a company limited by guarantee and having no share capital. The signatories to the memorandum of Association were: William Boosey, H. S. J. Booth, Oliver Hawkes, Lionel

"IT'S ALL RIGHT, OFFICER. . . ."

"I WAS THE FIRST MOVING PIANIST"

"IT'S FOR YOU, SIR"
(Sketches by Bert Thomas)

Monckton, Arthur R. Ropes ("Adrian Ross"), David Day and Charles Volkert, all of whom have since passed away.

"On April 1, 1914, the first general meeting of the members, numbering then thirty-nine, was held, and among those present were Paul Rubens, Howard Talbot, Liza Lehmann, Oliver Hawkes, David Day, Madame Teresa del Riego, Percy Greenbank, Hermann Löhr and other well-known figures in the musical world. The late Mr. William Boosey was in the chair.

"The Society had been born at a troublous time in the world's affairs, and its early history is a story of expedients to tide over difficulties. Notwithstanding these difficulties a start was made and the foundation laid of what was soon an established concern. Among the earliest licensees of the Society, it is interesting to note, were Moss Empires, and Stoll Music Halls, the National Sunday League, Messrs. J. Lyons and Company Ltd., the Savoy, Berkeley and and Claridge's Hotels, the Gordon Hotels, and a number of municipal corporations such as Bournemouth, Brighton and Eastbourne.

"The Society grants licences to the proprietors of premises in which music is publicly performed. Licences have been issued in respect of theatres, music halls, cinemas, hotels, restaurants, tea rooms, piers, public houses, clubs, dance halls, concert halls, church and parish halls, liners and other passenger vessels, as well as to municipal corporations, district councils and other corporate bodies. The total number of premises covered by the Society's licence in Great Britain is nearly twenty-five thousand.

"The Society is not a profit-earning organisation; in effect it acts as a collecting agency, and its entire net income, after deducting administration expenses, is distributed among its members in accordance with the extent to which their works are performed."

The board of directors consists of twenty-four members, half of them composers and authors and the other half publishers.

To-day the Society has twelve hundred members. Nearly every British composer, author and music publisher belongs to it. And it controls the performing right in some two million pieces of music.

As you have just read, William Boosey had a prominent part in the founding of the Performing Rights Society. One of my memories of him is an early morning one: he was looking very glum, and remarked: "Herman, I've a dreadful headache . . . and I haven't earned it!"

After that interpellation, we will return to performing rights. A. P. Herbert, always ready to wield a pen brilliantly in a good cause, recently wrote an article in *Punch* called "Up, the Music-Makers!"—an article behind which, I like to think, my inspiration was not lacking. A. P. H. roundly declared that the composer was not being sufficiently well paid for works broadcast, though for this he did not blame the B.B.C., since, he pointed out, the State appropriates nearly half the Corporation's income.

". . . think about the composer, the silly long-haired fellow," he wrote. "For many years he has been pursued by one mechanical enemy after another. In the good old days he won sufficient bread by the sale of 'sheet-music.' Those were the days when men bought 'The Trumpeter' and 'King Charles' and bellowed them in drawing-rooms: and young ladies bought sonatas and 'pieces' and obliged with them on the home piano. But now the domestic tenor is heard no more, and even the grandest piano is more often used as a sideboard than as a musical instrument. The gramophone was at first a new friend to the composer (though even there he was subjected to the unique imposition of a statutory wage or royalty); and while the bands still played in the cinemas, sheet-music still brought in a little bread. But the talkies and the wireless sprang up like great mechanical mushrooms; and soon sheet-music was almost dead and even the gramophone was not what it was. The last, or best, hope of the music-maker is his 'performing rights,' and there are those who are jealous even of these. The infamous Twopenny

Bill was thrown out (it proposed that on payment of 2d. any person should have the right to perform any piece of music in perpetuity without further charge !), but its spirit survives among some of the ' music-users '—the old English notion that composers and authors have not got ordinary stomachs and can exist on air and ideals. In a recent year a certain group of hotels is said to have paid £96,000 in fees to bands ; for the same period the composers of the music played received £6000. The B.B.C., which owes even more to music, should be enabled to be more generous. For, wide and various though the B.B.C.'s activities are, we do not think that all those millions would continue to pay for licences if they got no music for their money ; and in that event all the fine fabric of political addresses and uplifting talks and Sunday sermons—yea, the great Panjandrum himself would crumble and fall."

CHAPTER X

CABIANA

WHEN I was paying off a cabman one night, I was very surprised to hear him address me by my name. "Have you driven me before?" I asked. "Do you know me?"

"Know yer, Mr. Finck!" he exclaimed. "Know yer? Why, lor bless yer, sir, you and me's 'ad many a bluddy row!"

I don't want to give the incorrect impression that I have habitually spent the late hours of the night having altercations, or, if you prefer it, rows, with cabmen: but drivers of horse cabs and taxicabs are entwined with my memories ever since I was a young man.

One of my early memories in which a cab played a big part was connected with the cycling craze in the 'nineties: the novelty of the cycle so attracted people that everyone rushed to take it up, and young men—and even young ladies ("Damn it, sir, what are things coming to?" as the Colonel remarked)—were hurtling along the roads at seven or eight miles an hour.

My friends and I were soon caught by the craze, and we went to a school of cycling—people are apparently born able to cycle in these days: I never hear of anyone taking lessons—run by a Frenchman. The cycling school was indoors, on the first floor, above a carriage builders'. There was a very large room with a circular track on which we were given our lessons.

After several lessons we all felt we were quite proficient enough to take to the open road—and cut a dash doing so as well. So we arranged to meet at the Palace Theatre stage door on the following Sunday morning, and then to cycle in a party to Hampstead. The assemblage at any rate took place according to programme. Then the party made a rather wobbly start; I found that mounting unaided was not as simple as I had imagined and by the time I was fairly in the saddle they were out of sight.

When I had travelled a few yards I made a terrible discovery. *I could only turn to the right.* Whenever I had ridden on the circular track I had always gone round that way, so that I had never learned to turn left. Consequently, whenever I saw a corner enabling me to turn right I had to go round it, although I really wanted to go in the opposite direction.

Before long I discovered—to my surprise—that I was near the British Museum, heading directly away from Hampstead. And I did not know how to get off. It was a time for Napoleonic measures: I took one. I saw a lamp-post and rode straight at it.

After an interval in which I seemed to hit things and things seemed to hit me, and then the ground got in my way, a policeman came to my aid. He helped me to my feet, and said: " Where are you trying to get to, sir ? "

" Hampstead," I replied. " But I can't turn to the left."

" Well, it's just the same as turning to the right except that you do it with the other hand," he said, gave me a swift lesson, helped me to mount—and away I went.

By this time I was determined to reach Hampstead at least as soon as the rest of my party, and was pedalling away for all I was worth. There even occurred to me the dark thought of bundling myself and my cycle into a fast cab, enabling me to await the others, in a superior sort of way, when they arrived, puffing and panting.

However, when pondering this scheme, I arrived at Great Portland Street, and was amazed to see all my party ahead—and all dismounted. One of the party was having a vigorous argument with a cabby; he was abusing the cabby right and left. When I managed to find out what the trouble was about, I learned that the cyclist had run into the back of the cab. The cab was parked in the proper place at the side of the road; the cyclist had the whole of the rest of Great Portland Street to pass it—but he was abusing the cabby for being in the way. There was nothing of the tight-rope technique about riding a bicycle in the 'nineties.

Another early memory of cabs brings in Charlie—Charles B.—Cochran. It was when I was in my twenties, and he was living in a flat in Victoria Street. One night it was raining so hard that several of us decided that the only thing to be done was to have a four-wheeled cab to take us home. Four of us sat down in the four seats and then C. B. Cochran climbed in. We started off and a few moments later, Charlie Cochran—then very slim and agile—shot through the window. We heard him moving about on the roof—and then he appeared at the opposite window, and entered the cab through it. You would have thought that one performance of this extraordinary feat would have satisfied any man, but—despite the continual torrents of rain—Cochran went round and round, through the window, on the roof, and through the window again, until it was time for us to drop him at his home.

The most unpleasant drive I ever had in a hired car—which is morally a cab, I submit—was from Eastbourne to Brighton during the War. That drive was the culmination of a chapter, almost a whole book, of accidents. The sad story started the previous night with me working very hard indeed in the furnished house I had taken at Eastbourne. I went to bed, eventually, meaning to get up early and do one of the less strenuous passages before breakfast, and was reading a book to bring a little peace to my mind by making me forget work and so, I hoped, go to sleep. While I was reading I heard a crunching sound on the gravel outside. I listened: it was repeated. A burglar, without doubt, for no one else would be abroad as late as that.

I climbed out of bed, and opened the window. In the darkness I could see someone was moving about in front of the house: "What do you want?" I challenged.

"Orright, guv'n'r; orright, guv'n'r," a low voice replied.

"It isn't all right. Go away—now," I said.

Then I went back to bed, but still the crunching went on. The man had evidently decided not to go away. He did eventually leave, however, but by that time it was so late that the disturbance, and the expectation that the man would return or that someone else would break into the house, had put us out of the mood for sleep. It was hours before we felt in the least like sleep, and when we eventually did begin to doze a little, an alarm went and we were wide awake again.

Very miserable I felt, too, after missing my night's rest on top of so much work. Still, I set off to catch the train. Only when I was actually at the station did I find that, although I was wearing the proper trousers and waistcoat, I had on a horrible old grey coat which I wore when I was at work in the house.

To have faced the people in the train, wearing this garment, was a depressing enough thought, but it was obviously out of the question to conduct at an important rehearsal looking such a terrible sight. By this time I was wandering through a kind of miasma, and feeling like a jellyfish after an argument with a battleship. I went into the Grand Hotel and ordered half a bottle of champagne; I felt that I might be able to sort my ideas out when I had had a tonic.

When I had had the champagne I realised that the only thing to do was to change my coat, and then hire a car to take me to Brighton, where I could catch a fast train to town.

The driver of the car which I had hired on several previous occasions, was in the grip of a war panic, and did not want to take me. " We shall never get through," he said. " We shall never get through."

" Nonsense," I said, and sat in the front seat beside him to egg him on. Before every corner, he imagined we should meet goodness knows what. And when we actually heard horses' hooves ahead, his heart sank into his boots. It turned out to be quite a small detachment, who shouted a cheery " Good morning " and left us plenty of room to pass. But I needed all my champagne-generated energy to deal with that driver and see he had me in Brighton in time to catch my train.

The " burglar " who started my troubles turned out to be a convalescent soldier, very " lit up," who had decided to call on our maid while on his way back to camp.

George, an Armenian cabman, was very interested in music, and one night I took him up to the Green Room Club. No one had any idea he was a cabman, but took him for a foreign diplomat.

When he eventually landed me on my doorstep, and I asked him what the fare was, he said: "Nothing at all. I have enjoyed myself among your artistic friends. I could not let you pay anything."

Knowing that if I saw him I should make another attempt to pay him, George kept out of my way for a week. Then I had a letter from him, telling me the telephone number which would find him if I ever wanted him to take me anywhere. And underneath his name he had written " music-lover."

One day I was going to Simpson's-in-the-Strand to have lunch with a friend. I arrived opposite Simpson's, to find the road so full of traffic that it was impossible to cross. The close stream of traffic would not stop while I stood impatiently waiting, so I called a cab.

" Simpson's," I said as I opened the door.

" The one in the City ? " asked the driver.

" No, the one the other side of the road," I replied.

So the driver duly drove me across the road, holding up all the traffic, and landed me on Simpson's doorstep. "How much?" I asked.

" Oh, I would not charge you for that," the cabman replied. " You've given me the best laugh I've had for months ! "

He got a shilling out of it, all the same.

Another day, the friend I had been going to meet when that happened—who was, by the way, extremely prosperous—offered to give me a lift in his car. When I walked out of the theatre I found myself looking at the most extraordinary motor car I have ever seen—and a Rolls Royce, too. Its owner, an enormous man, was already standing beside it, and his wife—even bigger than himself—was there, too.

Evidently he felt that his motor car needed some explanation, for he began to tell me its history. "One day my good lady said she would like a motor car. 'Right you are, my dear,' I said, 'you shall have a motor car, and you shall have the best. Not only that, but we'll have a comfortable one while we're about it.' So we went along to the showrooms, and I said to the young man there, 'You can see what size we are. Now, you measure us both, and then make a car to fit us.' And that was what they did."

I thought the result was excellent. It was the only car I have ever seen where you could open the door and walk right in; which is, to my mind, the ideal, instead of imitating a crocodile. Cars are too small; loss of dignity, loss of hat, loss of temper and a scalp wound are caused by them; I have a big scar through being driven home by Valentine Williams, who put us in the back which was more like a gas oven than a comfortable seat. Is that what they call the " tonneau ? "

Charles (" Jock ") Prentice, the present conductor at Drury Lane, came to see me at the theatre one night when I was just departing to visit a friend who had newly become manager of the Curzon Hotel.

"You must come along with me," I said to Prentice, and we climbed into a cab.

Prentice had a big bag with him—and the driver was drunk. The two facts may sound queer in the same sentence, but we found when we alighted that they were closely connected, because the drunken driver swore that the bag was a third passenger and we should have to pay " his fare."

Naturally, we refused to pay this " fare "—especially to a driver who had imperilled our lives by his alcoholic driving. And we went into the Curzon.

When we had been in the hotel for a minute or two, Jock exclaimed : " Great Scott. In the argument, we forgot the bag. It's in that cab, and there's all the music for to-morrow's rehearsal in it."

Both of us rushed out of the hotel, and shouted after the taxi-driver, running as hard as we could. But he must have thought that we were putting the police on his track, for he deliberately accelerated. Some fifty yards further on he was caught in a traffic block and we rescued the bag after all.

There is, too, the case of the man who (I was told) had gone off in a huff.

"It looked like a cab to me," I replied.

Bill Eykin, a popular member of the Stock Exchange, as he climbed into a cab, said to the driver: "Waterloo."

"The station, sir?" asked the taximan.

"No, the battlefield, you fool," replied Eykin.

Lewis Sydney, of the Follies, and I, with both our wives, took a cab homeward one night. The driver was undoubtedly drunk, and when we dropped the Sydneys in Blenheim Road, he turned round near Lord's cricket ground in such a remarkable way that it was a wonder we were not thrown out—or that the cab did not overturn.

We reached our house in Hampstead and my wife walked towards the steps up to the front door, while I pulled out money to pay the fare. The driver then declared that there had been five of us, and not four, in the taxi.

"Nonsense," I said.

"Well, look at that," he replied, pointing to my wife. "There are two people walking up those steps now!"

I telephoned for the police, and the driver tried to get away, but, despite a clear stretch of road, he was unable to avoid a pillar-box on the pavement. Shortly afterwards a policeman arrived and took him quietly away; but at breakfast-time the next morning the taxi was still there, with a policeman solemnly mounting guard over it.

When we were expecting a new maid from the country my wife wrote to the girl to tell her that the other maid would meet her at the station, and explained how they would identify each other. "Send your luggage by Carter Paterson," she added.

The girl replied: "Dear Madam, Thank you very much for arranging for me to be met at the station. But I am rather worried about my luggage. How shall I know Carter Paterson when I see him?"

CHAPTER XI

IN CLUBLAND

IN my time I have been a member of many clubs and a guest at more; but the one I know best and like best, the one in which I have spent the most happy hours with my friends, is the Savage, of which I am a trustee.

Thirty-six years have passed since I became a member of the Savage, and naturally enough my memories of the place are bound up not with the present premises in Carlton House Terrace, to which the club moved only at the end of March this year, but with the delightful old building in what was the quiet backwater of Adelphi Terrace where, for more than fifty years, the heart of the Savage Club beat high and with generous good fellowship. During those fifty years thousands of men, celebrated in the creative side of art, writing, the drama, music and science, looked out from the Adam rooms on to the Thames; talked, sang, ate, drank and made merry. Nearly all of them had a real affection for that building and its associations—but the seal of doom was placed on Adelphi Terrace and the club had to move to new quarters.

Still, that was not the first time the club had changed its headquarters without losing its rare spirit. When it was founded in 1857 its premises were in Vinegar Yard, Drury Lane, and thither went a little band of authors and artists who felt the need of a place of meeting where, in their leisure, they could gather together and avoid the publicity of the coffee house. Some of the first members were Tom Robertson, Henry J. Byron, W. S. Gilbert, George Grossmith the elder, G. Manville Fenn, German Reed, Dion Boucicault, George du Maurier, Cruikshank, Gustave Doré, Artemus Ward, Clement Scott and George Augustus Sala, of whom I have an original caricature, published in *Vanity Fair*, by Pellegrini (Ape), the man who practically founded Pagani's.

There must have been musicians, too, but I am not old enough to remember them. After I joined, musicians who were members included Sir Frederick Cowen, Alfred Cellier, Walter Slaughter, that fine pianist, John Liddell, Dr. John Ivimey and Seymour Dicker.

And I must not forget Courtice Pounds, who was always the joy of an evening party at which he sang—and he sang in the Savage practically every night. Harold Samuel accompanied him, and afterwards played solos, but not Bach on those nights. Space alone prevents me from giving an enormous list of the people who helped to make those entertaining late evenings which we used to have before the licensing laws stopped them.

Why " Savage " was chosen as the name of the club is always a matter of argument and discussion; one theory is that the members regarded themselves as somewhat " wild " men; another that the name was suggested—and accepted—on the spur of the moment when several names had been rejected. I believe that actually the foundation of the club was decided at a memorial gathering to a journalist named Savage who fell down dead in Covent Garden. All the strange savage trophies—the spears, boomerangs, the tom-tom which is beaten to call Savages to dinner on Saturday nights, the club which the chairman at house dinners uses instead of a gavel—have accumulated as they have been given to the club from time to time.

In the beginning the ordinary " dinner " consisted of bread and cheese (2d.), half a pot of porter (1d.), and a screw of tobacco (1d.). Whatever we may think of such rations, members of the club then had liberty. They could meet together after their day's work was done, and please themselves how long they sat up for talk and refreshment. And why not ? Most of them were men whose work kept them busy while the people they amused and entertained were at leisure. Many of them were not free until midnight. Nowadays, of course, grandmotherly legislation ordains that you cannot have a drink or a meal in your club after twelve o'clock. You may be hungry and thirsty after your evening's acting or singing or conducting or writing or editing, but off to bed Grandma Dora would bundle you. Even granting the necessity of "closing-time" laws, I maintain that it is fantastic to apply the same regulations to men who finish work

A SATURDAY NIGHT MENU

at midnight and men who finish work at five-thirty or six o'clock in the evening.

The Savage "Saturday Nights" are wonderful; no management could afford to put on the programmes usually seen and heard at them, as guests who have had the good fortune to be present on a Saturday night will doubtless allow. Sometimes, if those contributing to the after-dinner entertainment were on salary, the cost would be £1000.

At one Savage Club house dinner at which I took the chair, in the B.B.B.C.—or Before British Broadcasting Corporation—ere, I hoaxed the assembled multitudes. I announced that I had arranged for a wireless transmission of Sterndale Bennett singing from the pier at Bournemouth. As it was about to start, I called for silence (stopped a singer), and added: "You can hear the waves...." Members heard a momentary buzzing sound, and then Sterndale Bennett's voice.

Everyone was well satisfied except George Tully, who said, in his obstinate, unbelieving Irish way: "I don't believe it. You can't do it. We're being hoaxed."

"Don't interrupt," I growled sternly and gave him a look of pained contempt to show what I thought of the man who doubted the greatest scientific achievement of the century.

When the song finished, George said: "Can we have another one?"

"I'm very much afraid it can't be arranged," I replied, "but what would you like if I find that we can do it?"

Later, George came to me and said: "Herman, old boy, I'm sorry.... I thought it was a fake, but now I've come to the conclusion that it really happened."

Sterndale Bennett helped me to produce some convincing evidence by sending me, from Bournemouth, this telegram:

"4.33   Bournemouth
Finick (*sic*) Savage Club London
ALL READY HERE TELL HURRY THREE SIX FOUR OVER SEVEN ZEYPHR WAVE NOT THREE OVER SEVEN ON EIGHT THIRTY STERNDALE."

Actually, all the transmission that had gone on had been from a gramophone upstairs, via a hole in the wall. It was most skilfully arranged by Colin Hurry. I have often been amused by the thought that only a short time after that it would have been far less trouble to arrange for the real thing than to fix up a fake broadcast as we did that night.

MacDonald Hastings—who, with the rest of the world to choose from—naturally lived at Hastings: I often thought of sending him a telegram addressed " Hastings, Hastings," to see whether it would arrive or whether the post office would think

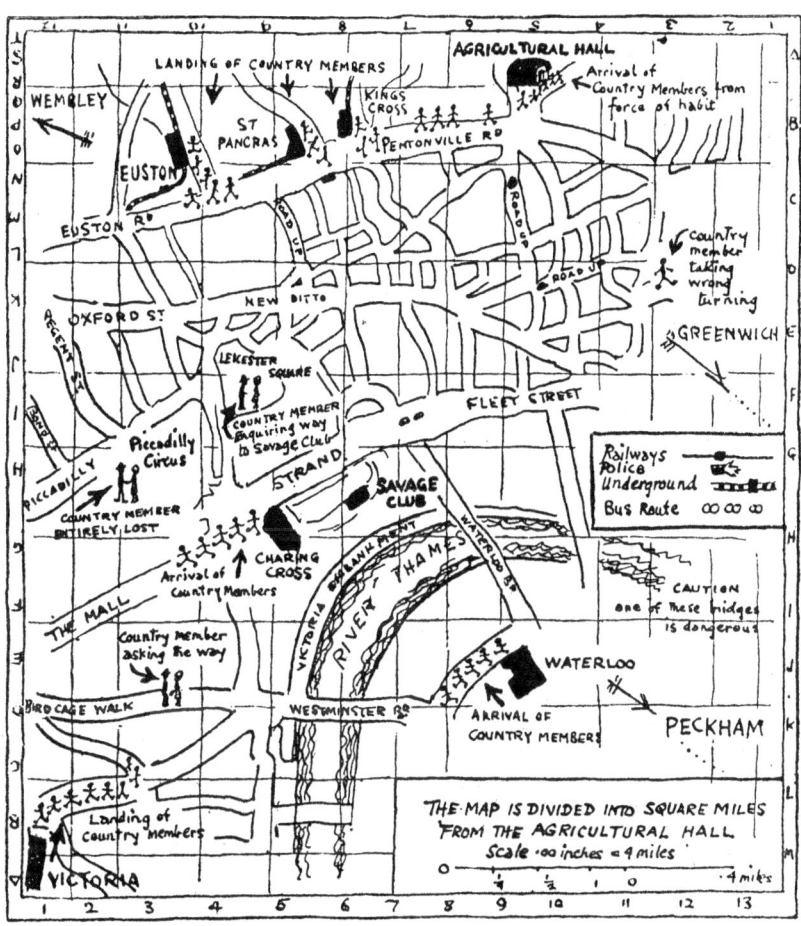

BUCOLIC NIGHT AT THE SAVAGE CLUB

they were seeing double or I was writing double—was always good for an evening's amusement when he was not writing his brilliant essays or his famous play, *The New Sin*. Being a country member because he lived at Hastings, he arranged a Bucolic Night at the Savage; he himself looked somewhat bucolic, much more like a farmer than a successful author. The club was soon filled with horsey-looking people, nearly all of whom would have been horrified if they had had to ride, for I have never seen any of them looking horsey either before that evening or since it. 'Peter' Page came as the "Village Idiot," and a large pile of smocks was kept near the door for members who had arrived not dressed for the part. All around the club were auctioneer's placards: "Sale of Cattle," "Sale of Pigs," or "Farm to be sold."

MacDonald Hastings had never been in the chair at a Savage Club dinner before, and I sat beside him in case he wanted a word of advice. When we had had "The King," I said quietly to Hastings: "Now you should say, 'Brother Savages and guests, you may smoke . . . but in view of the bucolic night it would be better if you said, 'Gentlemen, you may smock.'"

He did, and there was a roar of laughter.

"That's not mine, that's Herman's," he protested.

Another day I was in the Savage with MacDonald Hastings and Gilbert Laye, father of Evelyn Laye. After lunch, Hastings asked Gilbert Laye what he would like to drink.

"Coffee, please," replied Gilbert Laye.

"Yes, but with or without milk?" asked MacDonald Hastings.

"Why, café au Laye, of course," I said.

"It's very funny, but I *hate* it," said—almost bellowed, in fact—MacDonald Hastings.

"You hate it because you didn't think of it." I replied.

Feeling someone pulling my hair and jabbing me in the ribs at the Savage one day a few weeks ago, I turned round to face Mark Hambourg.

"All right, Herman," he said, "have a drink . . . what would you like?"

"Hollands, with a little bitters," I replied.

"Why are you drinking that?" he asked.

"Because I've a touch of lumbago."

"Then, there's only one thing you must drink—water!" And he walked away to his lunch.

IN CLUBLAND

I thought of the words of Henry Carey, author of "Sally in our Alley" and "God Save the King," who wrote:

> "Genteel in personage,
> Conduct and equipage
> Noble by heritage
> Generous and Free."

Nansen, the great polar explorer, was a guest at the Savage Club house dinner on February 5th, 1897. During the evening he told us about adventures and hardships in the Arctic; how he and his companions, when travelling over the ice, went for days without any change of clothes—they dared not remove undergarments for fear of frost-bite; how a polar bear waited for him outside his tent for hours, attracted by the scent of seal-oil; and many other incidents.

He said the Eskimos were a most hospitable people and very fond of dancing, and that if there was anyone in the room who could play some Eskimo music he would give us an idea of the way they danced.

There were loud calls for "Ivimey"—Dr. John Ivimey was accompanist at the club from 1896 to 1915—and he went to the piano and conferred with Nansen about it.

The farthest north Ivimey could go musically was Norway, and he played snatches of Grieg, in various rhythms, to Nansen, but none of them would do. Then Ivimey had an inspiration and tried Scotch (usually a safe thing at the Savage). When Nansen heard a few bars of "The Keel Row," he said: "That's it!" and for some minutes he danced an Eskimo fling to that old Scottish or Northumbrian tune.

In "My Sweetheart" there was a song written and sung by Charles Arnold, who was a very popular member of the Savage. He was asked to sing a song there one Saturday night. He sang one verse and there was a burst of applause as he finished it. He began the next verse—and dropped dead.

Some years ago George Grossmith—a magnificent after-dinner speaker and one of the finest fellows that ever lived—said to me at the annual dinner of the Savage: "They've invited me here to-night, and I shall have to make a speech. Can you tell me anything about the club?"

"One thing that I can tell you about it is that your grandfather fell dead here one night when he was singing a song," I said. And so it was, though I have always been amazed that George did not know it until I told him.

This grandfather was the magistrate's clerk at Bow Street, and therefore a *bon viveur* and most amusing companion. His son, and George Grossmith's father, was, of course, the creator of all the principal comedy parts in the Gilbert and Sullivan operas when they were first produced. He was also known as the "Society Clown"; he would receive as much for one night's performance in a private house as for a week's work on the stage, and his song, "See Me Dance a Polka," was a sure success anywhere. He also, with his brother Weedon, wrote that delightful little work—a prince among bedside books, I think—*The Diary of a Nobody*.

George Grossmith's brother, Lawrence, was nearly always in America, but I remember one curious incident in which he figured when in England. The Grossmiths lived in Dorset Square in their early days. Lawrence, for old times' sake, took rooms there during a short visit and one night he said to me: "You live in Hampstead, and so my place is on your way.... Let's go along together, and have a chat and a drink before you go home."

Lawrence brought a playwright with him too, and, after we had been at his home for a short time, the conversation turned on Dickens and Thackeray. "Oh, I can't read Dickens," said the playwright contemptuously.

If you had jabbed Lawrence Grossmith in the ribs with a red-hot poker, the effects would not have been so dramatic. He jumped up and shouted: "Get out! How dare you insult names like Dickens and Thackeray? How dare you?" For a moment I thought the wretched playwright was going to be thrown out of the window, but eventually I hustled him into a cab outside and the evening ended without serious harm being done to anyone.

The most moving scene I can ever remember in a club was the

last Savage Saturday night in the old Adelphi building. C. E. Lawrence, chairman of the committee, who is literary adviser to Murray's, the publishers, presided. Joseph Batten, who has been organising Saturday Nights for some years past, decided that the motto of that last evening should be, "We mustn't leave our ghosts behind," the last line of a poem written by Reginald Arkell not long before. So Batten arranged a Cavalcade of Ghosts. He collected gramophone records of the voices of nearly all the most famous Savages of the past few decades, and these were played upstairs and relayed through loud-speakers to the dining-room.

The Cavalcade of Ghosts opened with the signature tune of the club, the "Savages' March," by C. A. Lidgey, a former honorary secretary, a solicitor and Wagnerite, and then came the great songs and choruses of Albert Chevalier, Sir Charles Santley, E. J. Odell, Hayden Coffin and other famous entertainers of the past, while somebody sang Behrend's "Daddy." We heard, too, the voices of Lord Roberts, Earl Jellicoe, Edgar Wallace, and Sir Edward Elgar. Compositions by Sir Edward Elgar and by Sir Alexander Mackenzie were played; anecdotes of the club were told, and told very well, by Major Jones and Nelson Jackson; and members sang the favourite songs of the few great singers and entertainers of whose voices no gramophone records could be found.

To many the Cavalcade of Ghosts was no doubt simply an intensely interesting and rather wistful delving into the past; but the voices we heard were in too many cases those of men whom I had numbered among my greatest friends; men whom I had known right up to the day of their death. . . . I was not sorry when a telephone call enabled me to slip out of the room and to stay out until it was all over.

Sorry though we were when the national sport of demolishing anything worth keeping forced the Savage Club to move from the Adelphi, I must admit that the move was in many ways a good one. If the Adelphi Terrace clubhouse was an Adams building, the Carlton House Terrace one (formerly it was the home of the late Lord Curzon) is a Nash building, so the club is still in a fine period house. There is, too, more room for the fine collection of pictures, and the lounge of the first floor has a view that is certainly the finest in London—over the Mall and St. James's Park with its lovely little lake, to the towers of Westminster beyond.

The Adams fireplace from the old dining-room is now in the main hall on the ground floor, and in the new dining-room has been placed a portion of wall from the old building on which were written some notable signatures. There are those of King George V (George P., 1909), the Duke of Windsor (Edward P., 1919) and the present King—all brother Savages at the time of their accessions; and of Peary and Nansen.

I have heard people who did not know enough about the matter say that the Savage, the Green Room, the Eccentric and the Garrick are very similar clubs. Certainly not! You might as well say that the Savage is like the Athenæum, which is now one of its neighbours.

In an evening at the Savage you can hear almost every subject under the sun expertly discussed. Everyone there is an authority on something.

One of the best clubs in London for food is the Eccentric, to which many important racing people belong; very eccentric it is (the club, not the food)—and most benevolent. Talking of the food there reminds me of the man for whom a party was specially given at the Eccentric—and who did not have a mouthful to eat. His name was Johnny Rogers—he always signed himself "Yours merrily, Jno Rogers," and was the husband and manager of a very beautiful actress, Minnie Palmer. Rogers was a very popular man, and when he was going back to his native America with a show in which his wife was appearing, it was thought essential to say good-bye to him in fitting style. I was asked to a farewell supper to him at the Eccentric, and, after I had been there for a short time, I said to the man sitting next to me: "This is a very pleasant supper party, but it's supposed to be a farewell to Johnny Rogers and there is no sign of him. Do you know where he is?"

"Shss . . . he went to a farewell lunch party and a farewell

IRVING—BY PHIL MAY

*To Herman —
I forced this
picture on
him.
He looks at
it through
blue
glasses*

Tom Neaster

dinner party, and did some informal saying good-bye in between ... and he's under the table.... We can't get him out without disturbing the whole room and letting everyone know.... If you move your foot you'll kick him!"

I saw the first woman enter the Eccentric Club, and very dramatically it happened, too. She was Lottie Collins, mother of José Collins.

Lottie Collins' husband then was an American named Cooney, a pleasant, quiet man, but completely unable to say " Boo " to a goose, or to anything else in the farmyard. One night he came into the club and, the admission of women being forbidden, he had left his wife in a cab down below. Once inside the club someone asked him to have a drink and, being such a mild-mannered man, he was afraid to offend anyone by saying: " No, I must be going." So he stayed. . . .

He stayed until an angry woman, followed by a distressed commissionaire, stalked into the Club and demanded: " Where's my husband?" So Cooney was led away.

Late one night, when the Eccentric Club was in Shaftesbury Avenue, I went there with a friend and found only three people in the place—Arthur Roberts, by himself, and two old gentlemen hidden behind weekly papers. Agreeing that something should be done to liven things up, Roberts and I started a double turn. He sang songs while I played the piano. The two old gentlemen behind the weekly papers took no notice for a time, but presently one of them whispered something to the other, and they both put down their papers and stole quietly out.

When they had gone, Roberts and I looked at each other questioningly, and I asked the friend whom I had brought in: " Did you happen to hear what was said?"

" Yes," he replied, " one of them said to the other, ' Excuse me, sir, but Mr. Roberts and Mr. Finck are evidently rehearsing something private, and I don't think that we should be here. . . . They might not like it.' "

I thought that that was the first sign of the death of Bohemia.

Arthur Roberts and I did a more successful piece of impromptu entertaining at the Savage one night. We did a spoof operatic scene (Roberts invented the word spoof). I played and Arthur —with his quick ear—followed impromptu any chord I struck. Fred Cheesewright, the bass, joined in—and that made it difficult for me to battle with the two of them. Our operatic scene went so well that several people asked me afterwards where it was

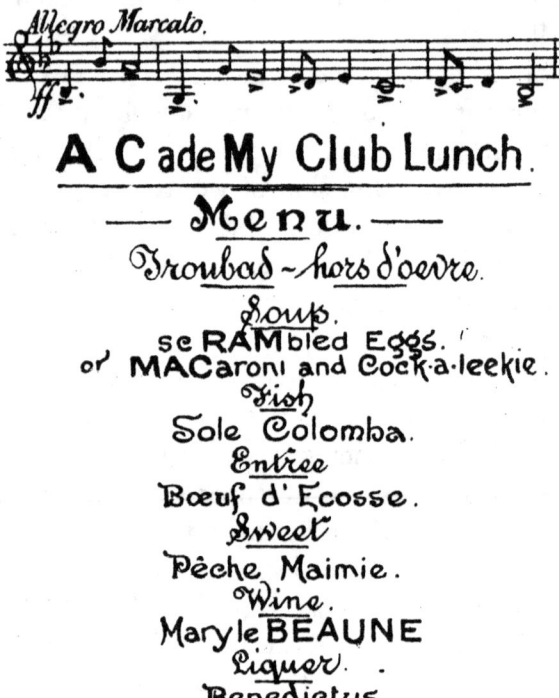

A.C.M. CLUB MENU WITH PUNS ON
MACKENZIE AND HIS WORKS

published! I laughed, for it had been done on the spur of the moment; it had never been written, far less published.

Incidentally, it was Arthur Roberts who founded the Savage Club Benevolent Fund with a gift of £100.

But the most exclusive club I have ever belonged to is the " A.C.M."

There were only four members of the "A.C.M." Club—Sir Alexander Mackenzie (hence the name), Sir Edward German, Lt.-Col. Mackenzie Rogan, who was the Master of Music of the Brigade of Guards, and myself. We formed it to lunch on our birthdays—though birthdays seemed to occur unusually frequently among us.

When Sir Alexander brought out his volume of memoirs, which he called *A Musician's Narrative*, he sent me a copy, inscribed, "To his dear friend Herman Finck, this volume of pure fiction, with sincerest good wishes from A. C. Mackenzie. A.C.M. Club, October 31st, 1927." And I found that he too had noticed the curious frequency with which we had birthdays, for, in the book, he says :

> "The A.C.M. Club, restricted to four members (including myself as President), was founded some years ago to celebrate the birthdays of Col. J. Mackenzie Rogan, Edward German and Herman Finck ; but our natal days occur too frequently to be reliable as to the accuracy of their dates."

All sorts of people wanted to join the A.C.M. Club, but we never would extend the membership, and now there is only one left, myself.

During my life I have often been taken to the Garrick Club, usually as the guest of Sir Alexander Mackenzie or of E. V. Lucas, who gave a birthday party in my honour there last year.

One day Cedric Hardwicke, when he had only recently achieved his great popularity, said to me : "I have just been made a member of the Garrick, but I hardly know anything about the place and feel most uncomfortable when I think of going there as a member for the first time. Will you come as my guest and show me round ? If you won't, I won't go in to the club."

So it fell to me, a non-member, to "do the honours" and show a new member round his club !

One member of the Garrick whom I occasionally met—he was pleasant to talk to—was Sir Squire Bancroft, husband of the famous Marie Wilton. He made so much money out of the theatre in the early years of his life that he spent the second half of it in leisure. He was also knighted, though I can see no great need to knight a man who is already a Squire—which shows what a start in life parents can give their children by judicious action at the christening: think of MAJOR Jones, EARL Carroll, or KING Bolton.

In the days of his leisure, Sir Squire Bancroft would, each morning, walk from his house in Berkeley Square to the Garrick Club. He had a tremendous amount of white hair, a big moustache, and wore a wide-brimmed hat at a jaunty angle, and an eye-glass with a black ribbon (if you wear a monocle you *must* wear a black ribbon, otherwise nine-tenths of the effect is lost). The result of all this was that everyone, from the inevitable boy in the street to the countess taking a morning drive, said: "*That* is Sir Squire Bancroft." He knew that he was being looked at as he went along, and his pomposity was almost absurd, although he was in other respects a very pleasant man.

One day Sir Squire was with Weedon Grossmith. The mischievous Weedon soon thought: "I must do something to puncture this mass of pomposity."

He said, with a deadly serious face: "You shave yourself, I suppose?"

"Oh, yes, I shave myself," Bancroft replied.

"How many strokes do you take with a razor in shaving?"

"About twenty-five to fifty, I should say."

"I am prepared to have a small bet with you that it is over three hundred. Try going over your face with the back of your fore-finger to find out."

So Bancroft did this... and if you know a way to make a man look sillier than to persuade him to throw back his head and "shave" himself with his fingers, counting each stroke the while, I don't. I have seen Weedon play the same trick on a hotel manager at Eastbourne.

There is another shaving story, however, which is at my expense. It starts from the most regrettable fact that I have never learnt to shave myself. One spring I went over to Paris to conduct a show for which I had written the music. There was a barber in the hotel where I stayed, but one Sunday I found several people waiting to be shaved, and as I had to go to a dress rehearsal, it was impossible for me to stay until the others had been shaved and my turn came. I went away unshaved. It was midnight before I was free, and when I got up in the morning, two-days' beard had made me look most fearsome.

"This won't do," I thought, "I must see the barber before I go to the last-minute rehearsal."

But when I reached the barber's shop it was closed (it was Easter Monday, but I had not realised that Paris barbers would shut on Easter Monday, so I was completely mystified).

Anyway, I could not spend my time looking for a barber then; I had to be at the rehearsal, and the rehearsal lasted until three or four in the afternoon. By the time I got away—with my beard still growing—a state of crisis was rapidly developing. I had to take a relative of mine, a lawyer, and his wife out to dinner and then go to the theatre for the opening of the show.

I went into hotels and anywhere else I thought I might be told where to get a shave. At last the idea occurred to me of calling a *fiacre*; I did, explained to the driver in my indifferent French what I wanted, and away we drove. . . . I have never seen as much of Paris as I saw that afternoon. Paris interests me enormously as a rule . . . but not on that terrible Easter Monday. The Tuileries or the Arc de Triomphe meant nothing to me; I hated the sight of them. What I wanted was a barber's shop; a barber's shop; a barber's shop. We found one at last, in a sinister, burglarious courtyard in Montmartre. Villainous-looking men, with beards even longer than mine, sat round the sordid little barber's shop; two unpleasant little boys glared at me shiftily . . . and the shaving staff was one old man (very slow).

Had I known enough French I would have tried to seduce him from the laws of professional etiquette. I would have said: "I know the other people came in first, but if you will shave me before you shave them I will give you more francs than you ever heard of. . . . I will take you to the theatre. . . . You can meet Sir Alfred Butt, Regine Flory, Sarah Bernhardt, Jack Hulbert . . . and Willie Clarkson."

Still, my French would not stand the strain; and the other people waiting did not look the kind to trifle with, so perhaps it was as well.

I sat and read E. V. Lucas' *A Wanderer in Paris*, looking up unhappily from time to time to see how things were going on.

Yes, I was shaved eventually. And I did arrive in time for dinner—just.

Charles Manners, a very good singer, was the original sentry in *Iolanthe*, and afterwards ran the Moody-Manners Opera Company, which carried out many successful tours, with his wife. Later, he retired to Ireland, but remained a member of the Green Room Club, and visited it whenever he was in London. Now, Charlie was bald—very bald—and would, for that reason, wear a hat at the most improbable times. One day, when he was over in London from Ireland, various members of the Green Room Club were appalled to see Charlie Manners eating boiled beef, carrots and suet dumpling—and wearing a bowler hat nearly as big as a bicycle track.

As he was so seldom in London, people did not know him, and one man asked me: "Who's that dreadful man sitting there having lunch and wearing a hat?"

The outraged members held a hurried and informal meeting in a corner of the dining-room, and eventually I suggested there was only one way to make him take his hat off. We began, right lustily, to sing the National Anthem. Charlie pushed the meal away from him, stood up, took off his hat and joined in the singing—singing far better than anyone else, in fact. "Good," thought the singers as the Anthem ended, "that achieved its object."

As soon as the last bar finished, Charlie sat down, pulled the boiled beef, carrots and dumpling towards him, ready to continue his meal—and crammed his vast bowler hat back on to his bald head!

At the Green Room Club one night I met Hannen Swaffer and Stanley Logan, who was then with us at the Palace, a good

STANLEY LOGAN DID THIS

actor, very amusing, clever and intelligent—but excitable. We three were chatting amiably over a round of drinks—lemonade for Swaffer, a teetotaller; beer for me; and a whisky and soda for Stanley—when the name of Fred Terry, the brother of Ellen Terry, was mentioned.

"I prefer him off the stage," said Swaffer casually, in a slightly superior way.

There would have been less dramatic results if he had squirted petrol into a blast furnace. Stanley flared up in fiery defence of Fred Terry; Swaffer refused to admit that his judgment of the man's abilities was wrong—and a big-scale battle developed rapidly. As each side brought up its dialectical heavy artillery, argumentative tanks and oral bombing planes, I wished I was out of the way. As I wasn't, the only thing I could think of was to persuade the combatants to leave the club, and eventually I lured them outside into the street.

Stanley was then staying at the Regent Palace Hotel in Piccadilly Circus, and we started to walk towards it. No sooner had we moved away from the Green Room Club than I realised that what I had imagined was a first-class wrangle was really only a few introductory remarks leading up to the real argument. Stanley lost his temper completely; he shouted; he waved his walking-stick to the infinite alarm of other pedestrians, who dodged rapidly.

Stanley's language became Shakespearian both in phrase and declamation. "How dare you, sir? How dare you?" he shouted. "I will smite you, sir. Be assured that I will smite you, sir."

To all this, Swaffer was replying, quietly but obstinately:

"But I still don't like his acting."

A crowd was by this time following us along the street, and, by way of advice to the two disputants—who were, in any case, much too preoccupied with their own argument to hear any remarks addressed to them—members of this crowd called out, encouragingly (whether to Logan or Swaffer, I cannot say):

"'It 'im in the jaw!"

"Go fer 'im, mite!"

" Don't you stand no nonsense. Let 'im 'ave one."

By the time we reached Piccadilly Circus both the crowd and the argument had thoroughly alarmed me. And the police noticed that something was happening, too. As soon as I saw a policeman approach with a " Now then, what's all this about ? " look in his eye, I decided that I must do something drastic to forestall the additional embarrassment of outside interference in the dispute. So I stepped swiftly up to the policeman and said, in a light-hearted sort of way : " It's all right, officer. They're rehearsing for a film ; it's going to be photographed here very shortly and they had to go through their parts beforehand, you know."

For a moment I waited in horrible suspense, feeling all shifty-eyed and wanting to shuffle my feet. Then the policeman decided to believe me. " Oh, really, sir ; that's very interesting," he said ; and, to the crowd : " Now then, move along there, what are you staring at ? "

A few minutes later they were safely across Piccadilly Circus, and Stanley disappeared into the Regent Palace Hotel.

I was left alone, on the pavement outside, with Swaffer. " I must go along to the *Weekly Dispatch* office," (he was the Editor then), he said. " Walk down there with me."

" It's not in the right direction for me," I protested. " Still, I'll walk part of the way with you."

A few yards farther on, Swaffer suddenly remarked : " I like that chap Logan . . . ask him to come to lunch at Simpson's to-morrow. . . . I'll bring Crosland."

So the next day I took Stanley Logan to Simpson's, and he and Swaffer got along splendidly together. So all went well that ended well.

Stanley Logan's first experience of a London club was an amazing one. His father, a wine merchant, had not, up to the time he was sixteen or seventeen—he was then, of course, away from home at school—taken a very close interest in his career, but one day he said to his wife : " How is Stanley getting on ? And what school is he at ? I pay the bills for him and I should like to have a look at him again."

So it was arranged that Stanley should meet his father at a club in Pall Mall, and he arrived there at the appointed time, and said: "I want to see Mr. Logan."

Mr. Logan was fetched, and remarked: "Oh, you're my son Stanley? You have grown . . . but you don't look too well. Come and have some lunch."

So Stanley was taken in to the club dining-room and his father gave him the same lunch as he had himself, starting with a sherry—a thing the boy had never tasted before. Then they had turbot and champagne.

"Like a cup of coffee?" asked Mr. Logan. "Good. We'll have a drop of old brandy with it." Then the old man began to talk about the boy's future—and gave him his first cigar. After that they both had a glass of port.

Mr. Logan senior thereafter went to sleep in the library. Stanley felt a bit drowsy, too, but he did not know what to do. He did not like to go to sleep in his father's club, so he determinedly refused to allow himself to go to sleep.

Half an hour later, Mr. Logan senior opened his eyes and looked at Stanley with some surprise. "I beg your pardon, sir," he said. "I did not know there was anyone sitting near me. I hope I did not cause you any annoyance by going off to sleep. My son's been lunching with me to-day. . . . I haven't seen him for years. He looks as though he will get on in life."

And the old man solemnly shook hands with Stanley and then walked out of the club. He did not know he was talking to his own son!

At many clubs it is the custom for members to present pieces of silver plate, and members of the Green Room give the club spoons, forks and so on from time to time.

I was there one day with George Tully, and another man who had only been a member for a few months. The comparatively new member, picking up a spoon when we sat down in the dining-room, said: "Why, that's the spoon I gave. Look, here are my initials on it."

"Curious," said George Tully, "I've never seen the one I gave."

"No, and I have never seen mine," I added.

So as soon as we had finished our meal—there was hardly anyone about by that time—we began to search for our spoons. We hunted through all the silver on the tables . . . we called the waiters in to help us in our search . . . we turned over vast piles of silver in the kitchen. Practically every piece in the club was gone through . . . and then, right at the end, we found our spoons.

I met the late Mr. Jerome K. Jerome—Jer 'OME SWEET Jer 'OME, as some shameless punster among his admirers might have said—at the St. John's Wood Art Club. At one time Jerome K. Jerome lived in the country, next door to W. W. Jacobs, whom he " found "; they were then both writing for *The Idler* and for *To-day*, which Jerome edited with, I believe, Eden Phillpotts. Eventually, Jerome went to Pinner and then to Belsize Grove or Road or Street or Crescent—there are so many Belsize addresses ! as bad as the Cadogans—and it was when living there that he joined the St. John's Wood Arts Club. Jerome, like most funny men, Gilbert, for instance, had the reputation of being a difficult man to deal with, and so some time after that I asked the secretary of the club: " How are you getting on with Jerome K. Jerome ? "

" Oh, he's resigned," said the secretary.

" Really," I replied. " Why ? "

" He says our bridge is so bad ! "

The Sports Club, originally the Corinthian, is one of the pleasantest clubs in town. It was there that we Savages found a place to lay our homeless heads during the week when our own club was moving from one building to another, and there we go during the cleaning time.

I am not a frequenter of the modern kind of supper club—partly because I am old-fashioned enough to think that a club is a place where men go to meet other men, not to take women—but I was a member of Murray's when it opened during the War. At the opening of it, Fay Compton came up to me and said: " Herman, nearly all the members here appear to be Jews. Why ? "

"Perhaps because it's in Beak Street," I suggested.

In a club at Brighton I several times met Sir Harry Poland, K.C.; he lived next door. Sir Harry was one of the worst-dressed men you could find anywhere, and one day a friend, who knew him extremely well, said: "Where on earth do you get your clothes? Why don't you go to Pooles and get a decent suit?"

"All right, I'll go there if you like," said Sir Harry amiably.

Sometime after this, Poland's friend walked into Pooles and asked: "Has Sir Harry Poland been here?"

"Yes, he came to us two or three weeks ago...."

"Well, what on earth do you mean by making him the villainously ill-fitting suit I've just seen him wearing. It's disgraceful; I recommended an eminent man to come here because your clothes are always so well cut, and then I see him wearing a perfectly terrible suit...."

"But, sir, how can you expect a suit to fit a man when he sits down in a chair as soon as he enters the shop and refuses to stand up to be measured?"

Of famous London restaurants I have perhaps even more memories than of clubs. There was, for instance, the day that George Edwardes—then at the height of his reputation—fell foul of Phillipe, proprietor of the Cavour, which is now the Café Anglais. Phillipe, when he died, left about £100,000, but he had not made it out of food: his policy was to cut the profits on meals down to the vanishing-point, and thus to attract customers who would make the place pay by the wines and cigars they bought.

One day, after lunch, George Edwardes pulled a cigar case out of his pocket and offered it to his friends.

"In future, Mr. Edwardes, you can have your food where you buy your cigars," said Phillipe.

Arthur Playfair, Morris Harvey and myself used to go to the Gambrinus Restaurant, next door to the Café Royal in Regent Street. Late one night, when the place was undergoing alterations, we were sitting in the centre of the room, but got up to leave and were going out by the back door—the front door was already closed. Near the back door was one little table, and someone remarked: "Let's sit down here and have another lager."

We sat down—and a moment later a great mass of plaster crashed from the ceiling on to the table we had just left. We had moved only just in time.

The old Long Bar at the Criterion was at one time haunted by a customer who had seen better days, and had formerly spent a good deal of money there. But evil times came upon him, and, while he could nearly always find enough money to pay for a drink—the poverty-stricken always can—food was undoubtedly scarce on his menu.

And so the old customer began to steal sandwiches. In the Long Bar the sandwiches were always placed at one end, and to obtain a drink for anyone who was taking a light snack the barmaid had to move a little way down the bar, and the lager beer pump was about half-way down the counter.

At the sandwich end of the bar this customer would ask for a small lager (it was threepence a glass in those days, even at the Long Bar), and, while the barmaid was fetching his drink, he would quickly whip off three or four sandwiches into the little brown bag which he always carried. He invariably chose the early part of the morning, when there were not many customers there, and if anyone had seen him taking the sandwiches it would doubtless have been thought that the customer was simply helping himself to food which he was going to pay for.

The taking of the sandwiches went on for some time, until the barmaid, or barmaids, found out what the man was doing. But they were kind-hearted, humorous girls, those tall fair-haired barmaids for which the Long Bar was noted, so they did not report the old customer, or let him know that they knew what he was doing.

However, the story leaked out somehow and it became a favourite pastime for a few of us to go into the bar and—unobserved and unsuspected—watch the marauder at work. After a time he grew careless, and also greedy, and one day he arrived with a larger brown bag, into which he popped a pork pie—

a *whole* pork pie, one of those long narrow ones with lofty walls of crust.

Now it was thought that this was a bit too thick. Sandwiches, two or three, or perhaps even four at a time—yes, that might be winked at, but a whole pork pie, for which the barmaid would have specially to account, was going a bit too far. The barmaid was determined to report the matter to the management this time, and have the old man watched.

But we thought of a better way. The " property man " at the Criterion Theatre where we were employed was approached, and a most beautiful pork pie was made. This dummy pork pie was then placed daily on the counter, and we wondered whether the old customer would fall to the temptation again.

Nearly a week went by, and every morning we watched to see if he would take the pie. But no! A sandwich or two, a hard-boiled egg, a sausage and roll—all these he fancied, but he left the pie alone. But at last, on the fifth day, the plot succeeded, and into the larger bag went the imitation pork pie—and away he went.

Poor old man. He never came back!

I think that the worst night I ever spent in an hotel was in Manchester—and that was not the fault of the hotel management. I was ill and miserable with an influenza cold, and the Town Hall clock solemnly striking the hours made it impossible for me to go to sleep. Every time I began to doze the clock struck and I was once more wide awake. Next day I protested violently about this: either people are out and too busy enjoying themselves to want a clock to strike at 3 a.m., or else they are in bed and anxious to sleep quietly, I said. But I was told that the Lord Mayor himself could not stop the clock striking, and that it would cost £150 to regulate it so that it did not strike during the night. " If you like to organise a fund," I said, " I will certainly subscribe. I am always hearing about the Manchester Watch Committee; what you want is a Clock Committee."

To another Manchester hotel went Hayden Coffin for the production of *Tom Jones*. And I realised that he had gone without paying me the three guineas which he owed me for orchestrating two pieces of music for him. So I sent a telegram to "The Executors of the late Hayden Coffin," requesting payment. Back came the reply:

"DEAR SIR,

"I regret to inform you that in your wire to our poor friend your misgivings were realised. In his last moments on the first night here of the new piece he desired me to send you enclosed cheque for £3 3s. and say he thanked you sincerely for all your kind help during his pleasant work at the Palace.

"The band parts of the two songs, of which enclosed is payment, were left with your boy for you to kindly put them right as so many changes were made at rehearsals for piano, etc. Kindly have this seen to. I shall be in London on the 15th and hope to see you in person to thank you again on behalf of our defuncted friend.

"Yours truly,
"TOM JONES.

"C. H. C. wished to be kindly remembered to all who thought well of him and forgive him for his love of stout and bitter."

Hayden certainly saw the joke that time. But I remember another occasion on which it completely missed him.

When the cigars appeared at a dinner-party one night—they were gorgeous things with magnificent bands—one of the men picked one up and put it to his ear and crackled it, in the way that connoisseurs affect.

"Why does a man always put a cigar to his ear like that?" asked one of the ladies.

"He's listening to the band," I answered, and approving chuckles followed the remark.

Shortly afterwards I was having dinner with Hayden Coffin, and all through the dinner it seemed as though we were doomed not to enjoy a laugh. At last the cigars appeared, and I told him my " listening to the band " joke. For some moments he looked puzzled, and then said, with a smile of relief at having at last seen the point, " I see, I see. And of course there was a band round the cigar then ? "

For a joke not to be understood is a terrible thing. I was sitting on the front at Folkestone with a friend one fine summer day in 1920 when, rather lugubriously, he said : " Seems almost wrong to be sitting here in this beautiful sunshine enjoying oneself with all these threats of coal strikes and electricians' strikes, and all sorts of labour troubles going on."

" Yes, bolshie far niente," I said.

I was rather pleased with this, and repeated it later on to another friend who looked puzzled for a second and then said apologetically : " Excuse me, Herman, but oughtn't it to be *dolce far niente?* "

He could not understand why I laughed louder still.

Sometimes when wit fails physical discomfiture will raise a laugh. This was evidently in the mind of a well-known song-writer who was present at a particularly dull supper-party given, after a performance, by the head of a famous concert-party. Everyone in that little company was a wit, but the theatre had not been well filled that evening, the best jokes had fallen flat, and everybody was worn out and depressed.

At last the song-writer, who had been doing his best to raise a smile, in sheer desperation took up a tureen of soup and poured it all over his head, face and shirt.

" Now, will you laugh some of you ! " he said.

And truly a smile was raised at the sight of this large person with soup-stained head and face and shirt-front.

One of the real old Bohemians who dined at Simpson's-in-the-Strand nearly every night was Sam Pallant, brother of Walter Pallant who was a director of the Gaiety and of the Empire.

Pallant used to give lavish bachelor parties in a house on the site which Dents, the publishers, now occupy. A man expressively referred to as The Lodger always presided over the drinks.

As I had to go off to the theatre immediately afterwards I

used to dread going to these parties, for the dinner was a really strenuous business. (The other members of the party, those who made an evening of it, would go without lunch in preparation.)

First came cold punch; then soup—mulligatawny or real turtle—and sherry. Cod fish and oyster sauce—everyone's portion contained at least half a dozen oysters—was washed down with chablis, and each course was discussed and analysed:

"Delicious, isn't it? Do have some more."

Then a bird, and next steak and kidney pudding.

At this point Pallant would remark: "When my brother died, he left me some wines. . . . Of course, the stock's dwindled, you know. . . ."

Then he would put out his foot, and lightly kick a bottle under the table.

"Oh, there's a bottle here," he would exclaim in mock surprise. "I thought they were all gone."

The Lodger came into action at this signal, brought the champagne out from under the table and uncorked it.

If the party were being given anywhere near Christmas time, there would be Christmas pudding and mince-pies. At other times of the year, there would be enormous sweets. With the coffee the cook came in to receive the congratulations of the guests: she was called Tottenham because she lived near Tottenham Court Road, and was assisted by a woman known as The Mad Hussy—because she was a nurse at a lunatic asylum.

At the coffee stage it was time for me to pack up—dinner had started at six o'clock—and go to the theatre. The others settled down to drink very old brandy, and to smoke cigars.

After a short time, all the guests would move towards card tables near the fire—ostensibly to play whist. But this was merely a pretence; actually they gradually dropped off to sleep. Many a time I have gone back to Pallant's house hours afterwards and found all his guests sound asleep, and with the cards still unplayed before them.

Of course the dinner was all very well for them: they slept it off. I had to conduct it off!

CHAPTER XII

KINGS AND QUEENS

I SUPPOSE that I have had the honour to turn my back to royalty more often than anyone else. I was about sixteen, and then a violinist when I first played before Queen Victoria. On that occasion I was a half-back, so to speak; my place was on the extreme left of the orchestra, a few yards from the Queen.

We were engaged to give a performance of Verdi's "Il Trovatore" in the Waterloo Chamber at Windsor Castle. The singer was Tamagno, the tenor. Tamagno was perfect for the Scala, Milan, or Covent Garden—he was about twice the size of Oscar Asche—but he was too much for the Waterloo Chamber. It met its Waterloo in him. He startled Her Majesty in the first act, which made me wonder what would happen when he sang his top C.

One thing I particularly remember about the occasion was the excited way in which the late Willie Clarkson bobbed about. Clarkson, with his wigs (he called them " vigs ") and his costumes, and so on, was always behind the scenes at these royal events, and he had a great fund of stories about what " Her Majesty " said to him and what he said to her.

Willie Clarkson, with his whiskers, his old-fashioned evening clothes and his minced way of speaking was one of the remarkable figures of the theatre. Everyone knew him and he knew everyone. King Edward VII, it would seem, knew him almost too well. Once, when Willie was rushing about at a royal entertainment, King Edward caught sight of him and said: " Oh, there's that silly old fool, Clarkson."

Willie, in relating the story—which he did with great glee and gusto (it was one of his best stories of what he called " the royals ")—always added as comment: " Wasn't it terribly nice of him."

Augustus Harris, the uncrowned king of Drury Lane, used to be responsible for arranging entertainments at Windsor. When Gus was asked why he gave up doing so, he replied: " I could not afford to keep them up."

There used to be an excellent band known as the Queen's Private Band. Its business was, when called upon, to play at Buckingham Palace or Windsor. All the members of the Queen's Private Band worked in other orchestras, and had to pay for deputies when the Queen required their services, much to their annoyance. They looked upon it as an annuity!

I followed my father when he died into the State Concert Orchestra (as an extra performer), and I remember how scornful I was when, after my performance at Buckingham Palace, I and the rest were regaled with some cold ham, boiled eggs, and tea (or beer if preferred).

For many years George Ashton, of the Bond Street firm, looked after all the arrangements for royal entertainments, and at one of them—a command performance at Sandringham on Queen Alexandra's birthday in 1905—I had the experience of having to run after the piano to play it. I was playing the music " off stage " of the Bioscope Pictures while " a change " was in progress on the stage when, to my sudden consternation, up came some men and began to shift the piano—an upright " cottage."

The scenes had to be shifted, and I and the piano were in the way. So there I was trying to play for a royal party while I followed the piano round the back of the stage, past scenes of Conway Castle and Brighton Pier. This occurred when " moving pictures " were being shown as a great novelty at the Palace Theatre. They were taken to Sandringham to be shown between scenes from a play and, of course, I had to play in the dark. If they were the first moving pictures, I was the first moving pianist.

When the scene shifters had done their very worst with me, and I was in a bath of perspiration, someone came up and said:

" What will you have to drink, sir ? We have some nice lemonade —some orangeade. . . ."

I was goaded to answer : " Give me some nice first-aid."

At that performance, the Follies, Harry Pélissier, Lewis Sydney, Dan Everard, Marjorie Napier, Ethel Allandale and Gwennie Mars regaled the King and Queen, several members of the Royal Family and the usual house-party of distinguished people, with their delightful burlesques.

King Edward VII was fond of music and he could play the banjo up to a point. I remember that there used to be a shop in Tottenham Court Road which had pictures in the window of him playing one. Which brings me to a story. I was one of an orchestra engaged to play for him at Deep Dene, near Guildford, where he was a guest. By this time I had risen to the height of being sub-conductor at the Palace (Theatre), but you can be sure that I was not averse from doing an extra job of this sort and adding a couple of guineas to my pocket. At the time, one of the most popular songs was May Yohe's " Honey, ma Honey," and King Edward was captivated by it. It was one of the first coon songs, one of the first of its kind to have a vogue in this country. (The words and music were by G. R. Sims and Ivan Caryll.)

There was a beautiful brunette in the party at Deep Dene— I don't think I ever knew her name—and both King Edward and she were very desirous that we should play " Honey, ma Honey." The idea was that the beautiful brunette should sing it. But unfortunately we had not the music of the song with us, and we were not so familiar with it as, I suppose, we should have been. We had a shot at playing it, but the King said : " No, no, not like that " (he had a very guttural voice)—" look, like this. . . . I'll show you."

Whereupon he seized my violin and, using it as a banjo, began to twang out something like the tune.

I naturally saw King Edward VII several times after that, but what will ever remain in my memory is that he had a particular liking for my " Melodious Memories." Whenever a programme of music was submitted to him for approval he always made a satisfied X against this selection if it were on the list.

KINGS AND QUEENS

SANDRINGHAM

PROGRAMME

DECEMBER 1ST, 1905

Mr. Charles Frohman's
Duke of York's Theatre Company

A play for an ancient family, in One Act, entitled

PANTALOON

By J. M. BARRIE.

CLOWN	-	Mr. A. W. BASKCOMB
PANTALOON	-	Mr. GERALD DU MAURIER
HARLEQUIN	-	Mr. WILLIE WARDE
THE CHILD	-	MISS ELA Q. MAY
COLUMBINE	-	MISS PAULINE CHASE

The Curtain will fall for a moment during the progress of the Act to indicate the passing of years.

The Play Produced by Mr. DION BOUCICAULT.
The Incidental Music Composed by Mr. JOHN CROOK.

Stage Director	DION BOUCICAULT
Musical Director	JOHN CROOK
Assistant Manager	R. M. EBERLE
Manager	JAMES W. MATHEWS

Concluding with **THE FOLLIES**

(a) "Our Canadian Canoe" (Duet)
(b) Mr. H. G. PELISSIER and Mr. LEWIS SYDNEY will sing to each other
(c) Burlesques of English Musical Comedy and Wagnerian Opera

The Follies and Bioscope
from the Palace Theatre, London

THE FOLLIES

In a Pierrot Playlet, entitled

O! PIERRETTA

Written and Composed by H. G. PELISSIER.
Lyrics by A. WIMPERIS.

CHARACTERS

PIERRETTA	MISS MAJORIE NAPIER
PIERREITE	MISS GWENNIE MARS
PIROUETTE	MISS ETHEL ALLANDALE
THE FAT PIERROT	Mr. H. G. PELISSIER
THE THIN PIERROT	Mr. LEWIS SYDNEY
THE LUCKY PIERROT	Mr. DAN EVERARD

Scene—Pierrot Land.

THE BIOSCOPE

The Incidental Bioscope Music composed and performed by
HERMAN FINCK, *Musical Director.*

Manager - - - ALFRED BUTT

Fortunately, King Edward never knew about a very rude message which I once "passed" in reply to a member of the Royal Family. I was playing at a State Ball at Buckingham Palace for John Liddell, a brilliant but autocratic Northumbrian who held the position of bandmaster at the Vice-Regal Lodge, Dublin. Liddell became very impatient because he kept getting requests to play a waltz instead of a polka. These requests —presumably from the Chamberlain—were "blown up" through a tube with a whistle, and, as the youngest member of Liddell's band, I had to take them and pass them on. Finally, exasperated, Liddell said to me, "I won't change any more—tell him to go to hell" . . . which I dutifully did. I am thankful that the person at the other end of the speaking tube could not see me.

King George and Queen Mary came to the first Music Hall command performance—an event which gave the Music Hall equal status with the legitimate stage—at the Palace in July, 1912. I arranged and conducted the entire musical programme.

A number of stage charities had been trying, through Lord Farquhar, to obtain royal patronage for various events organised to help Variety artistes who had fallen on bad times. Eventually King George sent a message to these various societies that if they would come together for the purpose, he and Queen Mary would be pleased to attend one command variety performance every year.

At the first command performance Pavlova danced, Harry Tate did his motoring sketch, George Robey was the Mayor of Mudcumdyke, and Harry Lauder sang, "Roamin' in the Gloamin'." In fact,—with the exception of Marie Lloyd— who was unable to be there—all the great stars of the day did their turns: Happy Fanny Fields and Little Tich, La Pia, Arthur Prince and Vesta Tilley.

Oswald Stoll, Walter de Frece, Walter Gibbons, George Ashton, then president of the Theatre Agents Association, were on the committee and Alfred Butt organised the whole affair.

George Ashton had to "edit" the performance of each artiste,

KINGS AND QUEENS

and he went through them all with a tooth-pick (metaphorical, as usual) to see that nothing which could possibly be construed as a breach of propriety, or which might in any way give offence, was included. But when the actual performance happened, George Robey was much too excited to remember all the things he had been told to do or not to do, and he gave his act just as usual.

As a matter of fact, I think that the turn that the King and Queen liked best was Harry Tate's; and I liked that best as well, because during his turn I did not have to supply any music. You are thankful for small mercies during a piece of marathon-music or endurance-test conducting like a programme of twenty-five turns!

Three or four thousand pounds were spent on decorations for the theatre alone, and we had to rehearse in a house that was a jungle of scaffold poles. One day—I must have been putting extra elbow-grease into it—I struck my baton against a pole and broke it (the baton). For the rest of that rehearsal I had to conduct with a piece of scaffolding!

My " Melodious Memories," which was the fifteenth item, was the first pot-pourri of popular airs ever played; I called it an anthology of melody. That idea has been widely copied since, but I don't think any of the imitators has yet got the right ingredients for this particular musical dish.

The most amusing memory I have of the first command performance is connected with Wilkie Bard. He sang such very long songs. But as each turn was not supposed to take more than five minutes we did not know what to do with his famous " Want to Sing in Opera " which was on the programme. He solved the difficulty himself by offering to do the " Night Watchman " instead. And then, when his turn came he went on the boards and the " Night Watchman " went on for nearly twenty minutes. The stage manager was in a frantic state. He had a clock which he used to wave to and fro from the wings at any artist who exceeded his time limit. He waved with the clock until he was dizzy but he never once caught Wilkie's eye. The audience, of course, knew nothing of this, and they were enjoying the turn thoroughly. But at the back the theatre officials were " throwing fits."

A royal message of congratulation sent after the performance ended with the words: " The King and Queen noted with pleasure that the audience testified by applause and enthusiasm their enjoyment of a variety programme which, if ever equalled, has certainly never been surpassed since Music Halls began."

What was to me a pleasant and interesting sequel to the performance was a letter from the bandmaster of the Scots Greys which I received:

> " H.R.H. Prince Arthur of Connaught desires me to write and ask if we can secure a set of parts of the pot-pourri of popular numbers you played at the command performance at the Palace Theatre. H.R.H. was very much struck with them and as he is a very enthusiastic and keen lover of music he has asked me as his Regimental Bandmaster to ask you about them."

Naturally, I arranged for the band parts to be sent, and Prince Arthur wrote to me that, " The orchestral parts of your popular pot-pourri ' Melodious Memories ' duly arrived and on behalf of the Officers of the Regiment, I wish to thank you for the same. It will be popularised as much as possible by our Orchestra, and will be a favourite number at our Officers' Mess."

During a series of three daily big shows given by theatrical stars to entertain wounded soldiers I was conducting " Melodious Memories " at the riding-school, Buckingham Palace (the coldest place I have ever conducted in) while waiting for King George V to arrive. Suddenly the most awful thought came into my mind. " Heaven help me, but I know what is going to happen," I thought. And it did happen . . . just as we got to " Hush, hush, here comes the bogey man," the King arrived. If the orchestra pit had been the bottomless pit, it could not have been too deep for me at that moment.

Before he came to the throne King George V—as were his sons the present King and the Duke of Windsor—was a member of the Savage Club. One evening he had been to the dinner of the club to the old Hotel Cecil (Shell Mex House is there now) and he popped round into the Adelphi to the Savage before going home. Like a good "Savage" he went into the bar (the North-West Room as we call it) and, to the great surprise of "Mac," who was behind the counter—and unaccustomed to such requests—the Prince said: "Give me a glass of hot milk."

Somehow hot milk was procured and somehow the story—a bit twisted—got out. It was printed in the *London Evening News*, I think. The result was that people began to ask for a "Prince of Wales Cocktail," and were not too pleased when they found themselves given a glass of hot milk pure and simple. They all thought there ought to be something in the milk to give it a kick, and would not believe that it was really milk alone that the Prince had drunk. But it was.

CHAPTER XIII

"IN THE SHADOWS"

WANTED: AN ERRAND BOY WHO DOES NOT WHISTLE "IN THE SHADOWS."

NOT merely did that notice appear in a shop window, but *somebody wrote to tell me about it*. As bad a case of man's inhumanity to man as I can remember.

"In The Shadows" may have been a sore point with the public who had to endure it so long—it was worse than *Chu Chin Chow* and the Children's Hour combined—but their soreness was not greater than mine. They only had to listen to it year after year, but I lost round about a million pennies through it.

The unhappy story starts in 1908, when I thought of a tune, and thought a great deal of it at the time. I just kept it in my head (a habit of mine with tunes), saying to myself: "Well, perhaps it will come in useful some day."

The chance to use it came in 1910, when old John Tiller wanted some music for a skipping-rope dance for the "Palace Girls." Tiller was really a Manchester cotton merchant, but he had a genius for organising and directing dancing troupes. He ordered everybody about in the most dictatorial way: but was a genial soul nevertheless.

Tiller once tried his hand at writing, and did the book of a piece which he called *Spanish Ballet*. He wanted me to do some music for it and showed me what he had written. "The Palace Girls," in those days one of the attractions of London, came to rehearse their skipping-rope turn with some dull lifeless sort of music. I could not do anything with it; neither could they.

"Wait a minute," I said, "I know a better tune than that,"

and I played the tune I was carrying about in my head. The girls loved it and did their dance to it.

It sounded a good tune and one that was likely to catch on, and so I went to see my publisher, Oliver Hawkes, about it. I will say for him that he did his best to squash it flat.

"I've got a tune for you," I said brightly.

"Well, I don't want it," he retorted in a teasing way. "I spent more than £100 on having plates engraved for that last tune of yours, 'The March of the Giants,' and no one is buying it. I am not very pleased with you, if you must know."

At that time, of course, sheet music was selling as gramophone records sell now. People played pianos and bought songs to sing.

John Hassall, the artist, had been partly responsible for getting me into bad books over "The March of the Giants." He heard it played somewhere, said how much he liked it, and went about whistling it at people. In gratitude, I got him to design a cover for it, but much good that did either of us, although John Hassall did receive twice as much "on account" as I did—ten guineas to my five.

Despite the fact that Hawkes had been teasing me, I played my tune over to him. He listened dolefully, and grudgingly said at the end: "Well, it's not too bad, and as I want you to do some more work for me, I will take it. But I am not going to give you a threepenny royalty this time; you'll have to be content with twopence a copy."

About a million copies of "In the Shadows" were sold while it was booming, and I received about a million pennies less than I should have done had I stuck out for a threepenny royalty! I did, however, get a substantial contract afterwards in which we both benefitted and there are now forte (sorry, forty) of my works in Boosey and Hawkes' catalogue.

The title came over lunch at the Café Royal; and "In The Shadows" caught on like wildfire, or hot cakes, or whatever the phrase is about music.

They could not print the copies fast enough, and at one time I had three men stamping as hard as they could all day long. A rubber stamp with your signature is used for the purpose, and they played a scurvy trick on us in America over this. We felt that our American returns should be much larger than they were stated to be, and so someone was sent over there to do a bit of secret spying. It was a very hot summer, and when our man inquired why he was discovering shop windows full of unstamped copies of " In The Shadows," he was unblushingly told that the heat had obliterated the rubber stamp signatures!

In France, too, where it was called " Dans Les Ombres," it sold and was played widely. I could have got another £5000 out of it if I had been a Frenchman and a member of that great French society, Société des Auteurs—but I was not. They tried to get me to Paris to " prove " that I was a musician by cross-examination as to my status and by harmonising a tune. Unable to bowl me out by these means, the committee came to the end of its time and a new Committee was appointed. I never came across so much manœuvring and side-stepping and obstruction in my life as I did over the matter.

An unfortunate music traveller got so excited about the overwhelming sales that he went mad; the tune was banned (I was not at all surprised at this) at a Sunday concert in Tottenham (I never knew why Tottenham of all places—perhaps they, too, were being driven mad by it there); and " pirates " started selling it in Walworth and Islington and such unsuspectedly musical districts for twopence a copy, thus defrauding both the publishers and myself.

These " pirates " were very active then—it was before the days of the Copyright Act—and from time to time some of us who suffered from them became infuriated to the point of organising physical violence raids upon them. Leslie Stuart, Walter Slaughter, who wrote, " The Dear Homeland," and other very popular songs, and I several times enlisted the services of two " chuckers-out " from the Empire and the Palace and of some fighting members of the National Sporting Club and the Eccentric Club, and descended in a band upon the " pirates." They always ran when they saw us coming; and before the bewildered police could interfere we had upset their barrows and

DAVID WILSON'S PORTRAIT OF MARK HAMBOURG

"I THOUGHT YOU SAID YOU DIDN'T GO TO NEVINSON'S PARTY," MY WIFE REMARKED

scattered their illicit wares. The trouble was that we never could find out where the pirated copies were printed. It may seem strange for writers of music to have been embroiled in such affairs, but there was nothing for it at that time but to take the law into our own hands.

"In the Shadows" went all over the world, torturing innocent people. Friends sent me gloating post-cards from Russia, Japan, Scandinavia, China and Australia to say they had heard it played. Thus, from St. Petersburg, came the message:

"Dear Finck,— Just a line to tell you that although I am very fond of 'In The Shadows,' I am bored stiff with the different versions of it I am constantly hearing in Russia. Everywhere one goes one hears it and it is always rapturously received. Every café orchestra and every theatre grinds it out."

From "Press Camp, Mysore," during the then Prince of Wales's Indian Tour in 1922, Sir Percival Phillips wrote:

"You may be interested in the enclosed (since lost, I regret to say) programme of orchestral music played during the State Banquet at the Palace here on Thursday night. You finished sixth, but were still a winner.

"I had another programme of music played by a comic Nepalese brass band of 73 pieces while H.R.H. was in the shooting camp in Nepal, but my flat-footed servant, who was instructed to put it aside to be posted to you, carefully threw it away, and he was executed the same day. (I kill him on an average three times a week). The real news item on the latter programme was 'In The Shadows' and I do not suppose it was ever played under more appropriate circumstances: the band stood in a big semi-circle under the trees (we were in the jungle) about 50 yards from the mess tent.

"Between the band and the tent were placed some trophies of the day: two rhino heads, a large, very dead tigress propped up on two bits of timber, a leopard and a live tiger cub—the effect being that of the fag end of a bankrupt circus.

The band played Finck in funeral time (you ought to hear the 'Mikado' done that way) and I am sure you would have been interested, although perhaps not pleased. Anyway, you can say that your compositions have penetrated even to the heart of the Nepalese jungle."

From Yokohama came the wail, "And once again 'Shadows.'" From Hong Kong, Fitzroy Gardner sent me a post card: "A Goanese (Indian-Portuguese) orchestra plays 'In The Shadows' in our theatre here every night. Doing huge business."

But a well-meant and pleasantly phrased letter from Lomagundi held in its depths the cruellest blow of all. It ran:

" You will be surprised to receive a letter from me.

" You will remember me when I remind you I was with Mr. Harwood and Mr. Roberts at Blackpool when yourself and Mr. Sturgess were there for the production of *Lovely Lucerne*.

" When I was coming out on the *Walmer Castle* recently I heard some of your music played.

" As I recognised it as some of your music, I enquired what piece it was, and found it was ' *Among the Swallows!* ' "

Well, I could not help it being played in far-away places—and anyhow, I never got any royalties, I am sure. But I got this cutting from a Sydney newspaper:

IN THE SHADOWS

The Greatest, Latest, And Most Successful Reverie for the Pianoforte

The sweetest MUSIC PIECE ever published; its bewitching strains charm humanity of all classes, positions, or ages. They all love IN THE SHADOWS because the melody haunts them. They rave over it, they play it, they sing, hum, or whistle the magic piano masterpiece, IN THE SHADOWS. Whenever this singularly pretty melody is featured, either as a Piano Solo or as a Duet, or as a Song, or on the Violin with

"IN THE SHADOWS"

Piano accompaniment, or played by the Band, or at the Pictures, in a Theatre, or in their Dreams, the performer and the listener—alike—get carried away into the seventh heaven and rave about it there.

If you have not heard it yet, then come to our Stores and we shall play or sing it for you, when you will freely admit that it is not only better, but also different to any music you are accustomed to; then, if you are INCLINED to buy it (we coerce no one), we shall courteously charge you Eighteen-pence for the piece (and, mind, nothing for the wrapper or for our trouble). Do you intend to give your girl, or yourself, a treat? Get IN THE SHADOWS. Come now. (If you cannot come we'll post it to you for 1/7). Miss a town luncheon; deny yourself a holiday outing; forgo an ocean home-trip, but buy a copy of IN THE SHADOWS from

J. ALBERT & SON, 137, King Street, Sydney.

One of my pleasanter memories in connection with " In The Shadows " is that the great ballerina, Adeline Genée wrote to me:

"I wonder if you have any objection to my using your music, ' Shadows '? When listening to it the other night an idea came into my head for my forthcoming visit to America and I thought I would write and ask you as I like it very much and should love to dance to it."

Naturally, I was very glad for that great artist to make use of the tune.

There was a distressing levity about some of the communications I received about " In The Shadows." Arthur E. Godfrey for instance, wrote:

> My poor Betty's broken-hearted,
> Of despair she's on the brink—
>   Yus, I don't fink!
> Tho' she's yearning for her album
> From annoying she will shrink—
>   Yus, I don't fink?

> In attempting to obtain it
> She has emptied pots of ink,
> And her language, once so maidenly,
> Is getting blue and pink,
> She's been playing " In the Shadows "
> Till she's driven me to drink ! ! !
>   Yus, I don't fink ! What fink ?
>   Why—H. Finck !

Or this, from a complete stranger in Brighton :

" To my Gramophone. Dear Mr. Finck,

" To-night at Palace Pier Theatre I had a long-felt want gratified—I saw *you ! ! !* You who so cheered and gratified my sense of hearing in three Continents ! ! ! My, yes ! ! ! I owe you surely a word of *thanks* and here it is ! I've been near you in town, but still you were " In The Shadows " there (it's a big place, I reckon) and so I had to take my husband's description of you, which ran thusly " he is fat and walks somewhat waddly, and though full of melody, and an excellent man in the *right* place, you would not look sideways at him " ! ! ! My ! I tell you again you have so cheered me in a " Deprofundis " mood, ever truly " In The Shadows." Now I wonder why you so named that haunting melody—*wrongly* named, I fancy, *n'est-ce-pas ?* Yet I don't know, it does entirely *shadow* one ! My sister (an Am*u*rrican) who sat next me at the Concert, said " Yes, Uncle Sam is quite wild about him too, but he can't be *English* ? Oh, no, for the English are not musical, leaving out Sullivan, Bishop and one or two minor folk. She is *right* : I don't wish to belittle them : I was born and ' raised ' in the ' North Countree,' though Thomas Moore the Irish poet was my great grandfather. Well may Byron call his *melodies* " tears of music." Some two weeks ago a woman singer sang ' She Is Far From The Land ' on the Palace Pier, and what's more she sang it *well ! !* I blessed Mr. Amers, the little darling, the idol of the ladies, great and small, indeed if my heart were not a purely blood circulating instrument only I'd join the crazy throng, still he has a beautiful and sweet wife and a woman who poaches on another's preserves is not worth her salt. Now Good-bye and thank you, dear *Gramophone*, for all the haunting melodies. Music exudes from your outspreading fingers."

But perhaps the final outrage on my sensibilities was this:

Extract from
" Your Piano as ' Doctor ' "
An article submitted to the Evening Standard.

In cases of flatulence, vertigo, back-ache, varicose veins and diabetes, one cannot do better than try Finck's " In The Shadows."

When the all-star Charles Dickens centenary performance was given at the Coliseum, Seymour Hicks invited about fifty of us concerned in it to supper at the usually very dignified Garrick Club. As the night wore on, it was felt that some music would be pleasant, but unfortunately the Garrick does not own a piano.

The company included Beerbohm Tree, Harry Pélissier, Edmund Payne from the Gaiety, Alexander Mackenzie, and we finally compromised by me whistling " In The Shadows " in minuet time while the guests gravely danced, with Hicks occasionally slapping Sir Alexander's bald head by way of comic relief.

A visitor to Harrogate, obviously moved to the point of desperation, defaced a poster relating to the local band. Across the announcements that " the Band will play from 8 to 9.30 and from 11 to 12.30; again in the afternoon and also in the evening," he took a pencil and gave full vent to his feelings by writing: " And it will play ' In The Shadows ' *all day long*."

The late J. M. (" Jimmy ") Glover was booked to give a recital at Newcastle-on-Tyne, and he sent me an unsigned post-card which he received: " God save us from ' In The Shadows.' Professor Hadow (a well-known critic and lecturer) says it is musically defective in the bass line. Don't tell Mr. Finck."

Actually the tune was a new "figure," as we say in music, but not everybody recognised that. Someone once wrote and asked me to "settle an argument" about it. "Is it a waltz?" he inquired. "You try to waltz to it," I replied.

Someone else whom I knew slightly asked me to let him have a free copy of it—they always ask for free copies, but I should be interested to hear what my tailor said if I asked him for a free suit of clothes. I forgot to send it and he wrote to me: "You haven't sent me that free copy yet."

"No," I replied, "I haven't bought it yet."

During the height of the tune's vogue I was staying for a weekend at the Grand Hotel, Eastbourne. The small daughter of my good friend Eeley, the managing director of the hotel, said: "Let's go on the balcony and listen to the orchestra." And when we got there she exclaimed: "Oh, Uncle Herman, there's nothing of yours on the programme. . . . Not even 'In The Shadows.'"

"I dare say they didn't know I was coming down," I said to satisfy the child, though, naturally enough, it was a relief to me not to have to listen to my own music.

But she still wasn't too happy about it. "What a pity you didn't write, 'God Save the King,'" she said. "Then you would *have* to be in every programme."

Another time I was at Brighton and met Billy Barrett, the famous flautist, who was a friend of Johnny Toole, a well-known member of the Savage and a fine musician. We dined at the old "Ship" and he insisted that I should go on to the Palace Pier with him to listen to the band.

"They've got a tune that I can't get out of my head," he said. "You know that I don't care much about anything but opera, but there is something about this tune they play that has got hold of me."

The tune was "In The Shadows." I let Billy Barrett take me to hear it and let him "enthuse" about it for some time, and then I thought that he had pulled my leg sufficiently.

"Oh, come and have a drink," I said. "You know perfectly well that I wrote it."

"*You* wrote it?" he answered with the utmost scorn. "Don't try to tell me that. *You* could never write a tune as good as that." It was just about the best back-handed compliment I have ever had.

Another time I was on the Palace Pier with Evelyn Laye, then aged about four or five, and her father, Gilbert Laye, who was manager there. It was a very wild day, the wind threatening to blow all of us into the sea at any moment, but to amuse Evelyn we began to dance when the band struck up "In The Shadows." Suddenly there came an extra strong gust.

"Look out," I said, "or we'll be out of 'In The Shadows' and into the shallows."

Marie Tempest liked the tune so much that she commissioned me to write the music to a mime play called *The Malingerer*.

A cabman who once drove me from a house I used to live in at Hampstead to dine at Pagani's was not so complimentary. All the way to the West End he whistled "In The Shadows"—whistled it till I would gladly have slain him on his box. When I got out of the cab I asked him: "What is that tune?"

"It's called 'In The Shadows' and my old mother plays it all day long at home," he replied with some heat.

"Then you must be sick of it?" I suggested.

"*Sick* . . ." he said, and spat venomously, as the old-fashioned cabman could. "*Sick*, guv'nor? Well, I tell you that if I only knew who wrote it, I'd . . ."

"Here, take this," I said quickly, pressing half a crown into his hand, and vanishing into the safety of Pagani's.

Then there was the man who (it was, of course, in the pre-talkie era) came to me and asked me if I would become musical director of a big London cinema.

"No thank you," I replied, "I may have written 'In The Shadows,' but I'm not going to conduct in the dark!"

Chirgwin, "the white-eyed Kaffir," put some words to the tune of "In The Shadows," and wanted to sing them. I don't know whether he was ever allowed to, and if so, how many times. He sent me the words for my approval:

> This hall's like—
>   Playing football,
> It's the goal of—
>   Many " scores."
> And our Man-a-ger
> As " ref-er-ee "
> Pays the " penaltee "
> Of pop-u-lari-tee.
> Our conductor's—
>   In the " centre,"
> His " full back "—
>   You have spied.
> I do many things—
>   When I leave these " wings,"
> But I never swank I'm " offside."

Poles apart from Chirgwin was the parson who wrote to me and said he would like to have the tune used at his bazaar, "but would you mind if we called it a skipping-rope 'exercise'" not a skipping-rope 'dance.'" There was supposed to be something a bit improper about dancing in those days.

I can, by the way, deny that that clergyman was the same one who said: " *Honestly*, we must have £50 for the organ fund. We must, honestly. And if we can't get it honestly, we'll hold a bazaar ! "

How things have changed since I wrote " In The Shadows." For the purpose of this chapter I have been looking up old documents relating to the piece. In a covering letter sent with a cheque for seven hundred odd pounds on account of some royalties, the publisher wrote: " . . . the sum includes £50 4s. 4d., being a first payment for mechanical rights . . . this item will no doubt interest you as an indication of the trend of things. . . ." £50 4s. 4d. for gramophone record royalties of a tune that was piling up a million sale !

All the same, if anyone offered me £50 I doubt very much if I could, offhand at this moment, sit down and play " In The Shadows " on the piano. And if I could—and did—most of those present would probably walk out of the room directly I began. Still, I will say for "In The Shadows" that it had melody. It was a tune that reached the public and that boys could whistle. The "high-brows" of to-day may sneer—but how many of their tunes can anyone remember? Perhaps, after all, it is better to become a nuisance than to be negligible.

And, of course, luck is the thing that gives a piece an extraordinary success. "In the Shadows" made me neither egotistical—nor rich!

CHAPTER XIV

MEN WHO DRAW

DURING 1936 I attended a very pleasant dinner at the Savage Club, at which Jimmy Greig, Art Editor of *The Morning Post*, was in the chair. The dinner was in celebration of something that had never happened before—the fact that six members of the Club, C. R. W. Nevinson, Alfred Praga, Albert Collins, William Hutchinson of Glasgow University, George Parlby and Albert Toft had paintings in the Academy. James Pryde and John Hassall were among the dazzling array of artists who assisted the celebration.

With that memory still fresh, I feel that this is a fitting time for me (since I have been a member of the Savage for so many years) to write about artists I have known. Not that I want to give either a lecture or a dissertation on art and artists. I merely intend to tell a few stories about friends of mine whose work adorns the pages of *Punch* and other periodicals and is found in Art Galleries up and down the country. John Hassall, for instance, has a beautiful work in the Walker Art Gallery at Liverpool; Dudley Hardy in the National Gallery.

One very notable thing is the number of artists who start by producing serious pictures and then, for economic reasons, drift into the lighter type of work. Hassall is one example. After beginning as a serious artist, he took to poster work, and then became a brilliant humorist.

Dudley Hardy, too, started as a serious painter. He was a great Bohemian and developed into one of the first poster artists—the "Yellow Girl," which made his name more than any other picture, was done to advertise a paper called *To-day* which was being run by Jerome K. Jerome. Hardy was brought up in a French school, and always looked like a Frenchman.

One day he came into the Savage dressed up in black coat and sponge-bag trousers; sponge-bag trousers look magnificent if a man can wear them successfully but, as George R. Sims once remarked to me, a man needs a very distinguished appearance before he can afford to wear them.

Hardy was sitting at the bar with a friend when another member he knew walked up to him and said: "Those are beautiful trousers you are wearing. I've been admiring them very much. I'm going to a rather swell affair this afternoon. Do you think that you could lend them to me for a couple of hours?"

"Certainly," said Hardy, and he immediately took off his trousers and sat down at the bar clad in immaculate black coat, perfectly cut waistcoat—underpants and sock suspenders Throughout the afternoon this state of affairs continued peacefully until suddenly Hardy exclaimed: "Good Heavens! It's half-past six. I must meet my wife at seven o'clock to take her to dinner at the Café Royal—and I haven't got my trousers back."

After some minutes of alarums and excursions I went down to the front hall of the club, and said to the commissionaire: "What about Mr. Hardy's trousers?"

"I don't know anything about his trousers," the man replied, "but there's a parcel here for him."

Without wasting a second I shot back upstairs with the parcel. We ripped it open, and inside were the missing garments, and a note: "Many thanks. The trousers were a great success." It was a good thing it occurred to me to inquire in the hall, or else Hardy might have been marooned trouserless in the bar all night.

One day I met Hardy in the Café Royal, and he said: "I don't think I can buy you a drink. I've only half a crown. I had ten shillings in my pocket this morning, but as I was passing a shop I noticed a little yellow bowl. It was seven and six, but it was so beautifully made I could not resist the temptation to buy it." He was like that: an artistic impulse put every other consideration into the background.

I met Phil May on various occasions at Romano's, but so much has been written about him that I don't think I need add much. He had erratic habits and no idea of the value of money. Even his wife, who adored him, remarked one day: "It isn't always easy to be married to a genius."

To-day, I am one of the very few who can remember when genial Leonard Raven-Hill wore a beard and drew for *Pick me up*, before going to *Punch*.

Raven-Hill and Sime both drew pictures for songs which Gus Moore asked me to write with him, songs consisting only of a melody, which seemed an absurd idea to me. I could not persuade the publishers to print the songs without accompaniments, so I facetiously wrote one in which the melody was the same throughout but the accompaniments were different. Of course, when played with the original harmonies the result was very effective.

One of the regrets of my life is that I only have met Bernard Partridge once, for he then seemed to me to be a man of extraordinary personal charm. Other brilliant artists are the late E. T. Reed and G. Denholm Armour, for forty years a contributor to *Punch* (of which, by the way, I have every number from the first to the current week's) and painter of superb pictures of horses. He has been commissioned to paint famous horses by most of the more distinguished owners.

No man has worked harder for a club than George Stampa has for the Savage; in fact he calls himself the club photographer, he has drawn so many portraits of members. Not only is he a fine and popular artist: he has a lovely tenor voice, and I delight in hearing him sing Sullivan's "The Pale Young Curate," from *The Sorcerer*. On the night when Sir Edward German was the guest of the evening and was made an honorary member of the club, and I was in the chair, Stampa wished to do something to please me. So he sang a song he very much liked from *Bric-à-Brac*—"Naughty, Naughty, One Gerrard" (Teddie Gerrard). That night Joe Batten, famous pianist, soul of popularity, organiser of club concerts and musician-in-chief to Columbia and His Master's Voice, played a selection of tunes by German and myself—Herman and German. I included a song in this selection specially for Stampa: we rehearsed it with him and told him when to come in—but when the moment arrived he could not remember the words.

Stampa wears a curious fringe of hair across his forehead, and so does Bert Thomas; I have often wondered whether this is due to their appreciation of the genius of Phil May, who had a similar fringe.

EXAMPLE OF WHAT GEORGE STAMPA WILL DO WHEN ROUSED

In his case the hair was worn like that, I was informed, to cover a scar.

I first met Bert Thomas in the days of the *World*, when he came to ask me if he might draw a portrait of me. " Certainly," I said, " but not now. I have to go into the orchestra."

" That's all right," he replied. " I have already done it." And a very good caricature it was.

Pellegrini (" Ape ") was once able, through a similar method of mental photography, to bring about the capture of a criminal. After travelling in the same carriage as the "wanted" man, Pellegrini drew a lightning portrait of him in the carriage on the way to Victoria Station. That portrait enabled the police to recognise and arrest the criminal.

Starr Wood—who says to me "I never could draw you"—has had white hair ever since I can remember him and, indeed, before that; for his hair went white in three days when he was only in his twenties. Once, when a debt collector in the East End, he was taken for Jack the Ripper because he was carrying a black bag; he had to flee for his life before a raging mob! As a young man he obtained a great deal of quiet amusement by going about, from time to time, dressed like a clergyman.

E. J. Sullivan once told me that he wanted to draw an orchestra at work and asked me if I could help him.

"I'm not conducting anything at the moment," I replied, "but at the Columbia studios there's an orchestra of seventy which is being conducted by Weingartner."

"Never heard of him. Who is he?" remarked Sullivan irreverently, and I explained to him that Weingartner is one of the greatest musicians of the day.

I took Sullivan round to the Columbia studios, explained who he was and what he wanted, and left him there. He was taken into the concert room by Joe Batten, and sat down to draw. All through the rehearsal Weingartner kept repeatedly looking at Sullivan. At first Sullivan thought that he must be annoyed because he was drawing the orchestra when they were rehearsing, but he soon concluded that that could not be the case, because when he caught his eye Weingartner smiled at him.

Eventually the rehearsal finished, and as soon as it did so, Weingartner rushed over to Sullivan and clasping him warmly said: "My old friend! I have not seen you for so many years. . . ."

Sullivan is still wondering who is his double—and where he is.

Tom Webster sat in the orchestra with me at a matinée for Arthur Roberts. At the end of the matinée things were becoming decidedly lighthearted, and I made Tom Webster stand up and conduct the orchestra. Fortunately, they took no notice of his conducting, and when he finished he turned to the audience and made a sweeping bow.

To his amazement, Tom Marlowe, Editor of the *Daily Mail*, rose from a seat in the front row of the stalls, and returned the bow.

Tom Webster was very depressed when he met me one evening because he was on his way to a party in Chelsea where, he said, he was sure there would only be light refreshments—and he had had no dinner, and had no time to have any.

" We can soon deal with that situation," I said. " Go to Rule's and buy a chop. Then, when you arrive at the party, say to the butler: ' Mr. Webster has arrived. He has had no dinner, and would be very much obliged if you would have this chop cooked for him.' "

And that was what Tom did.

One day I was with " Poy " and Joe Wilson, manager of the Tivoli Music Hall in the great days. " Poy " asked us to have a drink, and we said we should like whisky.

" *Avec* soda ? " " Poy " asked.

" No, *avec l'eau*," replied Wilson.

" Not *avec* Low, *avec* ' Poy,' " I remarked.

Then there are Maurice Griefenhagen, with whom I foregather at the St. John's Wood Arts Club, and Cecil Baumer.

The late Edwin Ward, for all that he was a magnificent painter, wrote a book about the Savage Club.

Caton Woodville was selected by Arthur Roberts, when they were in a club one night, as a suitable victim for the game of " spoof," which he invented. Roberts began to murmur a tune—the band would take it up in due course—and after a few moments he would shout " Coats," and all the young men there would rip off their coats; then " Waistcoats " . . . " Ties " . . . " Collars " . . . and so on. The thing to do was to see if you could rip off your clothes more quickly than the other man—if you were foolish enough to be involved, of course.

When Roberts began his " Spoof," Caton Woodville did not

realise what was happening, but he saw the other men tear off their coats. So he did the same. Then his waistcoat. Then his tie. . . .

"Collars," shouted Arthur Roberts.

Caton Woodville was wearing a shirt and collar all in one. He ripped off his collar and his shirt came with it—so he won the prize!

Julian Price, who did portraits and pictures of nudes, was the author of a book called *My Bohemian Days in Paris*. This volume was, when it was written, considered very daring, the kind of thing to clutch away from your daughters if they started to peep into it. Looking back on it, I am puzzled to know what anyone found "daring" about the book; it seems a most innocuous volume to me. He painted all the celebrities of the Eccentric Club of those days, and they still adorn the walls.

When I was at Eastbourne, in connexion with the organisation of some concerts recently, a man said to me: "My name's Herman Finck. What's your's?"

Unfortunately I did not know the answer until he told me. It was Arthur Ferrier, one of the most successful—perhaps the most successful—newspaper and magazine artist of the day.

One artist, and a well known one, returned from a trip to America and entered the bar of the Savage. A number of people were there, and one member turned round and made a little "welcome home" speech.

Nothing happened.

So the member who had made the "welcome home" speech, left his seat and, imitating the manner of returned traveller, said: "It's awfully nice of you to welcome me back like this. I hope you'll all have a drink with me. What is it to be? . . ."

And at that the wanderer did arise and stand a round of drinks.

C. R. W. Nevinson asked me to one of his parties which I was unable to attend.

A few days later, my wife said to me: "I thought you said that you didn't go to Nevinson's party?"

"No, I didn't go," I said.

JIMMY PRYDE'S PORTRAIT OF IRVING IN "LYONS MAIL"

LANCE THACKERAY'S PORTRAIT OF SEYMOUR HICKS IN
THE DRUNKEN SCENE FROM "DAVID GARRICK"

" Then how do you account for this ? " she asked, and handed me a copy of the *Bystander*. There, across two pages was spread a drawing of Nevinson's party by George Whitelaw, and showing me talking to an attractive girl!

George Whitelaw had thought I ought to be at the party, so willy-nilly he had drawn me in.

For the better comprehension of the drawing (which is reproduced (facing page 233) I give the caption written at the time by George Whitelaw himself:

" The above represents the ante-room to the ' studio ' of C. R. W. Nevinson, the well-known artist, during one of his famous bottle parties. Dancing is going on in the studio, but on your left Sir Herbert Morgan, R. J. Minney, co-author of *Clive of India* and Ronny Squire are listening to the singing of Carlo Norway, the artist. In the centre Mrs. Nevinson is offering ' hot dogs ' to Wilenski, the critic and artist; Miles Malleson, the playwright, helps himself in front of her; Mark Hambourg is enjoying his, but Morris Harvey prefers a cigar. Behind Mrs. Nevinson is Nevinson himself telling H. G. Wells a story, and behind looms the eupeptic figure of Aubrey Hammond the artist. In the foreground on the right Selwyn Jepson endeavours to elicit from Michael Arlen the secret of writing a best seller, and Miss Farmer listens with bated breath. Behind them Herman Finck and David Whitelaw (no relation—got it in first this time !) are amusing three of Nevinson's models; and on the extreme right, helping himself to another, is an artist of sorts whom modesty forbids me to mention."

At an exhibition of the work of the late David Wilson at the Leicester Square Galleries, I noticed two portraits unsold— one of Lord Northcliffe and the other of Mark Hambourg. Each was priced twenty-five guineas. When I saw the artist's brother, I said : " Look here, nobody seems to be buying that portrait of Mark Hambourg. I should like it, but neither can nor will pay twenty-five guineas for it."

" Oh, we shouldn't expect a price like that from a musician," he said. "I'll have a word with my brother, and we will see what we can do." The upshot of the conversation was that I bought the portrait (reproduced facing page 232) for three guineas. It hangs in my flat with originals of Cecil Aldin, Barribal, Tom Browne, Hassall, Haselden, E. T. Reed and George Stampa.

Jimmy Pryde gave me one of the very few prints made from a portrait of Irving which he did (reproduced facing page 248). I have a letter in which Pryde says:

> "I was glad that you accepted my print from the portrait I painted of Sir Henry Irving as Dubosc in the *Lyons Mail*, not only because you were so very appreciative but because of our old and valued friendship.
>
> "The great man never sat to me—I didn't want him to, I knew him so well it would only have hampered me. He was painted and drawn by many distinguished artists as you know and I was very proud of the fact that H. B. (Henry Irving's son) preferred my presentation to others."

The artistic Frenchman Palleologue painted a beautiful group of nudes—about five and half acres of canvas—which was hung in the Eccentric Club before they moved to their present premises.

Yeend King, of the Royal Institute, was very fond of the Savage and served on innumerable committees of the club; served very well, too, for he was a most reliable man. Before Saturday night dinners he would produce a beautiful old silver snuff box, and offer it to members—especially to those not accustomed to taking snuff. The sneezes of the tyros invariably infuriated Mostyn Pigott. "Blast this snuff!" he would say, giving ferocious twiddles to his big moustache.

The snuff box was left to the club when Yeend King died, but was afterwards stolen.

Frank Reynolds used to be art editor of *Punch*, but now prefers only to draw for the paper. Another *Punch* artist was Tom Browne. My great friend Albert Toft, the sculptor, has done a statue of King George V which has been bought by the

Eastbourne Corporation. I wrote the music for a gorgeous set of living pictures he did for the Hippodrome.

Before going home to dress between a matinée and an evening performance at the Palace, I dropped into the Café Royal with George Belcher.

"Stay and have some dinner," he said, when we had had a cocktail.

"I must go home to dress," I replied.

"Why don't you keep a suit of evening clothes at the theatre?"

"I do, but that suit has gone to be cleaned."

Anyway, I did stay for dinner, and sent a boy from the Café Royal in a cab to fetch my clothes from home. When the boy came back we drove to the stage door in the same cab. Neither Belcher nor myself had any change, so I went to ask Blake, the stage-door keeper, to change a note for me, or it may have been a gold coin in those beautiful days. When I arrived back with the silver and paid the cabman, he immediately drove off—with my clothes still inside the cab.

So after all that trouble, I still had no evening dress. The theatre wardrobe eventually fixed me up. They said I looked fine. But I took one glance at myself in a mirror and decided not to go round to the front of the house that night.

James Gunn will always be known for the deservedly famous "Conversation Piece" which he painted two or three years ago. Ernest Coffin, painter of architectural subjects, was, despite sponge bag trousers, the most dazzling Bohemian I have ever known. And Aubrey Hammond (who would not hurt a fly, formidable though his size makes him look), who did the "Grill Room" mask reproduced on page 107, is among my closest friends.

I can Sidney Strube, "Dr." Strube; and this is why. One autumn my wife was ill in bed with influenza, and although it had been dragging on for some little time, she did not seem to get better. While things were still in this unsatisfactory state, I arrived home one night with a drawing which Strube had done for a November 5 dinner at the Savage. When I showed this to my wife she laughed and laughed ... and when she had finished laughing the influenza fled defeated, and did not return.

Victor MacClure is an artist, novelist, scene painter, actor, a very good cook ... and anything else you may want to ask him to turn his hand to.

David Whitelaw used to work with Penrhyn Stanlaws. He also used to draw illustrations for books. But after a time he realised that he was making very little out of the illustrations, in comparison with what the authors were paid.

THIS DRAWING CURED INFLUENZA

" I'll write books myself," he said. He did—and now he only draws cheques. For many years he was editor of the *London* magazine, and he is still a successful writer of novels.

The doyen of the last generation of scene painters was Joseph Harker, who painted scenery for Tree, for the Lyceum and every other theatre. When he died I took his place as trustee of the Savage Club. His sons, who include Gordon Harker, the film comedian, are all very dear boys.

Their father would give a tremendous number of parties on a Sunday. He wanted me to go to his supper-parties occasionally, but I said I was accustomed to taking my beef quietly at home on a Sunday. Finally, one day, he said to me : " Look here, Herman, you bring your wife round to our place on Sunday. It's just a small family party. There'll be only sixteen there."

So we went to the " small family party " of sixteen.

Harker was fond of organising home theatricals, but when he played in them himself he often missed his cue. One night he determined to end this fault; and throughout the play he was so anxious not to miss his cue that he repeatedly came on too soon.

Lance Thackeray drew, and gave to me, the picture of Seymour Hicks, facing page 249. He was far from strong, but was determined to go to the front, and did so: poor fellow, he did not return from the War.

CHAPTER XV

AUTHORS AND OTHERS

AT one time Arnold Bennett had a pronounced girth. I thought it spoke of a just appreciation of some of the finer pleasures of life. But to Arnold Bennett it was no source for satisfaction, but for constant worry. He longed for a slender lissom figure, and he tried one treatment after another.

Persistence will achieve most things if carried on long enough, and eventually Arnold Bennett discovered a system that made his girth melt away. He decided that the good news about girth-control was too exciting and important to be kept to himself. So he sent me a book called *The Culture of the Abdomen*. There were diagrams and drawings of men with two tummies (the " before using " one represented by a dotted line) doing strenuous-looking exercises.

With the book was a letter from Arnold Bennett in which he said: " Dear Herman, This system has done wonders for me. It will abolish your ' tummy,' if only you will use a little persistence."

But I replied: " Dear Arnold, If I lost my ' tummy ' I should have to have new clothes and new photographs. No one would recognise me from my caricatures, and my career would be ruined."

So, I am happy to say, my abdomen remains uncultured.

That is one amusing memory of a great author, but I have many more: I suppose the fact that words and music are so closely allied may explain why I do know and have known so many authors—and of all sorts. Poets (I suppose they come first), novelists, dramatists, essayists, journalists. . . . I have not, of course, collaborated with all the authors I have known.

For instance, among those I know or have known, without collaborating with them, are H. G. Wells, Oscar Wilde, George Augustus Sala, George Moore, Lord Alfred Douglas, Hubert Henry Davies, Noel Coward and A. S. M. Hutchinson, author of *If Winter Comes*.

Among those with whom I *have* worked, and happily, are J. M. Barrie and E. V. Lucas. Then there are George R. Sims, C. H. E. Brookfield, Adrian Ross, C. S. Maclennen (who wrote *The Belle of New York*), Edgar Wallace, Basil MacDonald Hastings, Edward Knoblock (who wrote *London Life* with Arnold Bennett), John Hastings Turner, Dion Clayton Calthrop, Captain Basil Hood, Captain Harry Graham, the late Keble Howard, Neil Lyons, and my old friend Arthur Wimperis. And I nearly forgot Arthur Binstead—*Tale Pitcher* of the late-lamented *Pink 'Un*.

I wrote some music for the first play of Eden Phillpotts—a one-act play produced at the Comedy many years ago.

A. P. Herbert, whose hair is even more unruly than my own, goes to the same barber as I do; and one day we were so interested in the conversation we had carried on while waiting that we walked out without remembering to have our hair cut.

On two occasions I met Pinero : I preferred his plays.

Mr. Compton Mackenzie I met a great deal before he became a " Herm-un " and later Capri-cious. And, by the way, Sax Rohmer used to write comic songs for George Robey.

Now I have given you some idea of what you are in for we will return to Arnold Bennett. He sent me a copy of *Mr. Prohack* when it was first published, and I began to read it in a taxi on my way to the Café Royal for lunch. I laid the book on the seat of the taxi when I got out and was bringing the fare out of my pocket. The moment he had the money, the taximan slammed the door and shot off along Regent Street (I wish they would always show the same speed when taking me to my destination). Anyway, I was left standing on the pavement, without my book. I shouted after the taxi, but the driver did not hear me.

This put me in an awkward position. I was afraid that

Bennett himself might climb into the same cab and find the book, or—much more probably—someone would find it had his signature inside and would send it back to him. Then, when we next met, he would give me a meaning look and say: " Well, Herman, and how did you like *Mr. Proback?* "

" Oh, very much, one of the best things you've done," I should say, fumbling guiltily with a walking-stick the while.

" You liar, you haven't read it," he would reply, and would produce the copy he had given me, with my bookmarker in page 5. " You lost it the very day I gave it to you."

However, containing my fears and annoyance, I had lunch at the Café Royal according to my original programme, and in due course went on to Drury Lane. On my arrival I found a note addressed to me : " Will you please ring up Scotland Yard ? "

So I rang up Scotland Yard, and the man at the other end of the line said : " We have some music of yours here, Mr. Finck. You left it in a taxi."

" Not music, a book," I replied.

" No, music," he replied, raising his voice a little.

" A book," I shouted, thinking he had not heard me.

" Music," he shouted, thinking I had not heard him.

The game was a draw up to this point. I did not try to argue any further, but said I would call round the following morning to collect my property. I was confident of my ultimate victory over the man who insisted on calling the book music.

There, sure enough, was the book. And, equally surely, there was some music of mine which I did not know I had lost. It was a score which I had crammed into my pocket when going home the previous evening and which had apparently been forced out, without my noticing the fact, when I sat down.

So I was able to read *Mr. Proback* and give Bennett an honest view next time I saw him. I also confessed my worst fears over the temporary loss, to his amusement.

Bennett was a fervent admirer of Russian novels and plays, and when a Russian play came to the Ambassadors, he and I and Duff Tayler (like Swinnerton, one of Bennett's executors) went to see it and sat in the front row of the stalls.

Duff Tayler and I were bored beyond measure, but we grimly sat through act after act, thinking that no doubt Bennett was seeing something in the play that was not apparent to us. When the end at last came, we waited to hear what Bennett would say. He closed his eyes (so great sometimes was the effort to speak for him) and began to stammer: " It's . . . it's . . ." We expected a wonderful piece of praise. Then Bennett tried again, and blurted out : " It's *no* good ! "

I dedicated my " Crusaders' March " to Arnold Bennett, a thing which, I believe, greatly pleased him. When he heard what I was doing he wrote to me :

> " Duff and I are trying to arrange a dinner to you at the Garrick some night at 7 sharp. But it won't be this week as I'm engaged nightly. I'll see the fellow to-day and decide summat if poss. I should think Wednesday 10th.
>
> " What is this startling and unnerving hint about the admirable Crusaders' March ? Thine, A. B."

One night, during the War, E. V. Lucas and Phillip Page were having supper at the Savoy when an air raid warning went. Simultaneously with the news that there was an air raid, E. V. ordered a roll.

As, after some minutes there was no response, he asked again for a roll.

" All right, sir, I get it. I get it," said the waiter, his English weakening under the strain of the air raid warning. " You know the warnings have gone . . ."

After another five minutes, there was still no bread, but the waiter was bustling aimlessly about saying : " It is terrible . . . it is terrible . . . they are dropping bombs all over the place."

E. V. gave the man a pained and weary look. " Bombs ? " he said, then hopefully : " I hope they are dropping rolls as well ! "

He was served.

E. V.'s letters (I have stacks of them, for he seldom uses the telephone) are written in a kind of triangle, each line shorter than the one above it. After practice in deciphering them, it is mere child's play to turn to a cuneiform, Sanskrit or Arabic inscription.

One of his peculiarities is that when he wants to meet you for lunch, E. V. always names some odd time, such as 1.21. He says that people remember times like that, but if you ask a man

Dear Herman, here is the new edition. Pocketable only if, as in your case, the reader doesn't care a damn for tailors.

E. V.

April 26 1921

E. V.'s NOTE

to have lunch with you at one o'clock, he will turn up half an hour late and say vaguely: "It was half-past one you said, wasn't it?" The theory is, I think, sound.

Here is one example of his bidding to lunch.

"Dear Herman. Come at 1.5 if you can. I open no paper now without seeing your name and mine, usually in conjunction."

A letter written years before that says:

"Coventry, on Wednesday night. . . . Don't ever forget, will you, that I have a reputation for being the 'best hidden man in London' and wish to retain it."

I fear that that reputation has been shattered, because in the years that have followed the writing of this letter E. V. has joined far too many clubs.

A few weeks ago I went with Lucas to a dinner at the Hind's Head Hotel, Bray, a "dinner given by a few of his friends to Charles Walter Berry," the wine merchant, who had just been made a *chevalier de la Légion d'Honneur*. At the end of the dinner, our *guest* gave each of his *hosts* a parcel in which was a bottle of superb 1858 brandy—so magnificent a gesture as to make our generosity look foolish.

Letters from E. V. are usually brief, but one he wrote me from abroad, on horrible Continental note-paper, ran to some six pages and then ended abruptly with the statement: "But this is developing into an article, and I charge for that."

In 1925 he wrote to me:

"To-morrow, Wednesday, Jan. 7, I shall have sat at the *Punch* table for twenty-one years. I am coming to see you after. Yours E."

So from that you can work out how long he has been with *Punch*.

Somewhat later, I received a letter saying:

"Dear Herman, I just found this, in Lamb: 'I never knew an enemy to puns who was not an ill-natured man' and it made me think of you who are a friend to them."

In 1921, E. V. gave me a "pocket" Lamb inscribed: "Here is the new edition, pocketable only if, as in your case, the reader does not care a damn for tailors."

Among various communications from "Dr." Lucas (as he now is, even if he does not call himself so) which I possess,

I find his report on essays and stories written by the children of a Church school in Rotherhithe. He had been persuaded by the late W. Pett Ridge to perform the task and obviously, as you will see, took his duties seriously—too seriously, as it turned out, for, as he afterwards told me, the children were far too excited to listen to a word that he tried to read and he therefore gracefully retired. The Vicar, in thanking E. V. L., said what a pleasure and honour it was to be in the presence of "Evoe" of *Punch*.

But here is the report:

"In the search for the best I have read a great number of essays and stories, and I have suggested a first and second prize in each case.

"The essays on the theme 'Why I like Rotherhithe' are very similar. Out of, say, fifteen statements about Rotherhithe every essay mentions thirteen; and as they nearly all begin the same way and many end in the same way, a judge becomes rather suspicious. He feels that the lessons upon which the essay was based must have been listened to, or even taken down, almost too intently.

"Although the essays are good, I should have liked more original observation in them. Rotherhithe must have a variegated life to-day which could yield as many reasons for liking to live there as the fact that it has a teeming history.

"I would suggest that next time the children are asked to draw on their own experience.

"Before coming to the essays themselves let me say that I congratulate the teachers of the schools on the admirable and very high standard of handwriting that has been reached. Practically every essay is beautifully transcribed. If I had time perhaps I ought to take lessons myself.

"The essays are in two groups and each group is the product, I assume, of listening to a distinct address on Rotherhithe by the teachers.

"In one group all the essays mention Nelson as a resident of Rotherhithe and refer to Téméraire Street. The Free

Library and the Public Baths are mentioned and there are many references to Rotherhithe's sociability. The people, says G. Dodd, are 'sociable and clean.'

"'A stranger to Rotherhithe,' says Albert Osmond, 'will find the people very sociable.'

"To their sociability they can add a philosophic calm. According to W. Slaughter, people here 'are quite satisfied to die in Rotherhithe when their time comes.'

"Another essayist, Caroline Smith, is possibly not free from irony when she says : 'We ought to be proud to live in Rotherhithe because it was one of the first places that bothered about education.'

"Then we come to the other group, in which nothing is said of Nelson, but all the emphasis is laid on the old street names and Queen Elizabeth and Lady Carr Gomm. In referring to Southwark Park all call it 'a lung.' All say that Paradise Street is not the Paradise it used to be.

"That these things should be mentioned generally is natural. What is less natural is that all or nearly all in this group begin by saying that they like Rotherhithe because their homes are there and there is no place like home, and all or nearly all end by saying that they like Rotherhithe not because the people are sociable—this group has not observed the tendency to sociability—but because they are law-abiding and peaceable.

"Now that is an idea that one gets from a teacher. Children prefer rowdiness.

"I will give an example of what I mean. Louisa Nayler, aged 13, says 'The reason why I like Rotherhithe is because I was born there, and there is nothing better than our homes.' She adds : 'The people who live in Rotherhithe are very law-abiding people.'

"Frances Foster, aged 12, says 'Although Rotherhithe is a drab and sordid place I like it. Home is the best place and Rotherhithe is my home. It is simply teeming with history and is pleasant and historical. . . . The people of Rotherhithe are law-abiding and peaceful.'

"Maud Deal, aged 13, says 'I like Rotherhithe because my home is there and home is the best place. Then also it has a teeming history and is very historical.' She goes on to remark: 'The streets are very drab and sordid but the people who live in them are peaceable and law-abiding.

"You can't get away from it!

"Mabel Barrett, aged 13, says 'I like Rotherhithe because my home is here and home is the best place there is. . . . The next reason is because it is teeming with history. Rotherhithe,' she concludes, 'is rather drab and sordid, but we like it all the same because of the peaceful and law-abiding people.'

"Freda Bavin, aged 13, says 'I like Rotherhithe because I was born here and my home and parents are here. . . . The streets are drab and sordid.' Freda gets out of one of her difficulties very cleverly. Having forgotten a name, this is how she covers her lapse. She writes: 'There was once a farm at the top of Albion Street and if you were to ask a very well-known man who lived there he would most likely tell you about it.'

"Beatrice Taylor, aged 13, says 'I like Rotherhithe because it is my birthplace. My home is here and home is the best place.' But Beatrice has this ingenious passage: 'Where our school now stands was a field where perhaps cattle grazed, and I expect when Queen Elizabeth rowed down the river she looked upon this field and never thought a school would be built there.'

"At the end Beatrice Taylor is careful to state that, 'though the streets are drab and sordid the people are peaceable and law-abiding.'

"Eleanor Birchall, aged 14, discriminates: 'Although Rotherhithe is a drab and sordid place,' she writes, 'most of the people are law-abiding and peaceable.' Not all, you see!

"The repetition of the statement gives me—a visitor to Rotherhithe—a comfortable feeling of security. It also suggests that the police here must die of inanition.

"Later on Eleanor Birchall returns to the matter with what might be considered a touch of irony. She writes: 'Many governesses, teachers, lightermen, etc., say they like Rotherhithe because the people are peaceable and the children are loving and obedient.'

"After mature consideration I find that the best essay is that written by Edith Robinson, aged 12. She seems to me to have a wider outlook than the others and her facts are more easily ordered. While she has observed that the streets are drab and sordid, she is alone in adding that that doesn't matter because there is plenty to interest everybody. The people of Rotherhithe, she adds, are law-abiding and peaceable, but she does not end on that.

"The second prize goes to Doris Smith, age not given.

"The stories are disappointing.

"Most of them are about fairies who live either by or in a lake; while several naturally have wood-cutters in them. There is a sprinkling of detective stories and stories of hidden treasure and ghosts. One story is about a cowboy, and I suspect the influence of the movies here.

"It is a rule with the stories to begin better than they end. But this can happen with professional writers. Mr. Pett Ridge has some quite good beginnings.

"The fairy stories are so much alike that I suspect that they grew from something that was read or related in class; but one story about a giant has so surprising a turn that I must read a little to you. The author is Blanche Reynolds, age 12. It begins: 'In a far-off country there lived a giant whose name was Bully. He was selfish and wicked and always causing trouble to the people.' So the King put up a notice: 'Anybody who can kill this giant shall have one thousand pounds and my daughter.'

"Various efforts to kill the giant failed and then the blacksmith's son tried. It is his method that is such a novelty in this kind of story. He began by secretly abstracting and hiding the giant's weapons. He then said to the giant: 'Don't you think you would be happier if you did not live by killing and stealing and try to live honestly?'

"This is all right as a question. But the surprising thing

about it is the contemptible result. For the giant 'sat down and thought over the words which the young man had said' and found that they were true, and the next morning he promised to mend and 'live honestly and be a loyal subject.'

"So the blacksmith's son married the King's daughter and the giant Bully was an 'honoured guest' at the wedding and, I assume, changed his name. Surely when I said 'contemptible' I was right.

"The detective stories are not very good. The mysteries are too easy. I will describe one, by Daisy Alexandra Cox, aged 10, which refers to the skill of Dick Daring, the great criminologist.

"The trouble was the kidnapping of the son of Mr. Coinage, and Dick Daring was called in.

"He went to the boy's bedroom.

"The first thing he noticed was that the handle knob had finger marks on it.

"He took out of his pocket his microscope and book of finger prints.

"'Please may I see your valet?' he asked.

"'Certainly,' said Mr. Coinage.

"Dick questioned the valet. 'Has anyone been here at all?'

"'No, sir,' said the valet.

"Dick dismissed him.

"'Have you any light on the case?' Mr. Coinage asked.

"'I am very suspicious of your valet,' replied the detective.

"'You see,' says the author, 'he had noticed the valet's fingers. The middle finger was missing!'

"Mr. Coinage's valet turned out to be no other than Morton Hastings, the famous criminal.

"The boy was found and became Dick Daring's assistant.

"In the stories a better result would have been obtained if the competitors had been asked to relate the most interesting or exciting thing that they personally had ever seen or done. Only one competitor—A. E. Adams—has told a story of his own experience, with Rotherhithe in it.

GEORGE R. SIMS

["Sunday Dispatch" Photograph

WHAT I REALLY LOOK LIKE

AUTHORS AND OTHERS

"We find, however, the pull of Rotherhithe's historical riches in the story called 'An Hero' by Ivy Bayly, aged 13.

"This is about an American boy who asked his father to let him go to London.

"The father replied, certainly not. 'London,' he said, 'is one of the most nasty and sordid places I ever heard of.'

"'Yes,' said the boy, 'I know that, but it is teeming with historical things, especially Rotherhithe.'

"So his father let him come, with his tutor.

"In the ship's bath he learned to swim, so that by the time he arrived in England he was an expert.

"As he walked along a country road he heard a cry for help and saw a small girl in a pond. He dived in and rescued her. The girl asked him to take her home. The boy was given £140. As he was a rich boy he gave it to the London Hospital. He stayed in London and when he was twenty he married—not the girl he had saved but an English lady—and lived happily till he was eighty years old.

"The prize for the best story goes to Alice Barrett, aged 14, for 'An Adventure in Elfland.'

"The second prize goes to Alice Birchall, aged 11, the author of 'Milly's Strange Ordeal.'"

All that was in 1923. I wonder what has become of the competitors. The winner of the prize for the best essay, Edith Robinson, aged twelve, I wonder where she is now? A well-known essayist, perhaps, even knocking at Dr. Lucas's door, or a law-abiding and peaceable beauty of Rotherhithe.

Some time ago E.V. sent me a German cartridge picked up unused in a belt after a Marne engagement and given to him by the French soldier who found it. The cartridge now has a blade attached, so I use it as a paper knife. I have always taken E. V.'s word for the fact that it will not go off. It has not disillusioned me . . . yet!

When E. V. went to America I christened the friends who

arranged a farewell party " The Lucastrians." (See Stampa's letter on page 267.)

Another man who had, like E. V., the curious trick of writing each line shorter than the line above was George R. Sims.

" Why do you do that ? " I asked him one day.

" I can write another line in the time it would take me to move my hand back ! " he replied.

With George R. Sims I wrote several ballets which were produced at Blackpool.

" Have you tried Blackpool sunsets with potted shrimps ? They are lovely. Ask Mr. Herman Finck when he comes back."

Thus he wrote in a newspaper, somewhat inconsequentially, after he and I had arrived late at Blackpool one evening, and toyed with potted shrimps while our steaks were grilling. Anyway, I disagree with him: I thought the potted shrimps were poor stuff.

For many years Sims wrote " Mustard and Cress " in the *Referee*, and wrote is as no one has written it since. Through his writings, in which he did not mince words when he wanted to expose evils, he did a great deal for the poor. He was a poet and great journalist—and what a humorist ! He was a criminologist of no mean merit, and the police would take him round with them. To prevent his presence arousing resentment, when they entered some slum dwelling, the police would say : " This is *Doctor* Sims."

One of Sims's many plays was *The Ever Open Door*, on which we collaborated. It was produced at the Aldwych Theatre by Sir Thomas Beecham's father.

When I was doing a selection of dance music I asked Sims to suggest a title. " Why ask me ? " he said. " You should ask *Terps*-Hickory Wood." (The writer of innumerable pantomimes.)

Another great journalist is Sir Percival Phillips. Without a thought he crosses forests, deserts, jungles, oceans, continents ... but I found him one Sunday badly delayed because

LETTER FROM STAMPA ABOUT FAREWELL TO
E. V. LUCAS

he had taken the Brighton train when he wanted to go to Margate!

In his flat in Chancery Lane he showed me one day a vast Chinese executioner's sword, a thing with an enormous curved blade, needing both hands, and plenty of strength. As I left I said: "By the way, could you spare that sword? As a baton it would be wonderful; it would only take a second to deal with any member of the orchestra who did not behave."

The first dramatic works of Edgar Wallace to be produced were three one-act plays for which I wrote the music; they were given at the Camden Theatre. Wallace was then on the *Daily Mail* and his great reputation as a novelist and playwright still had to be made. A thing few people seem to realise is that he was the author of a very good comic song called: "A sort of a, kind of a. . . ." Wallace wrote the song for Arthur Roberts.

MacDonald Hastings and I wrote together a vocal ballet called "The Jackdaw of Rheims," which was based on the Ingoldsby Legend and in which the part of the jackdaw was taken by a dancer.

Hastings always had remarkable notepaper. Where on earth he bought it I cannot imagine: it always had strange Victorian drawings printed on the top. And the letters underneath were often charmingly inconsequential. For example, underneath "Sea Side Sketches, No. 2. The Pleasure Party," was this epistle:

DEAR HERMAN,

You may not have heard that
(then a newspaper cutting stuck on)
Herr Muck, the musical director, who has returned to Berlin from internment in America, intends to establish himself permanently in Switzerland.

Not that it matters, of course.
Yours,
B. MACH.

LETTER FROM BASIL MACDONALD HASTINGS

With C. S. Maclennen I wrote " Round the Map," which was played at the Alhambra. He was very anxious that I should go to America with him for the production, but I said it was impossible as I had to conduct a first night at the Palace before I should be able to return. Still persistent, he tried to " kidnap " me by luring me on to the boat train on the pretext that I must have a final drink with him. But I was too quick for him, and jumped off a moment before the train started!

I don't know how many years have passed since I first met Jimmy Heddle, for so long managing-editor of the Hulton group of papers, and the man who first brought Dean Inge into the *Evening Standard*.

Anyway, it was in my Palace days. Heddle was having a fight with the theatrical managers over a monopoly in the photographs of first-night productions in the West End theatres. He had founded the *Daily Sketch* and Hulton decided that success in the North of England was not enough, and that simultaneous production in London was essential. So, following the precedent of Northcliffe who duplicated the *Daily Mail* in London and Manchester, Hulton reversed the process; he took the *Daily Sketch* to London.

The fight against a photographic monopoly was one of many hard contests. They ended for ever when Hulton sold out to Rothermere and Beaverbrook.

I have a copy, given me by the author, of David Hodge's great success " The Quest of the Gilt-Edged Girl," a skit of Le Gallienne's " The Golden Girl."

Hodge, as a special constable in London during the War, was told that if any suspicious character resisted arrest he was to be struck a sharp blow on the shins with a baton. " That's all right," David muttered, " but as far as I'm concerned the suspicious character to be struck will have to be a consenting party."

David was a very canny Scot. He was the prototype of Barrie's famous journalist, Noble Sims. Wherever he went he got copy. He never made what he called a " purchase " without getting his money's worth in goods and a profit, large or small, in the salesman's talk. On one occasion he went into a jeweller's on Ludgate Hill to buy a watch-key. He heard a noise like the roar of a lion. He inquired. He was shown into the workshop behind, an expansive place. At one bench he saw a man pulling hard at a piece of catgut protruding from the works of a clock. Every pull brought a startling roar. The clock was being made as a present for an Indian prince. Instead of striking the hours by a gong or a bell there came a roar, loud enough to startle customers near the traffic of Ludgate Hill. David's story of that clock went round the world. "It made quite a good article, and it paid for my key anyway," he said.

A. E. W. Mason once wrote to me:

"I do not know whether you would be inclined to consider a wordless play, with a view to writing the music for it. I ought to say at once that it demands considerable scenic effects, and that condition would no doubt limit the opportunities of production. It is modern, but gives at the same time scope for picturesque dresses and dancing. It is meant to be rather a strong, and in some points sensational story enclosed within a sort of fantasy. It's called *The Opium Pipe*. I have the scenario completely mapped out, with the actions of the characters, and if you think it worth while, I should be very happy to send it to you for your consideration."

Within a few months the War was upon us and the scheme was never carried through.

A certain musician, who was supposed to be writing the music for a play by Brookfield (he wrote it for Hawtrey, who appeared in it as Oscar Wilde), commissioned me to do the work for him. In short, I was his "ghost."

Brookfield, however, was shrewd enough quickly to realise where the music was coming from, and insisted on making all his requests direct to me.

"Oh, by the way," he would say, "I want something Irish. . . ."

"Certainly," I replied, "I will tell Mr. X."

"How soon can you do this? We should like it to-morrow."

"I will tell Mr. X. I think that you will be able to have it to-morrow."

Brookfield, when making these requests, would never refer to the man who was really supposed to be writing the music, and I would never admit that I was doing the work.

I regret to say that I was never paid for my work, and after his death the play was found among the books of the man who had commissioned me to write the music. I bought it—bought my own work for which I had never been paid—for a guinea!

Sir James Barrie and I co-operated on a wordless play called *The Origin of Harlequin*, and he wrote me a charming letter afterwards in which he said:

> "I thought your part of the wordless play so delightful that very probably in about a week's time I shall begin to pretend that I wrote the music and end by believing it. So this is just to thank you warmly before these events come about."

Hastings Turner wrote a play, for which Captain Harry Graham did the lyrics, called *Merely Molly*. I wrote music for that and for a play written by the industrious Caltrop—author of so many plays, and now living peacefully in Devonshire—for Gaby Deslys. Basil Hood was part author of the Palace revue *Bric-à-Brac*, and it was with him that I wrote *The Optimist and the Pessimist*, to which I have referred elsewhere. I have also collaborated with Reginald Arkell, who adapted 1066 *and All That* for the stage.

Keble Howard, prolific novelist and editor of the weekly *Sketch*, wrote, with me, a sketch for Courtice Pounds. Poor old Courtice Pounds! I remember that when he was terribly ill a committee to give him a little help was formed by Oscar Asche, who was chairman, Robert Courtneidge, Anthony Prinsep, Oscar Barrett and H. S. Lambert.

> ADELPHI TERRACE HOUSE,
> STRAND, W.C.
>
> 19 Feb. 1917
>
> Dear Mr Finck,
>
> I thought your putting the wordless play so delightful that very probably in a short time I shall begin to pretend I wrote the music and and by believing it. So this is just to thank for warning before these events have time to come about.
>
> Yours sincerely
> J. M. Barrie

SIR JAMES BARRIE'S LETTER

Basil Macdonald Hastings wrote this charming, if saddening, tribute:

"'Youth's a stuff will not endure,' and one who has given us fifty years of song (lyrics by Shakespeare and Gilbert) finds himself at the age of sixty-five out in 'the rain that raineth every day.'

"Charles Courtice Pounds, gay of heart and art, is ill, and so placed (or, marry, displaced, but that's all one) that we are asking his friends in the world, and that's the whole pack of you, to tear a sheet from your cheque-books and write upon it the name of a sum that will stand in full grace for measure of the love you have for him and the joy he has given you.

"Think first of him in Gilbert and Sullivan (he is one of the five original Savoyards still with us), then in *La Poupée* and as the Clown in Tree's *Twelfth Night*. Recall his exquisite singing and acting in *The Duchess of Dantzic*, *The Blue Moon*, *The Cherry Girl* and *The Belle of Mayfair*. How often did you hear him in *Chu Chin Chow*? Finally there came his greatest triumph as an artist, his playing and singing of Franz Schubert in *Lilac Time*.

"It is hoped to add to our testimonial to this good fellow, the very mention of whose name recalls melody, dancing and delight, the proceeds of a gleeful matinée, quite unlike any former 'bespeak,' to be given on a date which will be announced later.

"But we are confident that you will wish to give now, so that the speed of your giving may warm the cockles of Charles's young heart, serving to bring our delightful friend quickly from bed to boards. Anthony Trollope wrote that 'it is self-evident that at sixty-five a man has done all he is fit to do.' Charles writes that down for nonsense. He protests on his sick bed that he will work again if the flesh should let him. That's pluck.

"Now that you have written out your cheque, may we ask you to take out *Twelfth Night* and read the epilogue so often sung by Charles.

"'When that I was a little tiny boy,' it begins. And the last stanza runs:

'A great while ago the world begun,
With hey, ho, the wind and the rain,
But that's all one, our play is done,
And we'll strive to please you every day.'

"Read it over in the quiet, and presently you will hear Charles singing it."

They spoke of Courtice Pound's pluck. And pluck he certainly had. He was going to be brought on to the stage in a bath-chair to sing at the benefit matinée. But he was dead before the matinée.

Then there is Neil Lyons, who first introduced me to H. G. Wells; Arthur Wimperis with whom I wrote the Palace revues; and J. B., or rather Johnny, Morton ("Beachcomber" of the *Daily Express*) whom I have known since childhood (his, not mine) and he has not grown up yet! My favourite among his books is *Hag's Harvest*, which is brilliantly funny but has never received from the public the appreciation it should have done.

Two other humorists I have known for many years are D. B. Wyndham Lewis, to whom I dedicated "Fairy Feet," and Maurice Lane Norcott, with whom I wrote a song. And then the lyricists: Harold Simpson, writer of so many plays, revues, ballets and songs; Desmond Carter and Frank Eyton who frequently work together.

C. H. Bovill, an official of the Lunacy Commission, used to write lyrics, and very amusing letters, as you can judge by this sample:

"Thanks for your letter. I am glad to hear that you propose to stir up the panting Hart.

"If he proposes to take either or both of the songs, for 'eving's sake get the doubloons out of him before the 'Blue Moon' begins to shed its fitful light on an uninterested world. I have doubts as to whether there will be any doubloons to get after that date.

"Can you, in the exercise of your discretionary kindness, as we say in balmy circles, manage to get two seats for me out of the magnanimous Miller? Don't bother about it if the mob are surging and clamouring round the doors every night, but if it *can* be done, I shall be immensikoffly obliged to you. I still have these American ladies of whom I told you on my hands to entertain, and money is tight both in balmy and lyrical circles.

"True, they will probably go off for a coaching trip in the Outer Hebrides, on the night I have with infinite trouble arranged for their entertainment, but that is no concern of mine."

Author, actor and stage-manager, Clifford Seyler—alas dead!—he was brother to Athene Seyler, the famous actress, was responsible for this particular lyric, dedicated to Nelson Keys, and called the " The Universal Provider."

> If you want an opera writing
> Or a co-respondent citing
> Or some new electric lighting
> Or a man to mend your sink,
> If you want a book well written
> If you want a dog or kitten
> Or a bungalow at Ditton
> Please apply to Herman Finck.
>
> If you want your horses backing
> If you want to do some packing
> If you've a cough that's racking
> And you want a soothing drink
> If you want a bill inspector
> Or a first-class vivisector
> Or a musical director
> Please apply to Herman Finck.
>
> If you suffer with a tumour,
> And to lose it—so says rumour
> You must get a *sense* of *humour*
> And to get it you must think
> That the best of wit is brevity
> Mixed with satire not severity
> And you'll get down to posterity
> If you follow Herman Finck.

And Frederick Lonsdale, who one New Year's day was in the Garrick Club when all the members were wishing each other the " compliments of the season." Lonsdale saw a very unpopular member coming towards him. "Hello," he said, "Happy New Year—but only one !"

Stephen Leacock, that scintillating University Professor, I took to the Savage Club one night; and an extremely funny speech he made. He has a wonderful speaking voice, one of the most remarkable I have ever heard; it has the tone qualities of a first-class tenor's voice. I think that what impressed Leacock most that night was a recitation by Stacy Aumonier.

Some ten years ago, when he was in Berkshire recuperating from an illness, Stacy wrote to me : " Life here is a placid symphony with a milk obligato."

I co-operated with Augustus Moore, brother of the late George Moore. George Moore's early books I liked, but as regards his later ones I completely agree with Swinburne's remark that he thought so much about style that he became almost unintelligible. Still, as I have first editions of nearly all his works, I hope to *value* them some day.

Talking of my books, reminds me of a remark by Arnold Bennett one day. "You're the only man I know who buys books," he said. And it is true that I have always believed that if a book is worth reading it is worth buying.

Authors, I have noticed, always expect the musicians they know to buy their books. But how many of them ever buy music ?

However, to complete my remarks about the authors with whom I have worked : there was Arthur Sturgess, who wrote so many pantomimes. He always wore the same costume : an unbrushed top hat, old-fashioned long frock coat and dark grey trousers. Even on a glorious summer day, when he came to the Blackpool railway station to see me off back to London, he was wearing his usual attire. It was a marvel to me that he was not mobbed as he wandered, in his top hat and frock coat, through the crowds of holiday-makers in the Blackpool streets.

Most authors and journalists, however quickly they may work, seem unable to start until the very last minute. I have, for instance, watched dear old Charlie Hands the war correspondent (who still, by the way, occasionally comes up to London from his country retreat—he is an Isle of Wight man) fiddling about with a pencil for a tremendous time, unable to strike the opening sentence he required. But once he started, his speed was wonderful.

My recollections include innumerable theatrical journalists. There was Chance Newton—"Carados" of the *Sunday Referee*—a man with an amazing memory who would write an article in a different paper every day but never, he once told me, made much more than £10 a week. Journalistic salaries were, of course, far lower than they are to-day.

Chance Newton once described me in the *Referee* as a Jew, so I wrote to him from Eastbourne:

"A cutting reached me here to-day containing an article of yours, wherein you place me among your Hebrew musical collaborators. But I am not a Jew, and after our close friendship of thirty-five years I thought you knew.

"I append (as you would say) a few biographical facts.

"1. I was born a few doors from Waterloo Bridge turnstile.

"2. I went to a protestant school and was baptised at St. John's Church, Waterloo Bridge Road (not far from the Old Vic).

"3. My father was a Dutchman, but not a Jew.

"4. My mother was born in Hereford (I have never heard of a Hereford Jewess).

"Then it must be my nose that has deceived you all this time! But Jimmy Glover has a nose three times the size of mine. Must he be a Jew?

"Perhaps it is that because I am in Eastbourne you conclude I am born of the East!

"I beg of you to fling me back among the Christians. Seriously, I wish I were a Jew. I would, by now, be a rich man."

Edward Michael was one day so struck with a society paragraph that he composed this one and sent it to me:

" Sir Herman and Lady Finck gave a dinner-party last night. *Among those invited* were The Mikado; Charles Bates, Junr.; the Dalai Lama; F.-M. Foch and the Right Hon. Mike Angel."

I have orchestrated a great deal of the work of Paul Rubens who wrote *Miss Hook of Holland*, *The Balkan Princess*, *Three Little Maids* and scores more. Rubens, seeking the right romantic atmosphere, decided to visit some of the Balkan countries—a rash thing to do for ants, sour bread and sheep's milk butter are things which seem to damp down romance when the Balkan countries are reached.

Rubens, however, went. He was changing trains at one railway station late at night, and as soon as he appeared on the platform there was a tremendous stir. A crowd collected quickly, but he tried to pretend not to notice anything. People shouted and cheered as he climbed into the train, and it steamed out with the station fairly reeling with joyful clamour.

The whole business puzzled Rubens. He could not believe that the people were cheering him; did not see how they could ever have heard of him, far less recognised him. Later he made extensive inquiries, and found that the crowd had mistaken him for ex-King Alfonso of Spain, whom he greatly resembled.

John F. Runciman, who was music critic of the *Saturday Review* in the days of its greatest prosperity, was completely responsible for the following written when he was in France:

>Twinkle, twinkle, Mister Finck;
> How I wonder what you drink
> In that damned, old, rotten, stink-
>   -ing place where we often sink
>So much cash on the delinq-
>   -uency of getting to the brink
>Of the state where everyone wink-
>   -s at the others when the pink
>Of all the party says he think-
>   -s all the rest have had enough drink.
>Twinkle, twinkle, Mister Finck.

> Twinkle, twinkle, Mister Finck!
>   What the devil do you think
> Of in that place where you do twink-
>   le? Oh! Why do you blink
> The fact of wasting little ink
>   On the man who's called here Rink-
> semong, who all day long does tink-
>   -er with his articles for the link-
>   -ed masterpieces that make wrink-
>   -le all his readers' brows. That minx
> Miss Dolly and all her high jink-
>   -s and flinbuinzees and trink-
>   -ets,—Oh! I know, Mister Finck
> Why you never of me think.
> Well, twinkle, twinkle, Mister Finck.

Arthur Binstead ("Pitcher") would rise at six each morning and work furiously for several hours so that he could spend the day in town as a gentleman of leisure.

Another journalist I know is toothless: and this is why. He had his teeth out and a beautiful set of false ones fitted. But after a "thick night" forty-eight hours later, he found that his false teeth were missing. So he went round to Scotland Yard and told them that he had lost his false teeth. Oh, come this way, sir," said the man to whom he applied. Then, the journalist relates: "I was taken into a room containing more teeth than I had ever seen before. I tried on thirty-eight sets, and none of them fitted, so I have decided to do without teeth for the rest of my life."

Fitzroy Gardner, now "the late" I am sorry to say, wrote a witty little book called *Pure Folly* which I have used to jog my memory on points connected with the story of the Follies.

The professional journalist is, I have found, usually a pleasant man to deal with—despite his habit of ringing one up at ungodly hours to ask for information: the amateur is frequently an impertinent nuisance. Let us take an example. An excellent musical critic, Filson Young, wrote me this letter:

> "The week before last I was at the Palace Theatre and heard some music, composed by you, which was played during the exhibition of the bioscope (that dates the letter!) describing winter bathing in America. It is a long time since I have heard

a piece of original, incidental music which has interested me so much; and as perhaps you may know my name in connecttion with musical criticism I am wondering if you would let me have a copy in close score of that particular piece of music. I will gladly pay your copyist the cost of transcribing it. I wish to keep it by me and to refer to it at some future date in something that I am writing about music."

Naturally I sent him what he wanted, and he replied:

"I am very much obliged to you for your letter; and it is most kind of you to arrange this piece of music for me. I can only assure you that my appreciation of it is based on very long and intimate acquaintance with music both from the inside and outside. When one considers the amount of rubbish that you are obliged to play at a music hall, I think it the more delightful and wonderful that you should preserve your interest in the real thing and produce such beautiful work as the movement in question.

"Perhaps you will accept as a slight return for the trouble I am giving you a little volume of musical essays by me."

Compare those letters, from a man of the status and accomplishments of Filson Young, with this epistle from a complete nobody:

"Mr. Herman Finck,
C/o B.B.C., London.
Dear Sir,
  Would you please have enclosed set to music, published and broadcast at your earliest convenience
                                        and oblige."

One of the things written about me which has amused me most was an "Impossible Interview" which appeared in the *Sunday Referee* some ten years ago. This is how it went:

"Notwithstanding the spread of Free Education, cheap meals at the Carlton, and the prolific cotton output in U.S.A., there may be certain benighted individuals in this happy land of ours who, even to-day, have never heard of Mr. Herman Finck. If so, it is not his fault. His first great success as a dramatist came like a flash with the charming comedy *Sunlight and Shadow*, for which that gifted composer Mr. R. C. Carton, wrote a melodious intermezzo entitled 'In The Shadows.' Mr. Finck, or 'Hard-boiled Herman' to his intimates (on account of his marked aversion to soft-boiled shirts), is a Constitutionalist on his mother's side, a Savage on his father's, a 'Pumpuritan' inside, and an Amateur Musician on the offside. His Rhapsody in A flat minor for the kazoo and his unfinished Symphony in Z sharp sergeant-major for the hoopoo are regarded in the best dress-circles as veritable hors d'œuvres.

"Knowing my quarry resided at Hampstead, where he pursues chemical research as a pastime between meals, and being pressed for time, I took the Southern Railway to Wimbledon and from there taxied across the main arteries and several subcutaneous blood-vessels of this great city. It happened to be Sunday, and knowing the maestro's desire for mental introspection far from the madding crowd, I pursued my lonely way across the Vale of Health until I caught sight of our celebrated numismatist whipping the pools (despite their noisy protests) for rock salmon. Then I recalled this weakness of his for hunting the land-shark as a relaxation from the painting of those delightful water-colours so much admired by (land) ladies and police women. I began to apply the torture :

"Me : Good morning, *cher Maître*. Tell me, what is your favourite air ?

"H. F. : Fresh.

"Me : Yes : but the music that fills your soul with yearning ?

"H. F. : The rustle of a Treasury note.

"Me : Who is your favourite character in history ?

"H. F. : King Alfred.

"Me : What is your favourite motto.

" H. F. : Butt me no Butts.
" Me : What is your favourite play ?
" H. F. : Poker.
" Me : What do you lack most in life ?
" H. F. : A sense of humour.
" Me : What is your favourite instrument ?
" H. F. : A corkscrew.
" Me : What would you do to make London brighter ?
" H. F. : Use lots of soap and water.
" Me : What is your favourite sport ?
" H. F. : Setting cheques to music in rag and bone time.
" Me : What is your greatest ambition—as a conductor ?
" H. F. : To conduct a Sevenoaks train to Blackpool.
" Me : Which is your most popular composition ?
" H. F. : Two parts French, one of Italian, and a spot of gin.
" Me : What is your favourite hobby ?
" H. F. : The slaying of interviewers with a Savage Club ! "

I am still appalled at the thought of the impression of me one of the " benighted individuals " mentioned above would have received from reading that interview.

I also recall with amusement a paragraph written by H. C. Hilliam (" Flotsam and Jetsam ") in the *Stage :*

> " During the hot weather rehearsals for *Merrie England* I found the conductor, Herman Finck, representing one of the principal character-names in the piece and having a Gill-All-Alone ! . . . There is no truth at all in the rumour that this musical presentation is to be advertised *Merrie Finckland* by Edward Herman."

CHAPTER XVI

DEAR OLD PALS

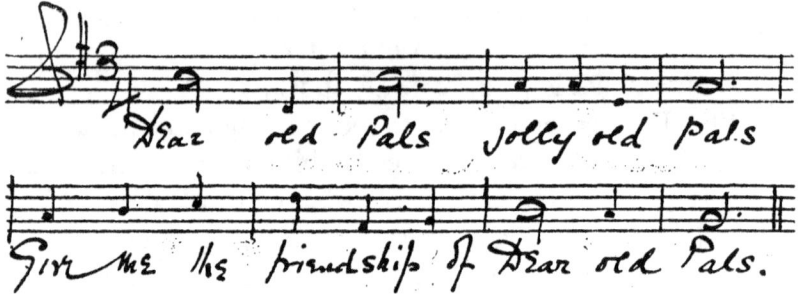

ONE day when I ripped open the envelope handed to me by a telegraph boy, I found that the message inside read:

"SEND FIVE POUNDS IMMEDIATE."

So I wired back:

"SEND TEN POUNDS URGENT."

I say that just to point out that some of the " dear old pals ... jolly old pals " I have known have been " very dear " to me—though in this case (one of the few in which I have managed to put my foot down) the only cost involved was that of sending a telegram.

Undoubtedly (confound it!) Charles Lamb, one of my favourite writers, is right when he says in his famous essay that there are two races, the borrowers and the lenders ; and that the borrowers constitute the great race and the lenders are born degraded. I must be very degraded.

The " dearest " old pal I ever had was a man who once asked me if I could put him up for the night and then stayed with my mother and myself (it was before I was married) for fifteen years. He never did any work and we could not get rid of him. Still he was a good fellow.

Once we went to Eastbourne for a fortnight, and while we were away a man came to cut off the water as the bill had arrived after I left and had not been sent to me. But even that did not get rid of him; half an hour afterwards another man came to the house and said: " You must turn on all the taps here and let them run—there is a fever epidemic in the district." And despite the water company the man received all the water he wanted and went on living in the house.

One man who owed me a considerable sum of money was always sending me letters of regret and appeals to our long friendship, but never any money. I wrote to him several times trying to obtain at least part of the money, and one day I nearly wrote: " The best of friends must *part*." But at the last minute, I relented and did not say it. Yes, there can be no doubt that *I was born degraded*.

But there have also been innumerable " deal old pals " in the real sense of the phrase—some of them no less dear because they are not named in this book—men whose companionship has added pleasure both to my working and to my leisure hours. And having been blessed with many friends, I always feel sorry for anyone who is lonely, and try to cheer them up. If, for instance, I see some temporary honorary member sitting all alone in the Savage Club, while all around are groups of friends enjoying themselves, I always go up to the lonely one, and say: " My name's Herman Finck. I'm an old member of this club, and a lot of people in London know me. So if you will let me help you to become at home in London I shall be very pleased to do so." (All real Savages have that feeling.)

More than once I have seen a man's face absolutely shine with pleasure at having someone to talk to. There is nothing that makes a man feel more completely alone, than to walk into a strange club in a strange city, with only a letter from the secretary of the club to tell him he is a temporary member.

To be all alone is terrible, but almost as annoying is to be among friends who will persistently interrupt while you are telling a story, instead of letting you finish and then saying what they have to say. Mark Hambourg will never hear me out—only the other night I never reached the end of a story because he began to talk about something completely different while I was in the middle of an anecdote—but the worst offenders are often professional comedians. They will seldom admit that anyone who is not a comedian can be amusing—especially a musician. Conversely, people seem to think it is amazing beyond belief that such a scintillating humorist as Ashley Sterne should be a composer of music.

Ashley Sterne discussed this very question in an amusing letter that he wrote to me recently, in which he said:

" My dear Herman,—I am so sorry that our conversation of yesterday afternoon was so rudely cut off at the main while there was still quite a lot of our shilling-in-the-slot unexpended. That's the tragedy of having a job of work to do: it so often interferes with one's job of pleasure.

" But I have since been thinking much on the main theme of our mutual discourse, and, at the risk of converting you into an artesian well by boring you profoundly, I would like to put the results of my cogitation into written words while they remain still hot and sizzling in my brain-pan.

" We agreed, I think that most people regard 'the musical composer with a strong sense of humour' as a contradiction in terms, while, at the same time, they allow that the possession of that same sense of humour is quite compatible with a man's being an artist or an author. Where they trip up, however, is that no composer as yet having had the temerity to term himself a 'humorous composer,' they therefore conclude that there ain't no such person. They postulate that Bateman will answer to the name of humorous artist and P. G. Wodehouse to that of humorous novelist, and hence there must be something awry somewhere if no composer has yet hypothecated unto himself the label of humorous composer.

" I suggest that in arriving at this conclusion they must have been studying the more austere-looking portraits of Bach and Handel, Brahms and Beethoven, and, begging the question, pronounced them incapable of cracking a gag either severally or jointly.

"Similarly they might ponder over the portraits of the spruce and genial-countenanced Edward Elgar or Hubert Parry, and thus deliver their verdict: 'Oh, yes! we can see the sense of humour here all well enough, but we'll wager a sovereign to a sausage that *these* birds are no composers!'

"In an attempt to sum up their difficulty in one significant phrase let me put it to you that *all* composers are humorists, but that they tell you so in a language of their own which is 'not understood of the people.' Having dabbled to some small extent both in the art of writing humour and in that of composing music, I am forced to the conclusion that one *has* to be a humorist first (or, at any rate, possess a practical sense of humour) before becoming a composer, otherwise one would never survive the manifold disappointments which, barring a fortunate few who would seem to have 'got away with it' as soon as the starting-gate flew up, appear to be the sorry lot of all who would aspire to woo the elusive Euterpe.

"As a young aspirant to musical honours, I slogged away for more years than I care to recall before finally and regretfully deciding that the pursuit of composition was the surest way to attain a state of premature *de*composition which any man could elect to follow. And it was, I know, my sense of humour which saved me from desperation during that period, and which ultimately urged me into adopting the writing of humour as a profession. Which, however, is the *true* Jekyll beneath my hide—the composer or the humorist—it defeats me to say. But I am convinced that a sense of humour goes hand in hand with a sense of composition, because otherwise it seems impossible to explain away Schubert and Bizet singing away so gloriously in their squalid poverty and sordid attics, and Beethoven enduring his Calvary of deafness the while he penned such brave and buoyant (I might legitimately add boyish) examples of sheer lightheartedness as his Seventh and Eighth Symphonies.

"But to those who won't take the trouble to learn the tongue which composers speak the composer must always appear as a somewhat ponderous old pundit, who may be clever enough to grind out with mathematical precision and accuracy an eight-part fugue or a six-part canon, but who couldn't say 'oboe to a Goossens,' or, in other words, crack a gag, even for all the cargo of Mr. Masefield's 'stately Spanish galleon.'

"Yet, my dear Herman, you don't need me to remind you that in every bar of the 'Cockaigne Overture' Elgar is handing out the gags for those who have ears to hear. There are quite a good few, too, in the 'Enigma Variations.' Beethoven's Symphonies are all punctuated liberally with 'em, as also are many of Richard Strauss's 'tone poems,' while I must have grossly misunderstood the score of ' The Master-singers ' if it is claimed to be absolutely gagless. Then what about old Bach with his 'Phœbus and Pan' and his 'Coffee Cantata'? I have often thought that had he had the resources of the modern orchestra, what a priceless riot his instrumentation might have been.

"To put my case in a converse way, by way of finale, let us assume that the works of P. G. Wodehouse are only accessible to you and me, both profound admirers of the Master of Woosterism and Jeevesiology, in the Chinese language. Right. We read P. G.—or rather run our eyes along the print so closely resembling a mass of debauched and disorderly Tonic Sol-fa—and we don't think him a bit funny! And why? *Because we are not familiar with the language*, and that, Herman, should form the basis of both a motto and a moral for those of whom I have been writing.

Ever yours,
Ashley Sterne."

The only humorists I cannot tolerate, and that is because they are not humorists at all—I have never heard a genuine joke from one—are those learned centenarians or bi-centenarians who deal justice to the King's subjects, and think it is consequently their

MY GREAT FRIEND, GEORGE BULL

ARTHUR WIMPERIS

prerogative to display an astounding ignorance and to make ridiculous remarks. Remarks which the judge thinks are funny, but which actually are merely brutal and incomprehensible insults to people already going through grave emotional trial, are frequently heard in our courts of law. The judge expects laughter at his preposterous attempts at humour, but if any of the really brilliant men who are often in the court dare to say something actually witty, and people laugh at it, the judge—gravely indignant at this infringement of his monopoly—angrily threatens to clear the court. (This does not, of course, include our amusing Lord Chief Justice Hewart, who is a Brother Savage.)

> "There's the *nisi prius* nuisance
>   Who just now is rather rife
> The judicial humourist
>   I've got him on the list. . . .
> They never would be missed."

One Christmas night, to fill in a few minutes before dinner, I played the overture from *The Mikado* (Gilbert, you see, knew what a plague a judge can make of himself) with Frank Tours, the conductor and writer of music to Kipling's "Mother o' Mine" and son of Berthold Tours, the distinguished Dutch musician. I am afraid our minds were more on the festivities than on the music—I was playing the treble and Frank the bass—*The Mikado* overture is done for four hands—and at the end, he said to me:

"I don't think you played that very well."

"Well, if it comes to that, your performance wasn't up to much," I replied.

"If that's how we both feel, we had better exchange parts," said Frank. So we did, and played it again that way.

Frank Tours, now in America, once had an enormous moustache. It was like a great floating banner, and gave you the impression of something missing until you realised that there was no word "WELCOME" written across it. In America, Frank joined the Lambs Club at which sketches and plays were given, and all the women's parts were taken by men. Frank wanted to take one of the principal girls' parts in a sketch they were producing, but he was told it was impossible for him to do so because of his moustache.

Next time the casting was being discussed, a voice said: " I'll take that girl's part."

The others looked at a strange man. " Who are you ? " he was asked—coldly.

" I'm Frank Tours," he replied.

" Impossible," they said, " he has an enormous moustache."

" So had I—once," replied Frank. And at last he was recognised. The fact was that no one had really known what he looked like before that. He had always appeared like a man seen through a forest.

Another " dear old pal " is Ben Davies. One night he was singing in *Carmen*—and walked up the stage followed by shrieks of laughter. Those last high notes had been too much for the hindermost seam of his trousers.

George Baker, just before his recent marriage to Olive Groves —they are very dear pals of mine—sang with his bride at a concert at Eastbourne during which I conducted " Eastbourniana," a selection of all the tunes I have written at Eastbourne.

Fred Terry, brother of Ellen Terry, Peter Dewar and Willie Harrison are among the finest friends anyone could have desired; and Bob Cunningham, the tenor who first sang in *La Bohème* in English, tells me the following stories about myself.

During the War, Raemaekers, the Dutch artist, was being discussed.

" What is he doing now ? " someone asked.

" Raemaking while the Hun shines," I answered.

Another day we saw, in the window of a photographer's premises, a basket of eggs for sale.

" That's curious," said my companion.

" It's where you would *expect* people to go for a sitting," I said.

Bob Cunningham is a man of great weight—in every sense of the word. One evening, in Regent Street he climbed into a cab on the seat of which I had placed a book I had been reading. " Don't sit on that book," I said, " or you'll stop the circulation."

Mostyn Pigott, fierce moustached, intolerant and sometimes with a tongue like a whip, was one of the real Bohemians of the last generation. He could—and did—write brilliant verse and lyrics. He was magnificently educated and a great clubman in the days—I should say the nights—when people stayed up later than they do now. How he and " Old " Odell could terrify new and nervous members of the Savage Club !

One day I said to Mostyn Pigott : " Look here, I can't call you Mos or Tyn—what does the T in your name stand for ? "

" Turtle," he replied. " But what possessed my father to give me a dam' name like that I don't know ! "

I began to see the night life of London when I was a young musician of about sixteen—I mentioned the evening engagements I had as a boy at the beginning of the book. Then, the night clubs were not a bit like those in the West End now. They were not " smart " dance places, but chiefly rendezvous for actors, writers, artists and such like who were in the habit of working late and in search of talk and drinks before finally turning in in the early hours of the morning.

Arthur Roberts once complained to me that he could not sleep. " Have you ever tried ? " I asked.

I don't think he ever, in his acting days, went to bed before 4 a.m.—and when he did he read books on botany. He had a theory that it was a mistake to take off your clothes to go to bed. " It only wakes you up," he explained in that staccato way of his.

Arthur's ideas about sleep were about as queer as those of another man on drink. This man told me that he had gone teetotal. " I haven't touched a glass of whisky for a fortnight," he said.

" What do you drink now ? " I asked.

" Only brandy," he said.

My first job in a night club was at a place called " The Gardenia " next door to the Alhambra. " The Gardenia " faded out because most of the people who were in the habit of frequenting it were stricken with typhoid. There was something wrong with the drains.

Looking back over late night sittings, I remember the time when C. B. Cochran used to be a very good dancer of the cakewalk for the entertainment of his friends—his agility as a cab passenger I have mentioned elsewhere.

Pélissier and I once shared in a remarkable entertainment. I happened to see an advertisement about a touring troupe calling themselves " The New Follies."

Pélissier's " The Follies " were then at the height of their vast popularity in town, and it was arranged that we should engage those so-called " New Follies " for a birthday party in a private room at Pagani's. All the real " Follies " sat and watched the programme, which was only just so-so, of course, and nothing was said till the end. Then Pélissier solemnly wrote out his cheque for the fee. Directly the wife of the man who was running the " New Follies " saw the name Harry Pélissier on the cheque she tumbled to what had happened.

" So you're all the ' Follies,' are you ? " she said, aggressively. " Well, if we had known that we wouldn't have come here."

I suppose she thought that she and the rest had been made fools of. But it was characteristic of Pélissier that he did not retort as he might have done; instead he wrote out a second cheque for an extra fee.

Shortly after I began to write this book I was bidden to lunch at the Ritz by Sir Harry Preston. I went and found E. V. Lucas, C. B. Cochran, Seymour Hicks, Gordon Selfridge (gloriously teetotal), but I still had no idea why the lunch was being held. Then, somewhat late, Leslie Hore-Belisha walked in . . . and I discovered that the lunch was being given in his honour. That was the last time I was to see Harry Preston.

William Murdoch, the pianist, each year sends me a calendar with daily quotations, prepared by a relative of his. The quotations are always very apt, as for example :

> " Now therefore keep thy sorrow to thyself, and bear with a good courage that which hath befallen thee."—
>
> 2 Esdras x, 15.

The day ? *Quarter Day.*

Brother-Savage Sir Stanley Woodwark—who is so tall that Starr Wood calls him "the length of Harley Street"—once gave evidence in a case where he had treated a man with a cut on the back of his head. The patient had quarrelled with a second man who had a hammer in his hand.

The question arose whether the cut was the result of a blow

THE LENGTH OF HARLEY STREET

(when there might be a case of attempted manslaughter) or whether the man had slipped and struck his head on the kerb.

Woodwark's evidence was that either of these causes was possible. The counsel laboured with him for a very long time, getting him to hold the hammer in his hand and asking him innumerable questions until at last he turned to the judge and said: "My Lord, I have been trying for the last five minutes to make it clear that there is no standard force with which a hammer can be used."

The Judge replied: "I have understood you perfectly for the last five minutes, Doctor, and I might add there is no standard thickness of skulls either."

"No offence meant, Mr. X.," the Judge added, turning to the Counsel.

Morris Harvey says he is my Boswell, and I do know that he somehow remembers more stories about me that I remember myself; while I shall always think of my great friends George Bull and Arthur Wimperis as two of the greatest wits I have known. For a revue in which "Teddie" Gerrard appeared Wimperis and I wrote a song I have already mentioned called: "Naughty, Naughty, One Gerrard." When I had the tune down he asked me for some " dummy " words of the verse to guide him over the metre. On the spur of the moment and over the telephone I gave him the following—with apologies to Alfred Butt:

> You like hal-i-but,
> So do I.
> Butt likes hal-i-but too.

I could go on interminably (perhaps I have!) about songs and singers and people who write them. Ada Reeve gave me a good laugh once. She was going to appear in some pantomime —I think it was at the old Grand Theatre, Islington—and she proposed to use a dance tune of mine to some song.

"But you can't," I tried to explain to her. "They don't fit, don't go together."

She picked up my dance music and the song, thought for a moment, and then said: "How do you mean they don't go together? Couldn't we paste them together, or sew them together?"

Another—perhaps less unconsciously funny remark that I remember was once made to me by George R. Sims. He was not well—he always said he was not very well—and one evening I went to see him at his house, "Opposite the Ducks," Regent's Park.

"Well, how are you?" I inquired.

"I've got double dyspepsia," he replied.

"Double dyspepsia? What on earth is that?" I very naturally asked.

"Well, people have double pneumonia and double vision, so why shouldn't I have double dyspepsia?" he demanded.

The Eccentric, the Savage, Romano's, Rule's, Pagani's, the Green Room, the Café Royal . . . you met everyone who was anyone in the circles I knew. Pagani's was "made" by Carlo Pellegrini who brought all the most famous Bohemians to the Artists' Room; and in the closing months of his life the great caricaturist was supported by a grateful Mario Pagani. Now the restaurant is in the hands of Arthur Meschini who tells me: "It is a joy to see you."

But to return to those Bohemian friends of the last generation, and the hansom cab days in which they lived. T. W. H. Crosland—that brilliant but eccentric poet and journalist, and writer of *The Unspeakable Scot* and other books—one wet night hailed a cab to take him from Piccadilly Circus to Pimlico, where he lived. There was a line of cabs waiting for fares, and Crosland, not wishing to get wet, insisted upon taking the nearest one—the last one in the line.

The driver was equally insistent that he must take the first one in the line. They argued for some time, Crosland and I (I was with him) both getting rained on, and finally he said: "Very well, then, I will take the whole lot—tell them to drive after us."

Whereupon we climbed into the cab and drove off to Pimlico with five or six other cabs following us empty in procession. It cost Crosland about a sovereign—but he had his own way, which was what mattered to him.

Crosland was, of course, a great poet, and once he fell in with the husband of a Music Hall star, who suggested that he should write a song "for the wife." It was arranged that the three of them should meet on the morrow, lunch and talk it over. Half-way through lunch, the star's husband inquired: "Well, what about that song—have you thought it over?"

"Thought it over?" said Crosland. "Why I've written it."

He produced the words which were read over and acclaimed as being fine—as they no doubt were.

"Now, about price?" it was suggested.

"Well, what do you usually pay?" asked Crosland, who knew nothing about that side of the Music Hall business, but who had visions of a ten-pound note coming his way.

"A guinea," said the star's husband.

"What?" almost yelled Crosland. "A guinea? Don't be silly—I could *borrow* that."

I have spoken at length about my Bohemian friends. . . . I must say something about those less noisy but not less pleasure-giving friends—my books. All around me, they are a goodly fellowship of biographies, memoirs, novels—novels like those of W. J. Locke and the great English classical writers; books that you want to read more than once, and that is in my opinion a vital test.

Reading is my only hobby, and books are to me my greatest "pals"; a book that I like gives me more pleasure than anything else in life. I still think that Mark Twain wrote the best bedside books—except for *The Diary of a Nobody*; though some day I may come to prefer *My Melodious Memories*." . . .

[CODA]

or, for unmusical readers,

[THE END]

INDEX OF
PEOPLE IN THE BOOK

A

Adams, A. E., 264
Agate, James, 143
Ainsworth, Alan (Tony), 131
Albani, Madame, 159, 160
Aldin, Cecil, 250
Alexander, George, 61
Alias, Charles, 128, 129
Allan, Maud, 53
Allandale, Ethel, 224
Anderson, Lawrence, 115, 181
Anderson, Mary, 115
Arditi, Luigi, 156, 157
Arkell, Reginald, 203, 272
Arlen, Michael, 249
Armour, G. Denholm, 244
Arnold, Charles, 201
Asche, Oscar, 127, 131, 133 et seq., 222, 272
Asher, Angelo, 36
Ashton, George, 222, 227
Ashwell, Lena, 67
Atkins, Robert, 138
Ayliff, H. K., 138
Aumonier, Stacy, 277

B

Baker, George, 290
Baker, John S., 149, 150
Bancroft, Sir Squire, 207, 208
Bard, Wilkie, 36, 122, 227
Baring, Hon. Maurice, 79
Barker, Granville, 130
Barrett, Alice, 265
Barrett, Mabel, 262
Barrett, Oscar, 34, 120, 121, 272
Barrett, William, 258
Barrett, Wilson, 18
Barribal, 250
Barrie, Sir James, 70, 255, 272
Barrington, Rutland, 93, 147
Batten, Joseph, 203, 244, 246
Baum, Vicki, 92
Baumer, Cecil, 247
Bavin, Freda, 262
Baylis, Lilian, 138
Bayly, Ivy, 265
Bax, Peter, 114
Beaverbrook, Lord, 270
Beckwith family, 27
Beecham, Sir Thomas, 121, 143, 157, 159
Beerbohm, Max, 34, 137
Behrend, 203
Belcher, George, 48, 251
Bell, Colonel Stanley, 67, 138
Bellew, Reverend J. M., 28
Bellew, Kyrle, 28, 29
Benjamin, Morris, 113
Bennett, Arnold, 88, 254 et seq., 277
Bennett, Sterndale, 198
Benson, Sir Frank, 115, 135
Bernhardt, Sarah, 210
Berry, C. W., 259
Best, Thomas, 58
Binstead, Arthur, 76, 255, 280
Birchall, Alice, 265
Birchall, Eleanor, 262
Black, George, 138
Blake, J. W., 62, 73, 74, 251
Blanchard, E. L., 119
Blanche, Marie, 70
Boisset, Frederick, 37, 38
Bolton, King, 208
Bond, Jessie, 53, 147
Boosey, William, 184, 186
Booth, H. S. J., 186
Boucicault, Dion, 137, 195

Bourchier, Arthur, 138
Bovill, C. H., 275
Bradley, H. D., 98, 99
Brandrum, Rosina, 180
Brayton, Lily, 136
Brogden, Gwennie, 68, 70
Brookfield, Charles, 20, 255, 271
Brough, Fanny, 81
Brough, Mary, 81
Brown-Potter, Mrs. Cora, 28, 29
Browne, Tom, 250
Bryan, Alfred, 33, 34
Bull, George, 294
Burke, Marie, 179
Burnand, F. C., 119, 130, 146
Butt, Sir Alfred, 87, 99, 100, 112, 140, 210, 227, 294
Byron, Henry J., 195

C

Calthrop, Dion Clayton, 54, 255, 272
Campbell, Herbert, 36, 121
Carroll, Earl, 208
Carroll, Sidney, 138
Carte, D'Oyly, 149
Carter, Desmond, 275
Cartwright, Charles, 18
Caryll, Ivan (*see* Tilkens, Felix)
Casson, Lewis, 138
Cecil, Arthur, 147
Cellier, Alfred, 125, 155, 156, 196
Cellier, François, 155
Cellier, Frank, 155
Champion, Harry, 40
Chaplin, Charles, 77
Chatterton, F. B., 120, 121
Cheesewright, F., 206
Chevalier, Albert, 36, 39, 57, 203
Chirgwin, George, 41, 239
Clarkson, Willie, 146, 210, 222
Coates, Albert, 143
Coates, Eric, 166
Cochran, C. B., 35, 84, 190, 292
Coffin, Ernest, 251
Coffin, Hayden, 203, 218, 219
Collins, Albert, 242
Collins, Arthur, 88, 92, 122, 123, 124
Collins, José, 135, 205

Collins, Lottie, 205
Compton, Fay, 215
Connaught, Prince Arthur of, 228
Conquest, George, 121
Cooney, ——, 205
Corbett, James J., 28
Courtneidge, Cicely, 81
Courtneidge, Robert, 81, 129, 130, 272
Coward, Noel, 137, 255
Cowen, Sir Frederick, 172, 196
Coyne, Joseph, 83
Cox, Daisy Alexandra, 264
Crook, John, 156, 182
Crosland, T. W. H., 295
Cross, Professor, 75
Cruikshank, 195
Cunningham, R., 290
Curzon, Frank, 90, 91
Curzon, Lord, 203

D

Dance, George, 148
Darran, Herbert, 103
Darrell, Frederick, 149
Davies, Ben, 60, 290
Davies, H. H., 255
Davies, Lilian, 125
Day, David, 185
Day, Edith, 96, 97
Deal, Maud, 262
Dean, Basil, 95, 101, 130
De Frece, Sir Walter, 227
Del Riego, Madame Teresa, 185
Delysia, Alice, 84
Dene, Dorothy, 18
Deslys, Gaby, 49, 54, 272
Dewar, Peter, 290
Dicker, Seymour, 196
Didcott, Hugh Jay, 39
Dodd, G., 261
Doré, Gustave, 195
Douglas, Lord Alfred, 255
Dresler, Marie, 81, 82
Du Calion, 80, 81
Dudley, Countess of (Gertie Millar), 24, 55
Du Maurier, Sir Gerald, 69, 137
Dunn, James, 48, 65

INDEX

E

Ediss, Connie, 81
Edouin, Willie, 76, 139
Edward VII, 24, 29, 53, 222, 224
Edwardes, Felix, 96, 114
Edwardes, George, 177, 216
Eeley, Samuel, 238
Elen, Gus, 49, 59
Elgar, Sir Edward, 69, 70
Ellis, Vivian, 83
Elsie, Lily, 83
Elvin, J., 36
Elwood, Arthur, 28, 29
Engel, Louis, 142
Evans, Edith, 95
Evans, Frederick, 118
Evans, Will, 118
Everard, Dan, 224
Evett, Robert, 135, 139
Eykin, William, 194
Eyton, Frank, 275

F

Fairbrother, Sidney, 81
Farnie, H. B., 128
Farquhar, Lord, 226
Fawn, James, 38, 121
Fenn, G. Manville, 195
Ferrier, Arthur, 248
Fields, Fanny, 226
Finck, Henry, 25
Finck, Herman (my uncle), 23
Fitzimmons, Bob, 28
Flory, Régine, 54, 84, 210
Fokine, Michael, 95
Foster, Frances, 261
Freer, Louie, 82
Friml, Rudolph, 177

G

Gardner, Fitzroy, 78, 234, 280
Genée, Adeline, 235
George V, 114, 204, 226 *et seq.*, 250
George VI, 204, 229

George, Muriel, 81
German, Sir Edward, 158, 174, 207, 244
Gerrard, Teddie, 244, 294
Gibbons, Walter, 227
Giddens, George, 22
Gilbert, Sir W. S., 62, 93, 126, 148, 156, 195, 215,
Girrard troupe, 119, 120
Glover, James, 20, 156, 182, 237, 278
Godfrey, Arthur, 157, 235
Godfrey, Charles, 157
Godfrey, Dan, 157
Godfrey, Sir Dan, 157
Godfrey, Herbert, 157
Graham, Harry, 255, 272
Graves, George, 78, 79, 122
Greenbank, Percy, 185
Greet, Sir Phillip Ben, 138
Grey, Eve, 125
Griefenhagen, Maurice, 247
Grieg, James, 242
Grimaldi, 119
Grineau, Charles (*see* Bryan, Alfred)
Grossmith, George (the elder), 195, 202
Grossmith, George, 201, 202
Grossmith, Lawrence, 202
Grossmith, Weedon, 208
Groves, Olive, 290
Gwenn, Edmund, 40, 83, 92, 135
Gye, Mr., 159

H

Hadow, Professor, 237
Hallam, Basil, 69
Hambourg, Mark, 58, 162, 163, 164, 200, 249, 285
Hammerstein, Oscar II, 96
Hammond, Aubrey, 108, 249, 251
Hands, Charlie, 278
Hanlon-Lees troupe, 110
Harding, L., 136
Hardwicke, Sir Cedric, 99, 131, 207
Hardy, Dudley, 242, 243
Hare, John, 74
Harker, Gordon, 252
Harker, Joseph, 252, 253

Harrington, Lord, 19
Harris, Sir Augustus, 119, 121, 122, 123, 130, 131, 222
Harrison, W., 290
Harty, Sir Hamilton, 143, 160, 162
Harvey, Morris, 72, 73, 81, 216, 249, 294
Haselden, W. K., 250
Hassall, John, 231, 242, 250
Hastings, Basil MacDonald, 199, 200, 255, 268
Hay, Ian, 88
Heddle, James, 270
Helmore, Arthur, 154
Henson, Leslie, 80, 83, 137
Herbert, A. P., 186, 255
Hewart, Lord Chief Justice, 289
Hicks, Sir Seymour, 79, 88, 124, 127, 128, 137, 159, 237, 253, 292
Hilliam, H. C., 283
Hodge, David, 270
Hood, Basil, 62, 255, 272
Hore-Belisha, Rt. Hon. Leslie, 292
Howard, Keble, 255, 272
Howes, Bobby, 83
Hulbert, Jack, 81, 84, 210
Hulton, Sir Edward, 82, 270
Hunter, Ian, 95, 104
Huntley, G. P., 76, 77
Hurry, Colin, 198
Hutchinson, A. S. M., 255
Hutchinson, William, 242
Hyde, Walter, 62
Hyson, Dorothy, 104

I

Inge, Rt. Rev. Dr. W. R., 270
Ivimey, Dr. John, 196, 201
Irving, Sir Henry, 38, 128, 135, 153, 155, 250
Irving, H. B., 250

J

Jackson, Barry, 138
Jackson, Bertrand, 97

Jackson, Nelson, 203
Jacobi, George, 45, 125, 182
Jacobi, Maurice, 182
Jacobs, W. W., 215
James, Cairns, 62
Janis, Elsie, 69, 83
Jeffreys, Ellis, 81
Jellicoe, Earl, 203
Jepson, Selwyn, 249
Jerome, Jerome K., 210, 242
Joel, Solly, 88
John, Augustus, 170
Jones, Edward, 125, 182
Jones, Major, 203, 208
Jones, Sidney, 182
June, 55

K

Kellie, Lawrence, 160
Kemble, Harry, 21
Kerker, Gustav, 177
Kern, Jerome, 177
Kerr, Lord Innes, 135
Keys, Nelson, 68 *et seq.*, 83, 276
King, Cecil, 138
King, Dennis, 93
King, Yeend, 250
Knoblock, E., 88, 255

L

Lambert, H. S., 272
Lane, Lupino, 83
Lang, Dr. Jackson, 133, 134
La Pia, 227
La Trobe, Charles, 101
Lauder, Sir Harry, 38, 226
Laurie, Charles, 119
Lawrence, C. E., 203
Laye, Evelyn, 83, 87, 102, 239
Laye, Gilbert, 200, 239
Leacock, Stephen, 277
Le Brunn, George, 42
Lee, Auriol, 138
Lehmann, Liza, 185
Leighton, Queenie, 55

INDEX

Leno, Dan, 36, 37, 42, 77, 121
Leontovitch, Eugenie, 131
Lester, Alfred, 77, 78
Leverton, William, 103
Levey, Ethel, 70
Lewis, D. B. Wyndham, 104, 275
Liddell, John, 196, 226
Lidgey, C. A., 203
Lind, Letty, 121
Lindon, Milly, 82
Lion, Leon M., 138
Livesey, Sam, 171, 172
Lloyd, Marie, 36, 49, 61, 121, 226
Lockhart's Elephants, 64
Löhr, Hermann, 185
Logan, Stanley, 21, 210, 212 et seq.
Lonnen, E. L., 144
Lonsdale, Frederick, 277
Loraine, Violet, 55, 70, 82
Lucas, E. V., 79, 124, 207, 210, 255, 257 et seq., 292
Lucas, Seymour, 124
Lupino, Stanley, 83, 84
Lutz, Meyer, 66, 143, 144 et seq.
Lynn, Ralph, 83, 87
Lyons, Neil, 115, 255, 275
Lytton, Henry A., 62

M

Macaire, Robert, 34
MacClure, Victor, 252
MacCormack, John, 165, 166
Maclennen, C. S., 255, 270
Mackenzie, Sir Alexander, 62, 70, 152, 153, 172, 175, 203, 207, 237
Mackenzie, Compton, 78, 255
Malleson, Miles, 249
Manners, Charles, 210
Manns, August, 26, 178
Marlowe, Tom, 247
Mars, Gwennie, 224
Martinetti, Paul, 34, 35
Martin-Harvey, Sir John, 170
Mason, A. E. W., 271
Maugham, Somerset, 131
May, Phil, 243, 245
Melville brothers, 125

Melvin, G. S., 105, 122
Merson, Billy, 83, 96
Meyder, Karl, 120
Millar Gertie (*see* Dudley, Countess of)
Miller, Joe, 108
Miller, Tom, 72
Minto, Dorothy, 70
Moiseiwitsch, Benno, 181
Mollison, Clifford, 139
Mollison, William, Junr., 139
Mollison, William, Senr., 139
Molloy, J. L., 125
Monckton, Lionel, 177, 184
Monkman, Phyllis, 10
Moore, Augustus, 53, 244, 277
Moore, George, 53, 252, 277
Moore, Mary (*see* Lady Wyndham)
Morden, S., & Co., 24
Mordkin, Michael, 51, 52
Morgan, Sir Herbert, 249
Morgan, Lou, 88
Mori, Nicholas, 180
Morton, Charles, 22, 35, 45, 46, 78, 137
Morton, J. B., 275
Morton, Leon, 84
Moscovitch, Maurice, 92
Murdoch, William, 292

N

Nansen, Fridtjof, 201, 204
Napier, Marjorie, 224
Nares, Owen, 69
Nash, John, 34
Nation, W. H. C., 139
Nayler, Louise, 261
Nevin, Ethelbert, 61
Nevinson, C. R. W., 242, 248, 249
Nevinson, Mrs. C. R. W., 249
Newton, H. Chance, 38, 278
Ney, Marie, 104
Nicholls, Harry, 119, 121
Nikisch, Arthur, 158
Norcott, Maurice Lane, 275
Northcliffe, Lord, 249, 270
Norway, Carlo, 249

O

Odell, E. J., 203, 291
Ogilvie, Stuart, 172
Oldham, Derek, 96, 97
O'Neil, Norman, 101, 102, 174
Orrell, George 108
Osmond, Albert, 261

P

Paderewski, Ignace, 58
Pagani, Mario, 295
Page, Phillip, 174, 175, 182, 200, 257
Palerme, Gina, 70
Pallant, Samuel, 220, 221
Pallant, Walter, 220
Parker, D. G., 166
Parker, Frank, 138
Parlby, George, 242
Partridge, Sir Bernard, 244
Paulo, Harry, 119
Pavlova, Anna, 49 et seq., 226
Payne, Edmund, 237
Payne, Harry, 118
Pearce, Vera, 55, 81, 102
Peary, Commander, 204
Pellegrini, Carlo, 196, 245, 246
Péllisier, H. G., 31, 32, 57, 85, 136, 137, 224, 237, 292
Pemberton, Sir Max, 130
Penley, W. S., 84
Percy, W. S., 111, 112
Perkins, Charles, 20
Philippe, 216
Phillips, Sir Percival, 233, 266
Phillpotts, Eden, 215, 255
Pigott, Mostyn T., 250, 291
Pilcer, Harry, 54
Pinero, 255
Pinkerton, Allan, 113
Playfair, Arthur, 68, 69, 216
Poland, Sir Harry, 216
Pounds, Courtice, 53, 196, 272, 274, 275
"Poy," 247
Praga, Alfred, 242
Prentice, Charles, ("Jock"), 193
Preston, Sir Harry, 292

Price, Julian, 248
Prince, Arthur, 227
Prinsep, Anthony, 83, 272
Pryde, James, 242, 250

Q

Queen Alexandra, 223
Queen Mary, 148, 226 et seq.
Queen Victoria, 222

R

Rachmaninoff, Sergei, 182
Raemaekers, 290
Raleigh, Cecil, 119
Randall, Harry, 85
Ravel, Maurice, 182
Raven-Hill, Leonard, 244
Rawlings, A., 153
Reader, Ralph, 138
Reed, E. T., 244, 250
Reed, German, 195
Reinhardt, Max, 137
Reynolds, Blanche, 263
Reynolds, Frank, 250
Richardson, Lady Constance Stewart, 53
Richter, Hans, 141 et seq.
Ridge, W. Pett, 260, 263
Riscoe, Arthur, 80
Roberts, Arthur, 38, 74, 75, 76, 79, 121, 205, 206, 234, 246, 247, 268, 291
Roberts, R. A., 49, 58
Roberts, Lord, 203
Robertson, Tom, 195
Robeson, Paul, 100, 101
Robey, George, 36, 83, 226, 227
Robinson, Edith, 263, 265
Robertson, Forbes, 138
Rogan, Lt.-Col. J. Mackenzie, 207
Rogers, John, 204
Rogers, Will, 70
Rohmer, Sax, 255
Rolls, Hon. C. S., 19
Romberg, Sigmund, 99

INDEX

Ronald, Sir Landon, 159, 171, 179
Ropes, Arthur R. (Adrian Ross), 185, 255
Rothermere, Lord, 270
Rothschild, Alfred, 168
Royce, F. H., 19
Royce, Teddy, 139
Rubens, Paul, 177, 185, 279
Runciman, J. F., 279
Russell, Frederick, 40
Russell, Lilian, 146
Russell, Mabel, 70

S

St. John, Florence, 129, 144
Sala, George Augustus, 195, 255
Samuel, Harold, 196
Santley, Sir Charles, 203
Sarony, Leslie, 104, 105
Saunders, Madge, 70
Saville, Lewis, 183
Schalkenbach, 35
Schonberg, Arnold, 175
Scott, Clement, 195
Selfridge, Gordon, 292
Seyler, Athene, 95, 275
Seyler, Clifford, 276
Sime, 244
Simpson, Harold, 159, 160, 275
Sims, George R., 67, 119, 144, 224, 243, 255, 266, 294
Slaughter, W., 261
Slaughter, Walter, 62, 196, 232
Smith, Caroline, 261
Smith, Doris, 262
Smyth, Dame Ethel, 157
Solomon, Edward, 125, 145, 146, 148 *et seq.*
Sousa, 156
Squire, Ronny, 249
Stanlaws, Penrhyn, 252
Stampa, George, 244, 245
Sterne, Ashley, 286
Stiles, Leslie, 62
Stoll, Sir Oswald, 59, 138, 227
Strauss, Richard, 178
Strop, Jacques, 34
Strube, Sidney, 251

Stuart, Leslie, 232
Sturgess, Arthur, 119, 234, 277
Sullivan, Sir Arthur, 23, 27, 146, 148 *et seq.*, 183, 236
Sullivan, E. J., 246
Swaffer, Hannen, 175, 210
Swinnerton, Frank, 256
Sydney, Lewis, 194

T

Tabrar, Joseph, 42
Tadema, Sir Alma, 21, 153
Talbot, Howard, 185
Tamagno, Francesco, 222
Tate, Harry, 84, 134, 226, 227
Tayler, Duff, 256, 257
Taylor, Beatrice, 262
Teck, Duke of, 148
Teck, Duchess of, 148
Tempest, Marie, 146, 239
Terry, Ellen, 212, 290
Terry, Fred, 212, 290
Thackeray, Lance, 253
Thomas, Bert, 245
Tich, Little (Harry Relph), 37, 38, 226
Tiller, John, 230
Tillett, Ben, 164
Tilley, Vesta, 36, 49, 55, 226
Tilkens, Felix (Ivan Caryll), 158, 159, 177, 182, 224
Toft, Albert, 242, 250
Toole, John, 238
Tours, Berthold, 289
Tours, Frank, 289, 290
Tree, Sir Herbert Beerbohm, 66, 67, 72, 128, 129, 138, 237, 252
Trevor, Spencer, 135
Tully, George, 68, 198, 214
Turner, J. H., 255, 272

V

Vanoni, 47
Venne, Lottie, 20, 81, 147
Venne, Topsy, 81

Vernon, Harriet, 55
Vokes, Fawdon, 119
Vokes, Fred, 119
Vokes, Mrs. Fred, 119
Vokes, Miss Jessie, 119
Vokes, Miss Victoria, 119
Volkert, Charles, 185
Vollmoeller, 138
Volny, Maurice, 54
Vosper, Frank, 95

W

Wadman, Miss, 121
Wallace, Edgar, 203, 252, 268
Wallace, Nellie, 81
Waller, Lewis, 173
Walker, Whimsical, 119
Ward, Artemus, 195
Ward, Edwin, 247
Warner, Charles, 18
Webster, Tom, 246, 247
Weingartner, Felix, 143, 246
Wenzel, Leopold, 76
Welch, James, 77
Wells, H. G., 249, 255, 275
West, Alfred H., 57
White, Jimmy, 127, 128
White, Fisher, 138
Whitelaw, David, 249
Whitelaw, George, 249, 252
Whiteman, Paul, 162, 163
Wieniawski, Henri, 19
Wilde, Oscar, 255, 271
Wilenski, R. H., 249
Williams, Valentine, 193
Wilson, David, 249
Wilson, Joe, 247
Wilson, William J., 140
Wimperis, Arthur, 68, 83, 130, 255, 275, 294
Windsor, Duke of, 204, 229, 233
Wood, Sir Henry, 143, 160
Wood, J. Hickory, 35, 119, 266
Wood, Mrs. John, 81
Wood, Starr, 240, 293
Woodville, Caton, 247, 248
Woodwark, Sir Stanley, 293
Wray, Maxwell, 138
Wylie, Julian, 117, 124, 138
Wyndham, Sir Charles, 22, 72, 137
Wyndham, Lady, 22

Y

Yohe, May, 224
Young, Filson, 280, 281

www.ingramcontent.com/pod-product-compliance
Lightning Source LLC
Chambersburg PA
CBHW071218080526
44587CB00013BA/1423